Criminal Justice

Recent Scholarship

Edited by
Marilyn McShane and Frank P. Williams III

A Series from LFB Scholarly

Contemporary Gangs
An Organizational Analysis

Deborah Lamm Weisel

LFB Scholarly Publishing LLC
New York 2002

Library of Congress Cataloging-in-Publication Data

Weisel, Deborah Lamm.
  Contemporary gangs : an organizational analysis / Deborah Lam[m]
Weisel.
    p. cm. -- (Criminal justice)
  Includes bibliographical references and index.
  ISBN 1-931202-30-3 (alk. paper)
  1. Gangs--United States--Case studies. 2.
Gangs--Illinois--Chicago--Case studies. 3. Gangs--California--San
Diego--Case studies. I. Title. II. Criminal justice (LFB Scholarly
Publishing LLC)
  HV6439.U5 W455 2002
  364.1'06'6--dc21

2002003818

ISBN 1-931202-30-3

Printed on acid-free 250-year-life paper.

Manufactured in the United States of America.

CHAPTER I: Introduction

CHAPTER II:
Understanding Gangs: Contributions of Research and Theory

CHAPTER III:
RESEARCH DESIGN AND METHODOLOGICAL APPROACH

CHAPTER IV:
AN ORGANIZATIONAL ANALYSIS OF FOUR GANGS.........

CHAPTER V: SUMMARY AND CONCLUSION

ACKNOWLEDGEMENTS

This book simply could not have been completed without the active involvement of numerous individuals. Scott Decker, University of Missouri at St. Louis, and Timothy S. Bynum, Michigan State University were involved in every phase of the research in this project; Susan Pennell of San Diego Association of Government and Arthur Lurigio, Loyola University, Chicago and director of research for the Cook County Probation Department, used creativity and persistence to get access to subjects for the interviews on which this study was based, and provided the students and staff who conducted the interviews. At the institutional level, the Cook County and San Diego County Probation Department, Illinois and California departments of corrections, and police departments of San Diego and Chicago were all valuable in identifying and accessing an appropriate sample. The research in this study was conducted under a grant to the Police Executive Research Forum in Washington, D.C. by the National Institute of Justice, U.S. Justice Department, grant #92-IJ-CX-KO36. Last, but not least, thanks to the members of my dissertation committee — Dennis Rosenbaum, Richard Ward, Timothy Bynum, Michael Vasu and, particularly, to Doris Graber at the University of Illinois at Chicago, who served as both chair and inspiration.

DLW

CHAPTER I:
INTRODUCTION

Although street gangs have been in existence since at least the turn of the century, concern about these criminal enterprises, often related to sensational media coverage of gang-related violence, rose dramatically throughout much of the 1990s. Research suggested that many gangs were undergoing significant changes. Some gangs were growing larger by recruiting and retaining more members over a wider age range, or merging with other gangs; some gangs were increasing their life span by decreasing rates of mortality; and gangs in some areas were becoming more numerous as rates of organizational founding rose, leading to increasing numbers of gangs in suburban areas and smaller cities.

Researchers also claimed that gang members had become more mobile, more highly organized and more violent than those of previous years (Hagedorn, 1988; Taylor, 1990b; Pennell, 1994; GAO, 1989). There were some indications of gang involvement in legitimate business enterprises, and with sophisticated criminal enterprises such as wholesaling drugs, laundering money and participating in financial crimes. Increasingly, researchers and criminal justice practitioners liken some criminal youth gangs to more traditional organized crime such as the Mafia and to highly-organized business enterprises. Most researchers recognize, however, that there are a wide variety of gangs and most of them participate primarily in social activities, such as partying, and minor crime, such as vandalism, rather than operating as sophisticated criminal enterprises.

NEED FOR RESEARCH

Despite some important research on gangs (Chin, 1990; Cummings and Monti, 1993; Jankowski, 1991; Moore, 1991, 1993; Hagedorn, 1988; Decker and Van Winkle, 1996), much is unknown about these criminal organizations. There is no reliable accounting of how many gangs exist and there has been no uniform standard to define a gang, gang member or a gang-related incident of crime (Esbensen et al, 2001; National Youth Gang Center, 2000; Ball and Curry, 1995; Curry, Ball and Fox, 1994; Curry, Ball and Decker, 1995). Consequently, there is no uniform method of counting or maintaining accurate files about gang membership across jurisdictions. Virtually nothing is known about features of some gangs which contribute to organizational longevity, what dynamics underlie organizational growth and – importantly – just how these organizations change over time. Because of the lack of cross-sectional and longitudinal studies of gangs, little theory has been developed to explain the growth or predict the future of gangs.

Research on the population of gangs and the organizational dynamics which affect gang prevalence, organizational density and mass has been needed to develop a conceptual model of gang evolution and growth. Such a model has practical implications for understanding and controlling the proliferation and harmful effects related to gangs. Current efforts to control gangs consume large amounts of public resources among law enforcement at the federal and state level. Gang-control efforts often disproportionately concentrate attention on the minority communities most troubled by gang problems, and gang prevalence exacerbates problems such as violence, property crime and drug-dealing. Educational and social intervention efforts to control gangs are often unfocused and ineffective. A conceptual model of gang evolution and growth has great promise for developing practical and effective policy approaches to gangs.

To date, much of the theoretical work on gangs reflects ideas about gang formation; underclass theories emphasizing "social dislocation" (Wilson, 1987; Huff, 1990) and a theory of subculture constitute the prevailing paradigm (Monti, 1993b; Huff, 1990; Goldstein and Huff, 1993). Related theoretical work on gangs has involved developing taxonomies for classifying gangs. Such taxonomies reflect the wide variation in types of gangs recognized by researchers. Most of these variations are based upon activities, motivations or structure of gangs. An understanding of these varying typologies has implications for learning more about specific types of gangs; perhaps more important is to develop an understanding of the relationship between different types of gangs.

Most gang researchers have typed or classified gangs into different groups. From the earliest gang study in Chicago, Thrasher (1963) described five distinctly different kinds of gangs – diffuse, solidified, conventionalized, criminal and secret society. In the ensuing years of gang research, other classification schemes were put forth by Coward and Ohlin (1960), Yablonsky (1962), Miller (1982), Fagan (1989, 1990), Taylor (1990a, 1990b), Jankowksi (1991), Huff (1989), Skolnick, Bluthenthal and Correl (1993); Klein (1995);and Rosenbaum (1983).

Distinguishing different types of gangs highlights variations in gangs that exist within cities and across the nation – all gangs are not created equal. In fact, each type may constitute a distinct population or subset of gangs, suggesting a differing growth trajectory, a distinct organizational structure, and differing effects of organizational dynamics. The classification schemes are inherently local, reflecting the diversity of gang types in a single or handful of cities. There is no consensus across the large number of gang-involved cities on types of gangs. And, importantly, the distinctions among types of gangs raised by Cloward and Ohlin, Miller, Taylor, Huff, Skolnick and others provide no conceptual or theoretical model about the processes of gang development. Despite some rank ordering of gang types from less serious to more serious – such as ranging from social to criminal gangs – these taxonomies offer no explanation of how gangs evolve as organizations. The authors, for example, make no claim that cultural gangs become opportunistic over time. Skolnick, Bluthenthal and Correl (1993) and Yablonsky (1962) raise the notion of a scale of behavior, with particular models representing end- or mid-points on that continuum. And Klein (1995) has suggested – but did not articulate how – that spontaneous gangs can over time become traditional gangs. But even these models are static, reflecting various gangs only at a specific point in time. Just how do gangs proceed from one model or type of gang to another? Increasingly, gang researchers widely use the term 'evolve' or its related terms – developed, matured, adapted, changed, grown and so forth – suggesting some widespread implicit agreement that contemporary gangs do grow and evolve over time. But the absence of a articulated conceptual model and theory of the process through which gangs evolve leaves a major gap in predicting the future of gangs in America.

In contrast to gangs, there are some theories about the evolution of organized crime groups. Phases or stages of organized crime groups are described by Block (1991), Lupsha (1991) and O'Kane (1992). But these models are not widely cited and have not been applied to gangs. As with gang literature, most of the theoretical literature related to organized crime involves thinking about how organized crime is formed. Continued research in the field of organized crime is scant; given the nature of the continuing controversy in the field regarding definition, structure, existence and demise, expectations about organized crime theory informing gang theory should be modest. Nonetheless, theorizing about organized crime stages raises questions as to whether there are any predictable patterns, stages or phases of gang development.

Organizational theory provides a promising avenue for understanding change and evolution in gangs. Among other theorists – Jackson, Morgan, and Paolillo (1986a), Kimberly, Miles and Associates (1980), Lippitt (1969), Greiner (1972), Schein (1985), Tushman and Romanelli (1990), Starbuck (1965), Freeman (1990), Aldrich and Staber (1988), Brittain and Freeman (1980), Daft (1986), Singh (1990), Singh and Baum (1994) and Staw and Cummings (1994) – all discuss the life cycle of an organization, evolving through different stages.   These concepts fit into the population ecology perspective in which organization formation and mortality and changing organizational form and size are analyzed to inform organizational growth trajectories, size distribution, organizational density and organizational mass. These concepts of organizational dynamics have promise for understanding the growth and rising prevalence of contemporary gangs.

RESEARCH DESIGN

It is quite likely that evolutionary processes occur in criminal groups such as gangs.   Among the wide range of types of gangs, gangs which are most successful – those which are large, long-lived, vertically-organized, highly criminal or entrepreneurial and thus closer to the endpoints on continuums of structure and behavior – are most likely to exhibit evidence of evolution. By documenting key characteristics of successful gangs, these gangs can be studied to learn more about their evolution.

The key research questions in this study include:

Should gangs be considered groups, informal or formal organizations? What organizational features distinguish between these different forms of social organization and how do these contribute to understanding the dynamics of contemporary gangs?

What organizational theories explain or contribute to understanding the form or structure and size of gangs, as well as the growth or rising prevalence of contemporary gangs?

Do organizational theories provide a relevant framework for describing and explaining the structure of successful gangs? What is the promise of such theories for explaining and predicting the growth and expansion of gangs?

Most information on gangs is criminal justice-based, involved in the counting of gangs, gang members and gang-related crimes for record keeping purposes (see Curry, Ball and Fox, 1994; Curry, Ball and Decker, 1995). Related studies on gangs, for example, look at drug involvement of gang members based on arrest data (Klein and Maxson, 1989) or cooffending of gang members, identified via arrest reports (Moore, 1993). Since police are concerned primarily with law-violating behavior, police information on gangs is limited (Monti, 1993a). But information from other sources about gangs, as with organized crime, is difficult to access. Gangs are secretive organizations whose rules, ethnic solidarity and involvement in criminal enterprise, make them difficult to penetrate.

Some researchers, however, have successfully studied gangs through interviews with individual gang members (Huff, 1990; Hagedorn, 1990; Jankowski, 1991; Pennell, 1994; Fagan, 1990; and others). The ethnographic method has proved useful for gaining general information about initiation and recruitment, rules and roles, criminal activity and attitudes about family, future and other issues. Most of these studies have either sampled gang membership identified through police or probation records or focused on individual accessible gangs. Snowballing techniques of identifying gang members are most commonly used.

To learn more about successful gangs, this study used field research as a means to gather information about organizational characteristics of successful gangs and elaborate on the evolution of these groups over time. Semi-structured face-to-face interviews were conducted with gang members to learn more about highly-organized gangs in Chicago and San Diego, comparing and contrasting two criminal gangs of African American and two of Latino heritage. Subject matter experts at the local, state and federal level were queried to identify two successful gangs in each of the cities. The Gangster Disciples and Latin Kings in Chicago and Syndo Mob and Logan gangs in San Diego were selected for study. The research focused on these four criminal gangs – examining their purpose, growth and changes over time in order to understand the process of their transformation into large and long-lived gangs.

The study consisted of a purposive sample of gang members, identified through probation and prison records, and selected based upon recommendations of probation officers and prison gang workers. Every effort was made to select gang members who had held named positions of leadership within their gang as these individuals were presumed to be most knowledgeable about the gang's organizational history and major changes in the gang over time.

To inform the basic research questions about gang evolution, the following information was collected about specific gangs:

Estimations of gang size and changes in size over time; age distribution; residence of membership; practices of recruitment; and evidence of maturation/exit from group participation;

Descriptive history of the gang, including specification of the time in which the gang was founded and a description of any organizational changes occurring over time;

Specification of the gang's goals and the individual gang member's objectives related to gang membership, and a description of any changes in goals occurring over time; and,

An assessment of the environment in which the gang operates and the gang's response to that environment.

These dimensions were evaluated using qualitative analysis methods and software to determine the unique characteristics of the gang and to identify the effects of different dimensions on the growth and proliferation of gangs. The study builds on the findings of Weisel, Decker and Bynum (1997) and Decker, Bynum and Weisel (1998) which used the data described in this study to describe the organizational structure of gangs including labor specialization; patterns of leadership; extent of hierarchy; occurrence of regular meetings, payment of dues, and adherence to rules, discipline and penalties. These descriptive dimensions of organizational structure are not addressed in this study; these dimensions are used to inform the basic research questions regarding organizational processes examined in this study.

The objective of the study described herein was to develop an understanding of the growth of contemporary gangs, with implications for estimating the population or eventual organizational density, mass and size distribution of gangs. This understanding draws upon extensive research in the field of organizational theory especially the field of population ecology. Chapter II of this study describes the criminological literature related to crime and delinquency as well as organized crime, and the range of related organizational theory literature in order to develop a framework for the analysis of data. Chapter III describes the research methodology and design of the study, including its limitations. Chapter IV details findings from interviews with gang members and analyzes how these data conform or differ from ideas of rising gang prevalence suggested by the organizational theory literature. Chapter V is a discussion of the significant findings in this study and points to directions for further research.

CHAPTER II:

Understanding Gangs: Contributions Of Research And Theory

Contemporary gangs constitute a pervasive problem in American society because of their involvement in homicide and other violent crime, drug dealing and use of weapons; their emergence in smaller cities, the increased participation of exceptionally youthful members and widely-held perceptions about the sheer growth in number and size of gangs. Growing variations between and within gangs relative to ethnic diversity, organizational structure and participation in criminal activity complicate understanding of these organizations (Cummings and Monti, 1993; Fagan, 1990; Taylor, 1990a, 1990b; Klein and Maxson, 1989; Hagedorn, 1990; Huff, 1990; Maxson and Klein, 1990; Miller, 1990; Conly, 1994). The rise in gang problems has contributed to a rise in research on gangs in the late 1980s – an increase which continues today – however, there is no generally accepted theory to explain gang formation and there has been no theoretical effort to explain the rising prevalence of gangs. Instead, most gang researchers have been involved in conducting descriptive research on individual gangs and pursuing specialized research interests (Huff, 1990; Horowitz, 1990; Miller, 1990; Hagedorn, 1990; Cohen, 1990; Covey, Menard and Franzese, 1992; Klein and Maxson, 1989).

Contemporary criminological theories to explain the formation and prevalence of gangs are grounded primarily in research conducted from the turn of the century to the mid-1900s. Two primary criminological theories emerge in most current gang research – underclass theory, which emphasizes the economic mismatch in low-income areas between the opportunities available to individuals and their aspirations, and subculture theory, which focuses on the culture of poverty areas as generating and reinforcing delinquent behavior (Miller, 1958; Huff, 1990; Horowitz, 1990). The underclass theory, put forth by Wilson (1987) in a general version, has become especially prominent in recent literature on gangs (Hagedorn, 1988; Padilla, 1993a, 1993b; Skolnick, Bluthenthal and Correl, 1993; Moore, 1993; Vigil, 1988; Cummings and Monti, 1993). Both sets of theories offer explanations for the formation of gangs but these theories have not been used to explain the rising prevalence of gangs. These theories offer both individual-level (social psychological) explanations for why individuals join or desist from gangs and macro-social level explanations of community conditions which give rise to the formation of gangs; there is also an extensive body of descriptive research on individual gangs, which has given way to theorizing at the small group or intra-organizational level. Absent from gang theorizing are attempts to explain gangs at the organization or population level, leaving unasked such basic questions as "How and why are gangs becoming larger and/or more numerous?"

These issues of gang formation and gang growth are related but quite different. As Klein (1995) points out: "...different facets of street gang formation – who joins, how gangs get going in a community, and how they are maintained once they have formed – are not necessarily determined by the same factors" (p. 203).

> Once formed, juvenile gangs may persist or disintegrate for reasons that may have little to do with why they formed in the first place. [a]

How can the phenomenon of growth in size and number of gangs be explained theoretically? This chapter reviews the historical development of criminological theories and the work of major gang theorists for their potential to explain the rising prevalence of gangs. Because these theories have limitations for explaining the tenacious persistence of some gangs, the emergence of new gangs in non-urban areas, and the general growth and rising persistence of gangs, organizational theory is examined for its value in explaining these trends. Indeed, several key concepts of organizational theory have great promise for understanding the rising prevalence of gangs. In particular, the population ecology perspective of organizational theory explains phenomena of organizational birth, growth and failure and concomitant changes in organization size, mass and density. These organizational processes are also illuminated through an examination of evolutionary or life cycle processes. Before applying organizational theory to gangs, however, its applicability to gangs must be evaluated. Since gangs are seldom considered as formal organizations, are concepts of organizational theory germane to our understanding of the population of gangs or individual gangs? Importantly, the relevance of organization theory to gangs is established in this chapter. In addition to defining characteristics of groups and organizations, different kinds of organizations are examined to identify models most promising for understanding contemporary gangs.

Once the relevance of organizational theory is established, several important questions about gangs can be asked. From an organizational theory perspective, what is currently known about prevalence and growth of gangs? How can perceptions of gang growth or rising gang prevalence be substantiated? How do individual gangs grow larger? How and why are gangs becoming more numerous? What factors contribute to the growth and persistence of some gangs, while others face eminent demise in the face of numerous threats to their existence? This chapter brings together organizational theory and current knowledge of gangs to explain rising prevalence of gangs in the nation – an issue of practical and theoretical interest. This application of theory then becomes a point of departure for extending knowledge of rising gang prevalence through organizational research on contemporary gangs.

THEORETICAL EXPLANATIONS OF GANGS

Current criminological theory related to gangs is well-grounded in historical and descriptive studies of delinquent boys that date to the turn of the century. Puffer (1912), for example, described the nature, organization and activities of 66 boys who were members of gangs; Asbury (1970, originally published in 1928) provided a descriptive social history of the gangs of New York; Thrasher's study (1963, originally published in 1927), looked at 1,313 gangs in Chicago over a period of seven years, raising numerous questions about juvenile delinquency and social pathology; and Whyte (1981, originally published 1943) provided an in-depth look at an Italian street gang.

These groundbreaking studies and those that followed (Shaw and McKay, 1969; Bloch, 1958; Cohen, 1955; Miller, 1858; Short and Strodtbeck, 1974; Yablonsky, 1962) resulted in the development of three major paradigms of juvenile delinquency and gang research explaining gang formation. These three classes of criminological theories – strain, control and subculture – represent the dominant views about gang formation. Despite their continued prominence in research on deviance, contemporary gang researchers recognize that all these major theories of delinquency and gangs have weaknesses.

Strain theory dominated gang theorizing in the 1960s and has enjoyed a resurgence in the late 1980s and 1990s in the form of underclass theory. Strain theory suggests that the difference between economic opportunity and individual aspirations is the root of criminal activity. The mismatch between these two factors leads to frustration and feelings of deprivation or discontent. The notion of strain theory dates to Robert K. Merton's 1938 article on anomie which suggested that the disjunction between

> what the culture extols – universal striving for success – and what the social structure makes possible – limited legitimate opportunities – thus places large segments of the American population in the strain-engendering position of desiring a goal that they cannot reach through conventional means.

As a consequences of this situation, there is an "intense pressure for deviation," sometimes through participation in criminal activity. Later elaborations of strain theory include Cohen's (1955) measuring rod and reactance theory and Cloward and Ohlin's (1960) differential opportunity theory; in the latter, blocked economic opportunity causes frustration which generates delinquent behavior through gang participation. Strain theory has not, however, been empirically verified (Shoemaker, 1990); indeed, most youths eventually mature out of gangs and delinquent behavior while not changing their economic status (Goldstein, 1991) and strain theory provides no explanation for this phenomenon. Goldstein (1991) noted that strain theory survives not as a general theory of delinquency but as part of an integrated understanding of delinquency as related to several causes. Strain theory has evolved into several forms of underclass theory incorporated into gang studies by Hagedorn, 1988; Padilla, 1993a, 1993b; Skolnick,

Bluthenthal and Correl, 1993; Moore, 1993; Vigil, 1988; Cummings and Monti, 1993. Currently, there is renewed interest in strain theory, as part of a general theory of crime expanding Merton's anomie paradigm (Lilly, Cullen and Ball, 1995). Persistent urban problems such as the growth of the underclass, rising conditions of social inequality, and urban decay contribute to interest in strain theory as an explanation of gang formation.

Control theories were common in the 1950s and early 1960s, a period in which gangs and juvenile delinquency were treated synonymously (Stafford, 1984). Control theory consists of two basic forms: individual or personal control and social control. The basic issue of personal control described by Reckless (1967) was the idea that self-concept is one's image of one's value to society or to others. Reckless' "containment perspective" suggested that "pulls" to delinquency exist which the individual must control in order to avoid delinquent behavior. Pulls consisted of unemployment, deviant friends, tension and frustration, among others. Negative self-concepts thus would contribute to delinquency while positive self-concept would provide insulation from the pulls to delinquency.   In contrast to individual control, social control theory suggests that individuals engage in criminal behavior because they have weak social bonds with family, school, community or other social structures (Hirschi, 1969). Strong social bonds, in contrast, include affective relationships with family, academic success, aspirations for jobs or education and the like. Hirschi (1969) considered social bonds as consisting of attachment, commitment, involvement and belief. The impact of weak social bonds on delinquency, according to Goldstein (1991), is supported by numerous studies linking delinquency with poor parental supervision, excessive parental drinking, poor parental discipline, less support and affection by parents and similar issues.

There is strong empirical support for control theories of delinquency. Numerous studies test the importance of family influences on the development of delinquency and find support for these explanations (Shoemaker, 1990). This conceptualization of control, however, refers to social bonds; Gottfredson and Hirschi (1990) proposed that an individualistic approach, self-control – or its absence – determines the propensity of individuals to desist or participate in criminal activity. Empirical tests of this theory of self-control are promising (Lilly, Cullen and Ball, 1995).

The roots of subculture or cultural deviance theories explaining gang formation can be found in the work of Shaw and McKay (1969, originally published in 1942). Shaw and McKay, in a continued the search for social causation, suggested that "culture conflict" and illicit means theory explained gang formation. In this conceptualization, the norms of delinquent youth conform to the social norms of the prevailing culture although these norms are often at odds with those of the larger society. Shaw and McKay claimed that social disorganization served as a basic underlying condition of delinquency rather than a causal explanation; economic instability and social pathology lead to conflicting moral value systems and often resulted in intergenerational transmission of criminality.

Miller (1958) echoed the subcultural theory that delinquency and involvement in gangs were simply an extension of the lower-class culture where gang youth lived – a generating milieu for delinquent behavior such that the predominant values and norms of the slum community shape delinquent behavior of boys. Subcultural theory was elaborated by Bloch (1958), Cohen (1955), and Sutherland (1934, 1970). Sutherland and Cressey (1970) developed the differential association theory which has been the most influential among the cultural deviance theories (Goldstein, 1991). Sutherland and Cressey suggested that delinquent behavior is learned and involves the same processes as other social behavior. Learning of delinquent behavior occurs in small group settings and develops from collective experiences and situational events (Shoemaker, 1990; Short and Strodtbeck, 1974, originally published in 1965).

Subcultural theories were popular in the 1950s and 1960s but provide no explanation for differences between individuals (Wilson and Hernnstein, 1985), thus failing to explain why some youths in these low income communities develop conventional values while others do not. Shoemaker (1990) noted that subculture as a theory of delinquency offers little explanation for ethnic or cultural variations that may affect delinquency within specific areas. Generally, subculture theories are viewed as accurate but incomplete and subculture remains a key portion of the etiology of deviance.

In addition to these three major theoretical streams, the theory of labeling refers to the stigmatization and reinforcement that occurs once youths become involved in the criminal justice system or in delinquent behavior. This theory of self-fulfilling prophecy, put forth by

Tannenbaum (1938), elaborated by Lemert (1951) and Becker (1973), has implications for gang research. Once labeled as a gang member, a youth may have difficulty shedding the group label or the delinquent activity associated with the gang.

> A final step in the career of a deviant is movement into an organized deviant group...the deviant who enters an organized and institutionalized deviant group is more likely than ever before to continue in his ways. He has learned, on the one hand, how to avoid trouble and, on the other hand, a rationale for continuing (Becker, 1973: 37-39).

Unlike the three major gang formation theories, labeling theory does not offer an explanation about the original cause of delinquent behavior, suggesting that such deviance "may be caused by any of a number of factors" (Shoemaker, 1990: 210); instead, it provides an explanation for the secondary and continued deviance that occurs once society has officially labeled an individual's primary deviant act. Empirical tests of labeling theory do not substantiate the theory. For example, an examination of official arrest data demonstrates that arrests of offenders peak around age 16 and then consistently decline over time (Steffensmeier, 1989; Snyder and Sickmund, 1995; Hirschi and Gottfredson, 1983), suggesting that formal contacts with the criminal justice system have minimal effects on subsequent criminal behavior. Research studying chronic offenders, and reoffense rates of juveniles sent to court show mixed results, making labeling theory questionable (Shoemaker, 1990). Sanders (1994) found effects of police labeling of gang members to be weak although Moore (1978) found that prison conditions tend to perpetuate gang membership and Jackson (1989) suggests institutional responses may contribute to labeling and, thus, maintenance of the gang.

Shoemaker (1990), noting that social class conditions do not change over time, asks: "Why, for example, do most delinquent youth, in gangs or otherwise, 'reform,' so to speak, and abstain from criminality when reaching young adulthood, as the theorists themselves suggest is the case?" Goldstein (1991), acknowledges the veracity of that claim: "Most low income youths eventually become law-abiding adults though their economic status often remains unchanged" (p. 12). This robust trend of declining participation in crime with age is perhaps the strongest correlation observed in the field of criminology (Hirschi and Gottfredson, 1983; Gottfredson and Hirschi, 1986, 1988; Blumstein, Cohen and Farrington, 1988).

Another subset of theories with potential for explaining gangs are those theories used to explain the formation and persistence of what is called "organized crime." The theory of ethnic succession (Bell, 1961; Ianni, 1969, 1972; O'Kane, 1992; Kelly, 1986) suggests that successive waves of immigration in the United States have fueled organized crime as these ethnic groups have used criminal organizations as a mechanism of social mobility, referred to by Bell as a "queer ladder" for social and economic progress out of poverty. Organized crime experts, who type Russian, Jamaican, Chinese and other ethnic gangs as organized crime, view the continuing immigration and criminal participation as support for the notion of ethnic succession. Indeed, O'Kane (1992), even explains participation of African-Americans in "emerging" organized crime activity as reflecting the de facto "immigration" of African-Americans from their dominant residence in the rural southern United States to the industrial and urban cities of other regions of the nation. The limitation of the ethnic succession theory, of course, is that not all immigrants of certain ethnic groups become part of organized crime (Kenney and Finckenauer, 1995).

Enterprise theory (Smith, 1980; Reuter, 1983; Smith, 1980) offers an alternative explanatory theory for organized crime, suggesting that organized crime "mirror[s] the legitimate business world" (Smith, 1980: 374) – crime develops when legitimate markets are unable to meet customers' needs for goods and services. Organized crime groups use economic laws of supply and demand, attenuated by practices such as violence and corruption to meet the demands of customers. Reuter points out that organized crime groups provide illegitimate opportunities – such as gambling or drug trafficking – for money and services to immigrants as both workers and customers. Smith (1980) integrated theories of enterprise and ethnicity describing criminals as entrepreneurial business people serving a wide range of customers in a marketplace stratified by varying levels of legitimacy.

There has been little empirical testing of theories of organized crime formation and perpetuation (Reuter, 1983). Because research on organized crime is even more difficult than research on gangs, due to oaths of secrecy and limited numbers of traditional organized crime groups, few empirical examinations of organized crime theories have been possible. Research has largely been limited to descriptive case studies, often drawn from court documents, and there is widespread agreement that no general theory of organized crime exists.

Need For Research

Gang theorizing has focused on gang formation but existing theories of gangs and juvenile delinquency are incomplete for understanding the apparent growth of gangs – bigger gangs, more numerous gangs, more problematic gangs and gang expansion or formation in suburban and small cities. With the exception of labeling theory – a theory with weak empirical support – none of the major criminological theories related to gangs have been used to explain what happens to gangs as groups or organizations once they are formed. Since the 1950s, no major theorizing about gangs has occurred (Miller, 1990: 271) yet evidence suggests that gangs have changed in significant ways during this theoretical lacuna. Since most contemporary gang researchers have focused on the behavior of individual gangs or groups of gangs, and the organizational structure (or lack thereof) within specific gangs, it is not surprising that these studies do not offer explanations for the growth of gangs – a phenomenon affecting the size of gangs and the number of gangs in the population.

Among the gang studies, Thrasher (1963) probably came closest to explaining gang growth. He identified features of formal organization in the gangs he studied – they were directed towards goals, they were internally stratified, there was a commitment to the group, and the gang as an organization outlived changes in leadership (Thrasher, 1963; Gottfredson and Hirschi, 1990: 205). In this way, Thrasher viewed gangs as no different from other organizations such as businesses or schools. Thrasher also recognized the adverse effects of labeling gang members (Shoemaker, 1990) and set the stage for further theory development by raising issues such as how 'play groups' evolve into 'delinquent groups (Monti, 1993b: 6). Each of these issues – organizational continuity, stigmatization of individuals and evolution into more goal-oriented groups over time suggests the phenomenon of gang persistence.

Strain theory is not incompatible with gang growth and persistence but offers an incomplete explanation. Strain theory, or its reconstituted version of underclass theory, draws upon the notion that conditions of poverty, segregation and economic dislocation of jobs from the inner city, is suggestive that gangs would have increasing persistence as jobs become increasingly less available. Although strain theory is not incongruous with the idea of individual gangs growing larger over time, for example, with gang members retaining gang membership as they become older and for the formation of more new gangs, it does not offer an explanation for gang formation in areas without underclass conditions – the middle-size and small cities and suburban areas in which gangs have appeared in recent years.

Control theory offers individual and social level explanation of gang formation. Without some additional explanation as to why the absence of effective social and individual control is becoming more symptomatic of life in America, this theory offers little for understanding the growth of gangs. Subculture theory, in which the norms of delinquent youth conform to the norms of subculture groups, provides an adequate explanation for why gangs may have grown within inner city areas but doesn't explain the incursion of gangs into small towns and cities.

None of these three criminological theories offer any understanding of the growth of individual gangs. As Covey, Menard and Franzese (1992:151) point out, there remains no generally accepted theory of gangs, which incorporates formation, persistence and disintegration of gangs, and uses multi-level explanations including influences at the community, organizational, small group, and individual level.

Historically, most research related to crime and deviance has occurred at the individual or social psychological level, attributing individual responsibility for the commission of criminal acts. Such explanations have ranged from body type (for example, Glueck and Glueck, 1950) to low intelligence to poor self-control to family, poverty, drug use, and low educational attainment (see Hawkins, 1996, and Rojek and Jensen, 1996, for a full description of this literature.) In a seminal work, Gottfredson and Hirschi (1990) state that the group context of crime is irrelevant since all crime is inherently individual.

There has been some research on the group perspective of gangs – see particularly Short and Strodtbeck (1974) and Goldstein (1991) – but such applications of organizational theory have largely been limited to examining group processes such as group formation and maintenance, cohesion, and leadership functions.

There is also a large body of work which uses a community-level explanation, for example, attributing delinquency to individuals conforming to the subculture of poverty in their community, suggesting that deviance is learned, attributing weak institutional or social bonds for failing to prevent the participation of individuals in delinquent or criminal behavior, and the dislocation between economic opportunity and availability – the subculture, social control and strain theories. Some authors, notably Klein (1995) integrate community-level and individual-level variables, to explain the formation or proliferation of new street gangs in communities.

The social organization perspective – an intermediate level of analysis between individual- and community-level perspectives – is a neglected perspective of gangs. Best and Luckinbill (1994) note that the social psychological and social structural levels of analysis – i.e., the individual level and community level – have traditionally dominated research on deviance. Indeed, the social organizational research on gangs has been left to a handful of criminologists including Best and Luckinbill (1994), Cressey (1972), and Kornhauser (1978). Cressey (1972) examined distinctions between formal and informal criminal organizations, classifying delinquent gangs as an example of an informal organization because of the absence of division of labor, behavior constrained by rules, and purposeful design. Thrasher (1963) also employed a social organization perspective but this was not the primary focus of his broad work on gangs. Organizational theorists have concentrated primarily on legitimate organizations, leaving organizational research on deviant groups to criminologists.

Jankowski (1991) points out that some newer studies of gangs include discussions of gang organization, "but they are not asking the question of what the nature of the organization is and what accounts for its successes and declines over time" (p. 327, fn 16). And he noted that "Although researchers have an intuitive understanding that the gang has organizational traits, for the most part, studies of gangs have not closely examined the nature, dynamic and impact of the gang's organizational qualities" (p. 5). Despite his urging for an organizational analysis of gangs, Jankowski's own organizational analysis is limited to a examination of the internal leadership structure of these organizations and does not examine the effects of organizational dynamics.

Contemporary gang research is increasingly demonstrating that group context is germane to understanding criminal behavior:

membership in a gang exacerbates both the frequency and seriousness of criminal acts (Esbensen and Huizinga, 1993; Thornberry et al, 1993; Jensen and Rojek, 1980; Warr, 1996; Maxson, Gordon and Klein, 1985; Morash, 1983; and see Spergel, 1990, for a detailed description of this literature). In this sense, the group context is an increasingly important dimension for understanding criminal behavior (Bursik and Grasmick, 1996; Spergel, 1990; Camp and Camp, 1988) as serious gang problems and crime are more likely to occur when gangs are larger and different gangs are concentrated in a small area.

To fill the theoretical gaps explaining rising gang prevalence, organizational theory provides both a rich context and useful mechanism for examining what happens to gangs after they are formed. Organizational theory has amassed a large body of descriptive and theoretical work on individual organizations and groups of organizations. Because of this work, an ecological approach can be employed to examine the organizational history of a population of gangs as well as individual gangs. This organizational-level approach is advocated by Freeman, 1978, 1990; Hannan and Freeman, 1989; Singh, 1990; Hannan and Carroll, 1992; Singh and Baum, 1994; Carroll, 1988; and others. The population ecology approach will illuminate issues about the growth and proliferation of gangs – issues previously obscured because of a dominant analytical focus on the individual- and community-level of analysis.[b]

ORGANIZATIONAL DYNAMICS: GROWTH AND CHANGE

Since criminological theory is limited in its ability to explain the rising prevalence of gangs – including growth in the number and size of contemporary gangs – key tenets of organizational theory are examined in this section for their relevance in explaining these phenomena. In particular, organizational life cycles are examined for their potential to describe and predict organizational stages of evolution – creation, growth or maturation and decline – through which organizations typically proceed. These life cycle models can aid in conceptualizing how gangs develop and change over time.

Population ecology, another specialty of organization theory, is also examined for its unique contribution to understanding gang growth. The population ecology perspective focuses on the reciprocal relationship between form and size of organizations and their environment – key features of rising gang prevalence. Thus, the ecological perspective provides a fertile mechanism to understand and evaluate changes in the population of contemporary gangs – including changes in the form or structure, number and size of gangs. These concepts of organizational theory are reviewed in detail in this section to provide a robust framework for analyzing the growth of gangs.

Organizational Life Cycles

It is widely acknowledged by organizational theorists that social organizations are not static entities but change in important ways over time. A widely-held notion is that organizations proceed through temporal and sequential stages of development, a process commonly known as an organizational life cycle (see, for example, Kimberly, Miles and Associates, 1980; Freeman, 1990; Jackson, Morgan and Paolillo, 1986; Lippitt, 1982; Greiner, 1972; Tushman and Romanelli, 1990; Starbuck, 1965; Schein, 1985). The use of the biological metaphor suggests that organizations are created, grow and, finally, face organizational decline, a process that may occur within a few years or over decades.

It should be noted that views making comparisons between organizations and organisms have been subject to criticism. Katz and Kahn (1966) are particularly strident in their negation of organic models: "This figurative type of thinking ignores the essential difference between the socially contrived nature of social systems and the physical structure of the machine or the human organism." (p. 31). Similarly, Pennings (1980) suggests that the wide range of organizational diversity is a fatal flaw of biological analogies of organizations. Such analogies are tempting "because it facilitates the reduction of social complexities to a few parsimonious ordering principles" (p. 135). Tichy (1980) also points out that organizations do not have predictable phases or linear stages through which they evolve; instead, organizations are more influenced by factors such as "environmental threats, opportunities, size, and technology than by unfolding maturational processes" (p. 165). The phases of organizations are cyclical processes based on dynamics of social systems not maturational processes, according to Tichy. Indeed, while death is an inevitability for organisms, this truism is not so for organizations; similarly there are no inevitable linear stages for organizations: "If there are laws that govern the development of organizations...they are yet to be discovered" (Kimberly, Miles and Associates, 1980: 7).

Despite these criticisms of life cycle models, the models are widely used to explain the organizational processes through which organizations proceed over time.   John Gardner (1912) had a classic observation about organizational life cycles: "Like people and plants, organizations have a life cycle. They have a green and supple youth, a time of flourishing strength, and a gnarled old age... An organization may go from youth to old age in two or three decades, or it may last for centuries" (p. 32).

Kimberly, Miles and Associates (1980) dedicate a full text to describing organizational features and processes relative to the life cycle, extending the biological metaphor. Such stages include organization creation and early development, organizational transformations, and organizational decline and termination. Despite their use of the biological metaphor, the authors acknowledge limitations in its applicability because organizational demise is not a certainty:

> Death is not an inevitable feature of organizational life...There is no inevitable linear sequence of stages in organizational life, although there may be remarkable similarities among the developmental patterns of certain clusters of organizations (p. 7).

The biological or organic conceptualization of organizations is well-grounded in classical organizational theory. Such theories are reinforced by parallels to life cycles of animals, plants and other organisms. In the sense of the birth metaphor, birth rates of organizations may be related to economic well-being or economic opportunity. For example, the rise of births for the 1950s baby boom occurred during a time of plenty; new organizations may be created when the economy can support their presence – during periods of "resource munificence," borrowing a term from Freeman (1990). Within the birth metaphor, new organizations may be considered fragile entities; they often begin as quite small in size, a parallel to newborn babies. Newborn organizations are highly vulnerable to external forces. In adolescence, the maturing process occurs as organizations become adaptive to the environment. In decline, organizations are again weak and vulnerable; change and adaptation may be difficult.

Differing models of organizational life cycle are described by different organizational theorists. Jackson, Morgan and Paolillo (1986) note that many organizational theorists suggest that organizations follow a predictable pattern consisting of three primary stages: formation and initial development; stabilization and dynamic equilibrium; and change or decline and dissolution. The developmental stages of the organizational life cycle are described by Lippitt (1982) as birth, during which creation and survival are critical concerns; youth, in which organizations gain stability, develop reputation and pride; and maturity, in which organizations tend to seek uniqueness and adaptability and make a contribution to society. Tushman and Romanelli (1990) describe an organizational life course known as a "punctuated equilibrium model" in which organizations evolve through relatively long periods of incremental change punctuated by reorientations which activate a subsequent period of convergence.

Greiner (1972) suggests a series of five distinct life cycle periods that occur within two critical organizational dimensions: age and size of the organization. Each sequential phase in Greiner's model begins with an evolutionary period and concludes with a revolutionary period in which a management crisis creates significant internal turmoil. Every phase is shaped by its predecessor. Greiner claimed that specific types of growth and crises are peculiar to the various stages of the life cycle: Sequential phases of growth are interrupted, sequentially, by differing crises. For example, crises of leadership occur early in the life cycle, when the organization is young and small, while crises of control and red tape characterize the latter stages of organizational development. Organizational size and age are the most important structural dimensions in Greiner's model for predicting growth of organizations: size is important because it relates to problems and solutions faced by the organization such as coordination and communication. Age is an important dimension because problems and decisions are rooted in time (Jackson, Morgan and Paolillo, 1986).

Starbuck (1965) describes several models of organizational growth, including a metamorphosis model, in which organizational growth is a process "marked by abrupt and discrete changes in the conditions for organizational persistence and in the structure appropriate to these conditions" (p. 486).   Starbuck also described a biologically-based cell division model in which an equation commonly incorporates organizational births and deaths at fixed frequency and incorporates a term proportionally decreasing the rate of growth as the total number of organizations in the organizational population becomes large; as more organizations constitute the organizational population of a certain form, the growth of individual organizations slows. This slowing of growth occurs as the number of organizations reach a level of organizational density, which shapes the growth trajectory of the organizational population (Baum and Powell, 1995; Hannan and Carroll, 1992, 1995).

Population: Number and Size of Organizations

Starbuck's biological model laid the groundwork for the notion of organizational population, suggesting that there is a set or number of organizations of a particular form and size which comprise a population of organizations at any given time.   More specifically, a population of organizations is   a group of organizations defined by patterned activities.   Another way to conceptualize the population is the group of organizations which are in competition with one another and using a similar strategy (Boeker, 1991).   Bidwell and Kasarda (1987) point out that the form and size of the population and the environment are features in an ecosystem which are related reciprocally in a continuing process of change.   Over time, the relationships between these features produce evolving population form and size such that a change in one has an effect on another.   And, as Freeman and Hannan (1989) point out, these changes in population continue over time because there is no fixed equilibrium point for the organizational population although the size of the population does tend to stabilize over time.

The total size of the population – and of organizations within the population – is most directly affected by the amount of resources available to those organizations.   Resource availability is a critical part of the environment in which organizations operate.   Hannan and Freeman (1989) explain that an expansion of the resources available to organizations "will often lead both to the growth of individual organizations and to growth in the population of organizations using those resources but [these authors note that] the relationships between the two kinds of growth processes are unknown" (p. 338).   Thus, the availability of more resources may suggest that individual organizations will grow larger and that larger organizations will constitute the population. Or, the availability of additional resources may result in the creation of new organizations, resulting in more numerous organizations in the population. Of course, both these phenomena may occur simultaneously.

Although resources in an environment may expand, there are also resource constraints or limits that exist and effectively limit the growth of the population and affect the growth of organizations within the population. These resource limitations are referred to as the carrying capacity of the environment for the activities in which the organization engages. Organizations operate in a fundamental niche that imposes limits on growth; this phenomenon is generally referred to as density dependence - a point beyond which the population cannot grow (McPherson and Smith-Lovin, 1988; Hannan and Freeman, 1988; Carroll and Hannan, 1992).

In general, organizational theorists agree that populations of organizations typically begin with slow rates of growth in terms of the number of organizations within the environment. In other words, when the organizational form is relatively new and new organizations are being created, growth in the number of organizations is somewhat slow. Over time, the rate of growth of organizations within a population speeds up and reaches a maximum rate. Growth then declines slowly – with some organizations dying out – until there is a stable number of organizations comprising the population (Tucker et al, 1988; Hannan and Freeman, 1987; Carroll and Hannan, 1992). Historically, however, the phenomenon of population growth is driven by organizational creation and dissolution; these two processes are much more common than the adaptation of organizations (Brittain and Wholey, 1989). Indeed, organizational failures within a population create an opportunity for new organizations, such that most organizational populations are replenished more or less continuously by an inflow of new members (Hannan and Freeman, 1989: 90).

As a population of organizations develops, the organizations which comprise the population have a tendency to look very similar; Hawley (1968: 334) claimed that, in the environment, one finds only the organizational form "optimally adapted to the demands of the environment." In particular, this observation suggests that organizations of a specific type will tend to be of a similar size.

Each [organization] experiences constraints that force it to resemble other [organizations] with the same set of constraints...[and] must submit to standard terms of communication and to standard procedures in consequence of which they develop similar internal arrangements within limits posed by their respective sizes (p. 143).

Organizations in the population which are significantly larger or smaller than others population in effect create a new organizational population, in which similar patterns of growth occur to determine efficient size relative to available resources. Hannan and Freeman (1978) point out that growth or movement of an organization from small size to large size is tantamount to death of the small organization and birth of the large organization. Small organizations do not typically compete with large ones, so large differences in organizational size suggest membership in differing organizational populations.

Founding rates of new organizations within a population typically occur in historical spurts, according to Stinchcombe (1965): "An examination of the history of almost any type of organization [population] shows that there are great spurts of foundation of organizations of the type, followed by periods of relatively slower growth, perhaps to be followed by new spurts, generally of a fundamentally different kind of organization in the same field" (p. 154). Stinchcombe called these spurts of growth waves of organizing. These waves occur because, according to ecological theory, of the logic of natural selection: organizations which have certain characteristics have advantages in some way that increases their likelihood of survival over organizations without those characteristics. An example of this selection process, according to Brittain and Freeman (1980: 292), suggests that bureaucratic organizations emerged because these organizations formed during a period when this type of organizational structure thrived for a specific population of organizations. Such a natural selection process is used to explain the dominance of specific types of organizations within specific fields.

Ecological theories of organizations suggest that there is a relatively stable number of organizations in the population, however, organizational theory has little to say about why new organizations come into being or why they cease to exist, according to Freeman

(1990: 16). In the organizational founding process, new and small organizations must compete with old organizations already in the population or, if the organization represents a new form of organization, it must create its own niche and address a host of barriers to entry. Thus, as Hannan and Freeman (1989) point out, "liabilities of age and size produce a slowly changing aggregate number of organizations" in the population; often a seemingly stable population is "supported by a highly volatile underlying process involving millions of organizational births and deaths and the creation of new forms" (p. 35).

Birth of New Organizations:
Proliferation through Imitation and Schism

Freeman's (1990) study of organizational populations filled a gap in organizational theory that had largely neglected the issue of organizational birth. Most often organizational founding has been studied through entrepreneurship, conceived as a psychological phenomenon related to risk aversion or achievement objectives of individuals (p. 16), rather than a population-level phenomenon. But organizations are created through a variety of mechanisms.

One of the common ways in which proliferation of organizations occurs is via organizational imitation. Such imitation increases the organization's chance of survival because new organizations copy existing organizations in most ways. Since existing organizations can be presumed to be successful in the prevailing environment, imitation increases the chances of success for a new organization. Simple prevalence of an organizational form gives that form legitimacy and these forms of organizations assume a "taken-for-granted" character that becomes known and widely imitated. Typically, organizational forms which are more widespread are considered legitimate forms of organization; their prevalence contributes to increased founding rates of organizations of a similar form (Hannan and Freeman, 1988: 21). The phenomenon of organizational schism also contributes to proliferation. Schism is an event that occurs when subgroups of an organization break away to create a new organization. This is a particularly useful way for proliferation to occur because members of the organization – insiders – may be the only ones with knowledge about a successful organization's strategies and structures. Such limited access to this knowledge

> is commonly the case when organizational functioning is shielded from public observation and when essential features of the organizational form have not been codified. In such situations, existing organizations are the only training grounds for knowledgeable organization builders (Hannan and Freeman, 1988: p. 21).

In other words, the organizational process of schism is perhaps the most successful means of imitating an existing organization's form and structure. Generally the success of new organizations is also related to the organizational experience of its founders. Stinchcombe (1965) points out that organization founders with previous experience in an organization which failed typically have higher rates of success with their "new" organizations.

New organizations will also be created and populations will become more dense when there are new resources or opportunities. Individuals who begin new ventures may be "stimulated to take action by factors such as the availability of new technologies, venture capital and unexploited markets" (Freeman, 1990: 16). Freeman also points out that new organizations and even new forms of organizations will come into being when there is political and economic turmoil in the organization base. Such turmoil creates new resource niches and can increase the viability of new organizational forms. When new forms of organizations appear successful, they are quickly replicated. And as new forms of organization appear in the environment, natural selection plays an important role in determining the number of new forms which will survive: organizations that are adaptive to the environment survive while others expire. And, as Aldrich and Auster (1990) point out, new organizations must undergo transformations to adjust to volatile environments or else they will be selected against and cease to exist. Since few organizational environments are static, such organizational transformation or adaptation is necessary for new organizations to persist.

Organizational Growth and Size

Much of the organizational theory literature is dedicated to analyzing growth and size of organizations, and the associated impact of these related phenomena on organizational structure. Growth of organizations is not an instantaneous occurrence, according to organizational theorists. Instead, growth typically occurs over periods of time since organizations generally start off as small entities:

> Large and complex organizations do not spring into existence full-blown but develop out of simpler ones (Blau and Scott, 1962: 224).

Measuring organizational size and changes in size over time – organizational growth or decline – is not a straightforward process; one could measure building size or height for an organization, the amount of learning that occurred in an educational setting, or a host of other output variables. Typically, however, organizational size is measured through productive capacity, number of personnel, some quantification of inputs or outputs (e.g., sales or students), or assets/profits. The most predominant measure of organizational size is the use of the number of members or employees to reflect the concept of size (Jackson, Morgan and Paolillo, 1986).

Organizational size is often highly correlated with age: older organizations are larger, as they have grown over time while young organizations are typically small, with few employees, students, members or the like. As organizations grow larger, they are believed to obtain increasing benefits – efficiency – from achieving greater specialization. The major outcome of movement toward an efficient structure is the presence of growth, according to Katz and Kahn (1966):

> The contribution of efficiency to growth is not a one-way or a one-time organizational event; it is a cycle which continues over a wide span of time and a wide range of organizational circumstances, sizes, and structures. Efficiency begets growth, but growth brings new gains in efficiency (p. 159).

Katz and Kahn note that there is some optimum efficient size for any organization and, theoretically, a point at which size becomes a handicap. There are also environmental conditions which can make efficiency irrelevant. Again, these ideas are reflected in the concept of natural selection as applied to organizations: organizations are selected against if they are not of the optimum size for the environment.

Changing Size and Organizational Structure

As organizations grow, they typically change – organizations cannot maintain their original form and continue to grow, claim Hannan and Freeman (1989). Whyte (1969) suggests that organizational growth – in terms of number of members – necessarily results in changes in formal organization structure and, particularly, in the patterns of interaction and activities of members. Indeed, it has been widely accepted that large changes in organizational size are accompanied by changes in structure or organizational form (Meyer and Associates, 1978: 151; Kasarda, 1974; Simel, 1902, 1903). Among organizations, larger size typically means that there is a more pronounced division of labor and greater hierarchical differentiation into numerous managerial levels and divisions. The increased specialization contributes to increases in standardization, formalization, and centralization (Blau and Schoenherr, 1971; Jackson, Morgan and Paolillo, 1986: 215).

These organizational changes occur because, for organizations, there are natural consequences to growth:

> Growth in size creates greater distance, both physical and psychological, among members of the organization, and this tendency is reinforced, in most cases, by the process of organizational subdivision. Thus, organizational growth, by itself, can have very powerful effects on both the various internal structures and processes that emerge within the organization and on the relative influences of those structures and processes versus the influence of the founder and core group (Kimberly, Miles and Associates, 1980: 435).

This concept of growing organizations suggests an organizational predisposition, under conditions of growth, towards bureaucracy. The result of organizational growth – organizations of large size – necessitates a shift toward more impersonal and formal interactions between organizational participants: it is simply not possibly to carry on face-to-face interactions between all members of the organization as it becomes larger (Hannan and Freeman, 1989; Blau and Schoenherr, 1971; Jackson, Morgan and Paolillo, 1986). The problems of management change significantly as organizational size increases and ultimately the organization's policies, procedures and structure must also change.

Organizational Decline

Organizational decline or mortality can occur for various reasons. Generally, organizations fail when they no longer fill the need they had created, "or when they cannot adapt to a changing set of conditions" (Jackson, Morgan and Paolillo, 1986: 334). This failure to adapt may be considered failure to adapt to either conditions internal to the organization or to external conditions. Organizational survival is dependent upon adaptability but organizational adaptability may be limited by resistance to change since some "organizational forms are inherently resistant to change" (p. 336). Organizational failure also occurs because organizations are unable to change. Organizations are "imprinted" at founding with social conditions prevalent at the time of their founding, according to Stinchcombe (1965) and they exhibit inertial properties which significantly limit their ability to change or adapt. They also continue over time to exhibit imprinted characteristics associated with their original founder.

Organizational failure may also be attributed to internal decay, i.e., a breakdown of the structure and policies within the organization, a mismatch between organizational goals and individual needs, inequitable distribution of power within the organization, and neglect of planning succession. External adaptability and internal flexibility and efficiency are not sufficient to stave off organizational decline. The approach with which the organization reacts to prospective decline has implications for the outcome of its efforts. A reactive response to prospective decline includes cuts and layoffs, retrenchment and weathering the storm. Generating or developing adaptive responses involves creating new organizations characterized by "experimentation, informal communication lines...tolerance for occasional failure, ad hoc jobs, frequent movement of personnel and high incidence of innovation to combat decline" (Jackson, Morgan and Paolillo, 1986: p. 341).

Although large size and age are characteristics which typically reduce the incidence of organizational mortality, there are some disadvantages or liabilities related to age and size: Aldrich and Auster (1990) suggest that two variables affect the ability of large organizations to adapt to changing conditions – internal inertia and external dependencies. Internal inertia occurs because information logjams sometimes occur in the hierarchy; rules and documentation requirements can slow adaptation, resulting in a mismatch between a changing environment and the organization's formal practices (Powell, 1990). Older and larger organizations attempt to cope with these limitations through emulation and exploitation; emulation refers to internal venturing and entrepreneurship while exploitation involves franchising, creating spin-offs and subcontracting. Participating in the exploitation strategies of large organizations offers benefits to small organizations because it shelters them from the liabilities traditionally associated with newness and smallness.

"Liability of newness" is a classic of organizational theory articulated by Stinchcombe (1965). He described conditions in which mortality rates appeared to decline as organizations aged. Organizational mortality declines for various reasons, including the inability of new organizations to mobilize resources because they lack legitimation as organizations. But organizational mortality rates are also high for new organizations for other reasons:

> Some organizations are little more than extensions of the wills of dominant coalitions or individuals; they have no lives of their own. Such organizations may change strategy and structure in response to environmental changes almost as quickly as the individuals who control them. Changes in populations of such organizations may operate as much by transformation as by selection (Hannan and Freeman, 1989: 81).

Mortality is often the fate of new organizations which fail to become formally organized and delegate responsibility as the organization grows larger. There is some critical organizational size in which the failure of leaders to delegate is fatal to the organization. Although that critical size varies by the form of organization and its age, the failure to delegate power in growing or large organizations inevitably limits the viability of the organization.

Usually, organizational mortality rates decline with age and size. Older and larger organizations fail less often since large organizations can often buffer themselves against effects of environmental change (Hannan and Freeman, 1989: 88). Generally, a high-rate of organizational attrition is associated with new organizations. Freeman (1990) points out that organizations which are already established have specific administrative advantages over newly-formed organizations. In new organizations, members must learn their roles and the organization's formal structure must be developed, a process which can only occur over time. If the new organization, however, contains veterans of other organizations, including failed organizations, these individuals can help socialize new members. Organizational mortality may be accelerated with the loss of an organization's founder or key members of the group during its early stages of formation or when the organization is undertaking new venture (Kimberly, Miles and Associates, 1980: 433).

Conclusion

This section has discussed the concept of organizational life cycles – developmental stages through which all organizations proceed – and the notion of organizational population. The parameters of the population are determined by the set of organizations, available resources, and the relevant stages of organizations in their life cycle. These two concepts are central to understanding the concept of organizational proliferation. Organizations proliferate, that is, the specific population becomes more dense or these organizations become larger – increasing organizational mass – when there are sufficient resources to make the organizational form and size efficient. New organizations tend to imitate the successful organizational form that comprises the population, creating a pull towards an equilibrium number of organizations of a similar size. What is the applicability of these concepts to gangs? The next section addresses the key linkages between gangs and organizational theory.

BUT ARE GANGS ORGANIZATIONS?

Gangs are typically considered as groups or informal organizations rather than formal organizations. But do contemporary gangs – or some of them – meet the definitional criteria of organizations? Since there are different kinds or types of gangs, this section examines the distinctive and defining characteristics of gangs and compares these basic features with those of formal organizations, informal organizations and groups. Just as there are different types of gangs, there are also different types of organizations. Although the bureaucratic form of formal organization is the most common and well-known, it is not the sole type of formal organization. Indeed, there is strong evidence that the forms of organizations which emerge are those which are uniquely suited to the existing organizational environment. Thus, distinctive organizational models are described in this section to illuminate the distinctions and similarities between different types of gangs and different types of organizations.

Defining a Gang

Efforts to establish a uniform definition of a gang suffer from a major dilemma – lack of consensus. "At no time, has there been anything close to consensus on what a gang might be – by scholars, by criminal justice workers, by the general public" (Miller, 1981). The large and growing numbers of gangs and an apparent wide variation between gangs from one region and city to another, and even within cities, suggests a difficult task in taming the definitional beast.

The term "gang," currently so widespread in its usage, was originally used to describe bands of outlaws in the settling of the western United States who engaged in robbing stages, banks and saloons; by the early 1920s and '30s, the term gang was used to describe the criminal groups that are currently known as organized crime (Jankowski, 1991: 2-4). Only later was the term gang was used to describe groups of delinquent youths, particularly those whom most Americans were exposed to with the film West Side Story.

Despite increased gang research for the last decade, there is still no consensus on gang definition and hence no standardized terminology (Esbensen et al, 2001; Pennell et al, 1994; Curry, Ball and Fox, 1994; Ball and Curry, 1995; Spergel, 1990; Miller, 1981; Decker and Kempf-

Leonard, 1995; Bursik and Grasmick, 1993, 1996). Conly (1994) suggests that the term gang is a meaningless label imposed on youth by adults. Horowitz (1990) suggests that the term remain locally defined in order to avoid unnecessarily limiting research on these types of groups.

Klein's (1971: 13) is perhaps the mostly widely used definition of gangs:

> Any denotable adolescent group of youngsters who (a) are generally perceived as a distinct aggregation by others in their neighborhood, (b) recognize themselves as a denotable group (almost always with a group name), and (c) have been involved in a sufficient number of delinquent incidents to call forth a consistent negative response from neighborhood residents and/or law enforcement agencies.

Miller's (1981) definition also is widely cited:

> A self-formed association of peers, bound together by mutual interest, with identifiable leadership, well-developed lines of authority, and other organizational features, who act in concert to achieve a specific purpose or purposes which generally include the conduct of illegal activity and control over a particular territory or type of enterprise.

Gang definitions are also complicated by a pull toward tautology (Ball and Curry, 1995; Bursik and Grasmick, 1995). Inclusion of criminal activity as a distinctive feature in distinguishing groups from gangs is circular logic that does not advance our understanding of gangs. "Using delinquent behavior as a criterion makes a possible outcome of gang activity one of the defining characteristics" (Bursik and Grasmick, 1995). But crime is often included in definitions of gang. Spergel (1990), for example, identifies continued participation in crime as preeminent characteristic of gang involvement.

Spergel (1990), distinguishing between gangs and groups of delinquent youth, noted that groups should be considered gangs "when they maintain a high profile, and engage in serious violence and crime, and when their primary reason for existence is symbolic or communal rather than economic" (p. 260). By inference, Spergel suggests that gangs with economic motivations are more closely akin to organized crime; he suggested that gangs significantly engaged in drug trafficking should not be considered gangs at all. Klein (1995) concurs.

Problems in defining gangs are compounded by what are viewed as relatively recent changes in the organization and activities of many gangs, suggested a wider range of organizational structures and a broadened range of gang activities, both legal and illegal. And research of the last decade, although limited, has identified significant differences between in individual gangs across and within cities and states, creating a consensus that gangs are diverse (Weisel and Painter, 1997; Cohen, 1990; Snyder and Sickmund, 1995; Huff, 1990; Fagan, 1990; Hagedorn, 1990). Since formulation of a meaningful definition of gangs involves specification of commonality, wide dissimilarity between entities commonly known as gangs suggests continuing difficulty in building definitional consensus. Ball and Curry (1995: 240) recommend a heuristic approach producing the following:

> The gang is a spontaneous, semisecret, interstitial, integrated but mutable social system whose members share common interests and that functions with relatively little regard for legality but regulates interaction among its members and features a leadership structure with processes of organizational maintenance and membership services and adaptive mechanism for dealing with other significant social systems in its environment.

Such a cumbersome definition is unlikely to have much practical value for either documentation of gangs, necessary for measuring growth, nor will it clarify discussion and debate about alternative features of contemporary gangs.

Kinds of Gangs

Defining "a gang" is complicated by the recognition that there are varying forms of gangs in the nation. Categorizing of different types of gangs has occurred since the earliest gang studies, and in some ways serves to accommodate the absence of a consensual definition. As early as 1927, Thrasher (1963) recognized varieties of gangs, including diffuse types, solidified types, conventionalized and criminal types.

Typing or classification of gangs generally is based upon the activities in which various gangs participate or, "closely related, the purpose (of the gang), its organizational structure or level of criminality" (Goldstein, 1991). The accuracy of some of these typologies, for example, relating to the type of criminal behavior in which specific gangs participate, is clouded by evidence indicating that gangs as organizations – and individuals within the gang – have great criminal versatility and do not specialize[c] in specific types of crime (Klein and Maxson, 1989; Weisel, Decker and Bynum, 1997; Farrington et al, 1988; Rankin and Wells, 1985; Gottfredson and Hirschi, 1990; Miller, 1972).

Cloward and Ohlin (1960) identified three types of gangs – criminal, violent and retreatist. Criminal gangs were recruiting grounds for adult criminal organizations; violent gangs existed in unstable slum areas; and retreatist gangs were drug-using youths who engaged in criminal activity for sport.

Yablonsky (1962) discussed three types of gangs as including social, delinquent and violent, with violent gangs constituting the primary problems for local law enforcement agencies. Miller (1981) categorized youth gangs as turf, fighting or gain-oriented; fighting, entrepreneurial and social were gang styles observed by others, according to Fagan (1990). Jankowksi (1991) observed three varieties of gang organization. He found that gangs were organized by vertical hierarchy, with clear patterns of authority and power; by horizontal "commission" with relatively equal roles among gang members; and influential, albeit informal, leadership roles. Klein (1995) classified gangs as either spontaneous or traditional; Rosenbaum (1983) described gangs as fighting or moneymaking.

Taylor (1990a, 1990b) characterized gangs as having either scavenger, territorial or corporate motivations. Scavengers engage in petty crime with gratuitous violence; territorial gangs identify specific areas which define their turf and engage in protective behaviors; organized or corporatist gangs have strong leaders and focus on illegal money-making ventures. Crimes, among this latter category, are serious and are committed for a purpose.

Huff (1989) classified gangs in the following manner: Informal or hedonistic gangs use drugs and engage only in minor property crime; instrumental gangs focus on concerns of economic issues and engage in more property crime, selling some drugs but not as an organized gang activity; predatory gangs commit robberies, muggings and other crimes, use addictive drugs, and often sell drugs to finance gun purchases, especially automatic weapons. He noted that predatory gangs "represent a ready-made 'target of exploitation' for organized crime" (p. 529).

Skolnick (n.d.) and Skolnick, Bluthenthal and Correl (1993) differentiate between cultural gangs and opportunistic gangs. Cultural gangs are traditional gangs, strongly grounded in neighborhood identity which may be involved with crime and drugs. These gangs have strong values of loyalty to the gang and the neighborhood; the gang is considered a tightly knit primary group or an extended family. In contrast, opportunistic gangs are organized primarily for the purpose of distributing drugs. They are considered organizations and operate as business organizations primarily to engage in criminal activities. The opportunistic gangs are also called "instrumental" or entrepreneurial gangs because loyalty of membership depends on the opportunities offered by leaders, such as a drug source connection. The organization is motivated by profits and market control, often of a specific area. The financial goals of this gang predominate; entry and loyalty of individuals to the gang is related to economic reasons.

Fagan (1989) studied gangs extensively, looking explicitly at participation by gangs in criminal activity and drugs. He grouped gangs as being party gangs, engaged in few nondrug criminal behaviors except vandalism; social gangs, which engaged in few delinquent activities; delinquent gangs , which engaged in violent and property crime although few drug sales; and organized gangs, the latter group getting extensively involved in the sale and use of drugs along with predatory crime.

With the exception of Fagan's (1989) study, little is known about the relative composition of gang types relative to the population of gangs. Fagan studied the four gang types in three cities. Social gangs accounted for 28 percent of the gangs; party gangs, accounted for 7 percent; serious delinquents constituted 37 percent; and "organization" gangs represented 28 percent of all gangs. But these proportions varied from one city to another. In the three cities, Chicago gangs were predominately serious delinquents and organized gangs; Los Angeles gangs were more social (38 percent) and serious delinquents (36 percent) while San Diego gangs consisted of more serious delinquents (39 percent) and organized gangs (31 percent). These variations in gang-type composition between cities is suggestive of great diversity in the types of gangs that can be observed in the rest of the nation, regardless of the typology employed to classify gangs.

The absence of consensus on gang definition and the verification of a wide range of "types" of gangs makes operationalizing the term "gang" quite difficult. Do gangs qualify as organizations? Do some gangs qualify as organizations? Or should gangs more appropriately be considered as groups?

Defining an Organization

To determine the appropriateness of labeling a gang as a group or an organization requires examining the definitional criteria for both entities. What is an organization? What is a group? And how are organizations distinguished from groups? Organizations, by definition, are social systems. A social system, according to Katz and Kahn (1966), "is a structuring of events or happenings rather than of physical parts and it therefore has no structure apart from its functioning" (p. 31). Blau and Scott (1962) further distinguish social organizations, which emerge spontaneously among people, from formal organizations, which are established deliberately.

The defining feature of organizations is the primacy of their orientation to goals (Parsons, 1987; Weber, 1947; Blau and Scott, 1962; Katz and Kahn, 1966; Lippitt, 1982; and others). Parsons (1987) considers that an organization is a social system that focuses on the attainment of specific goals and contributes, in turn, to the accomplishment of goals of a more comprehensive system, such as the larger society. Weber (1964: 151) stated that "An organization is a system of continuous purposeful activity of a specified kind"; Blau and Scott (1962) define the organization as a social unit "established for the explicit purpose of achieving certain goals" (p. 1). Stinchcombe (1965) defined the organization as "a set of stable social relations deliberately created, with the explicit intention of continuously accomplishing some specific goals or purposes" (p. 142).

In addition to goal orientation, these definitions suggest that formation of an organization is intentional and purposeful, there is some process of continuity within the organization, and that goal orientation consists of a collective effort or coordination of some activity directed at achieving the goal.

Blau and Scott (1962) point out that social organization emerges as a natural consequence of people living together; in contrast, formal organizations have been deliberately established for a certain purpose:

> If the accomplishment of an objective requires collective effort, men set up an organization designed to coordinate the activities of many persons and to furnish incentives for others to join them for this purpose...Since the distinctive characteristics of these organizations is that they have been formally established for the explicit purpose of achieving certain goals, the term 'formal organization' is used to designate them (p. 5).

In addition to these basic definitional elements of the organization, other theorists are more detailed and include additional traits. For example, Daft (1986) specifies that "organizations are social entities that are goal-directed, deliberately structured activity systems with an identifiable boundary" (p. 9). The latter element – boundaries – emphasizes the distinctiveness of membership of an organization and differentiation of the organization from the larger community. Jackson, Morgan and Paolillo (1986: 2) add that:

> Organizations ...have distinct structures; they have rules, organizational norms, and cultures that have developed over time; they have life cycles of their own that go beyond the lives of individuals; and they have goals, policies, procedures, and practices.

Organizational theorists have invested a great deal of effort to distinguish between the organization and group. Typically, definitions of group are absent the purposeful goal orientation and reflect more informal operations than do organizations. But it is important to recognize two critical phenomena that link groups and organizations: First, organizations typically include groups and organizations can evolve from groups. These two phenomena often blur the distinctions between the two organizational forms.

Most theorists recognize that organizations are comprised of groups. Lippitt (1982) stated that organizations are simply systems of overlapping groups. He distinguishes groups as subsystems of the organization:

> An organization is usually comprised of two or more groups having a more or less common reason for working together, although an organization can at any time consist of only a single group (p. 34).

These groups within the organization – but independent of the structure of the larger organization – are also known as peer groups (Blau and Scott, 1962); autonomous groups (Whyte, 1969); and informal organizations (Vasu, Stewart and Garson, 1990). The informal organization has an important role within the formal organization for it serves to enhance communication between individual members, generate cohesiveness by contributing to team spirit, and provides a form of support between members, enhancing their self-respect.

According to Meyer and Rowan (1992), researchers have long recognized the distinctions between the formal operations of an organization – as represented by an organizational chart, rules, formalized procedures and articulated goals – and the informal organization or group which is responsible for carrying out the day-to-day operations of an organization: "Structural elements are only loosely linked to each other and to activities, rules are often violated, decisions are often unimplemented..." (p. 24). But Schein (1989) suggests that informal groups often serve both the needs of the individual and the larger, formal organization of which groups are part. Members may join a group to achieve outlets for affiliation needs; as a means of developing or maintaining self-esteem; or to increase security and cope with a common threat. Hechter (1987) adds that cohesion develops between group members and norms are established to provide standards for behavior within the group.

Regarding the evolution of groups into organizations, theorists suggest that groups can become formalized into organization. Whyte (1969) stated that over time, when three or more individuals interact, "the group tends to develop a structure" (p. 201). Blau and Scott (1962) point out that as groups become larger and seek to accomplish more complex tasks, there are increasing pressures to become explicitly organized: "Once a group of boys who merely used to hang around a drugstore decide to participate in the local baseball league, they must organize a team" (p. 7). Since organizations do not spring forth in a mature form, this logical understanding of the relationship between organizations and groups suggests a sequential process related to time and size.

In contrast to the definition of the formal organization, a group is typically defined in a simpler way. Berne (1966) defines the group as "...Any social aggregation that has an external boundary and at least one internal boundary" (54-55). This definition suggests that a group need only distinguish between members and non-members and contain at least two levels – leadership and membership. While Berne claimed there is no need to distinguish between organization and group, his definition does not contain the threshold motivation of the organization toward a specific purpose.

Other definitions of groups are also absent goal orientation. Goldstein (1991) lists definitions as including the following: "two or more people who share a common social identification of themselves"; "a collection of people who experience their collective existence as reinforcing"; "two or more individuals sharing a common fate"; and, "a set of persons who interact with one another in such a way that each influences and is influenced by every other person" (p. 78).

These definitions and others imply that size is a defining feature of groups since a group consists of any number of individuals who interact with each other and perceive themselves to be a group (Whyte, 1969; Schein, 1989). In this rather consistent view, the size of the group becomes a delimiting factor because its membership can be observed through frequency of interaction between individuals. In large organizations, individuals cannot routinely interact and be aware of each other. But groups must be large enough to include at least two or three members. In other words, groups have minimum and maximum size requirements: there must be at least two members and the group must be small enough to allow for routine face-to-face interaction.

In contrast to organizations, groups may not be intentionally organized to achieve goals however groups do form around affiliation needs such as friendship and support (Schein, 1989), around common or mutual interests, to pursue common objectives and may offer group membership incentives such as sharing of collective goods (Hechter, 1987). Blau and Scott, for example, characterize as a formal organization recurrent fishing trips carried out in nonliterate tribes

(1962: 224). Although the objectives of such an organization are rudimentary, formally established procedures are required to accomplish the tasks.

The establishment of formal procedures to accomplish objectives typically refers to the articulation of both rules and roles. Both organizations and groups are influenced by norms and values, reflecting the subculture of members, and structure and roles. Rules and roles are defined differently for small groups than in larger, formal organizations. (Lippitt, 1982: 35). Within a small group, roles are often interchangeable and there is usually no sharp distinction between different roles. People in specific roles can move into and out of specific roles with ease and their behavior is easily observed by other members of the group. In the formal organization, roles usually are not interchangeable since they are distinguished for purposes of efficiency and role assignments contribute to organizational stability albeit at the cost of organizational flexibility.

To carry out explicit goals, formal organizations are required to have "explicit rules and regulations, and a formal status structure with clearly marked lines of communication and authority," according to Blau and Scott (1962: 14). Starbuck (1965) agrees that organizational commitment to achieving goals requires "explicit and stable structure of task allocations, roles and responsibilities" (p. 452). This requirement, according to Starbuck, "excludes mobs and informal social groups as organizations and permits social and service clubs, like Rotary and Kiwanis, [to be considered as] organizations only part of the time."

Despite the centrality of goals as a defining feature of organizations, organizational theorists recognize that goals are not always clearly discernible. Most organizations "substitute some type of covert goal for the publicly stated goals. That is, they all realize that what the organization tells the world it is trying to do may differ from what it is really trying to do. This may be because the organization has a hidden agenda of goals that it cannot legitimate in the broader society or because covert goals are developed through machinations of the dominant management group" (Freeman, 1990: 26). According to Freeman, numerous researchers "step back from the usual functionalist argument that organizations are structured so as to maximize the attainment of explicit goals." There is a well-developed body of literature which supports the idea that the objectives of organizations are "often ambiguous, fluid, multiple, conflicting, and only loosely coupled with the action of the organization" (Popielarz and McPherson, 1995; Scott, 1993).

Lippitt (1982) suggests that every subsystem has certain goals toward which its behavior is directed. The conscious or unconscious perception of these goals may range from clear to vague. They may be short range or long range, fixed or flexible, explicit or implicit. In formal organizations, goals are the rationally contrived purposed of the organizational entity.

Kinds of Organizations

Just as there are different types of gangs, there are different types or forms of organizations. Two organizational models are commonly discussed, however, the focus on one – the bureaucratic model – is discussed so prominently that its features seem ubiquitous in descriptions of organizations. However, another model – the organic model – is increasingly used to describe the form of contemporary organizations.[d]

Bureaucracy

Among organizational theorists, the concept of bureaucracy is a classical theory, descriptive of a fundamental organizational form. Much of the vast literature on organizational theory thus relates to characteristics of bureaucracies. Weber (1947) studied bureaucratic organizations, which he identified by characteristics such as specialization, division of labor, formal hierarchy, written rules, and so forth. Importantly, Weber viewed these bureaucratic characteristics as a means to identify the primary distinctions between organizations; he did not advocate these characteristics be pursued as normative goals. Instead, they represented an ideal-type of highly-developed organization and were not a depiction of reality (Shafritz and Ott, 1987; Weber, 1947; Weiss, 1983). Nonetheless, bureaucracies erroneously came to be seen as models of efficiency; rational control and decision making were viewed as the foundation for these organizations.

Weber's views of bureaucracy were related to those of earlier theorists who advocated the principles of scientific management, which viewed organizations as machines (Durkheim, 1933; Fayol, 1949; Taylor, 1911) – maximizing efficiency in order to achieve organizational goals. The concept of organizations as machines was advanced through Frederick Taylor's work on "scientific management principles," which inferred that there is a single best method of reaching organizational goals.

> Workers were not viewed as individuals but as interchangeable parts in an industrial machine whose parts were made of flesh only when it was impractical to make them of steel ... Organizations, it was thought, should work like machines, using people, capital, and machines as their parts (Shafritz and Ott, 1987: 21).

Burns and Stalker (1961) described organizations in stable environments as mechanistic: these organizations were formalized, centralized, characterized by a proliferation of rules and a clear hierarchy, consistent with the seven characteristics of bureaucratic organizations described by Weber: presence of rules and standard operating procedures to regulate work; clear division of labor; hierarchy of authority; professionalism and technical competence of staff members; separation of ownership from production and administration to maintain impersonal efficiency and formal conduct, insuring that employment and promotion occur on the basis of performance and competency; objectivity and task-oriented management; administrative records are maintained (1947: 330-340).

A brief explanation of these dimensions is necessary for understanding their value in describing organizations.

The notion of formalization refers to the extent to which employees or members of the organization are controlled by specific rules. Usually these rules are written down in formal organizations, however, the degree with which an organization's members comply with the rules is variable. Often the level of formalization may be inferred by the sheer volume or number of pages of written rules: the thicker the pile, the more highly formalized the organization.

The term division of labor refers to the amount of specialization in an organization. Do group members perform only a single activity or a narrow range of tasks in their jobs? Organizations which are highly specialized have their members perform only a single or perhaps a few discrete tasks. Organizations reflect various levels of hierarchy of authority. This concept is also referred to as span of control, scalar chain or chain of command. When a span of control is wide, the hierarchy is shorter and individuals have greater autonomy; when span of control is narrow or limited, the organization will have a steeply vertical hierarchy. The notion of centralization also reflects the degree of autonomy people have within the organization. If decision making is the province of only a few people at the top of the organization, the organization is considered highly centralized. Personnel configuration refers to the division of organizational activity by types of groups. For example, the administrative ratio of an organization (in comparison to professional or other staff) is an important dimension of organizations. As with complexity, organizations tend to develop larger administrative ratios as they grow larger, creating a need for keeping administrative records and information (Weber, 1947; Blau and Scott, 1962; Daft, 1986; Shafritz and Ott, 1987; Vasu, Stewart and Garson, 1990). Typically, bureaucratic forms of organization measure high on each of these dimensions – many rules, specialized labor, steep hierarchy, concentrated leadership, and high administrative ratios.

In recent years, bureaucracy has come under widespread criticism for its inefficiency, inability to adapt to changing conditions, and impersonal approach to employees and clients. Heckscher (1994) believes the most central failure of the bureaucracy is role specialization, such that people are only responsible for their own jobs in the organization. This specialization wastes the intelligence of individuals, serves to artificially separate the formal organization from the informal organization, and limits the adaptability of the organization to changes in its environment. Bennis (1993) attributes the demise of bureaucratic organizations to their inability to mediate between the inherent conflict between individual and management goals, so that the needs of both are satisfied. "Organizations...are hardly mechanical devices. They are owned, designed and managed by people. As such, they possess most of the limitations and potential that people have. Organizations are fluid and dynamic: they move in time and in space; they act and react" (Kimberly, Miles and Associates, 1980). Blau and Scott (1962) point out that "it became evident that scientific management's conception of workers as rational machines could not adequately account for their behavior..."(p. 87). Other researchers point out that the bureaucratic or mechanistic model is dysfunctional because of its procedures "designed to control the activities of organization members" (March and Simon, 1978: 146-147).

Despite widespread criticism, much of the lore of bureaucracy remains intact and organizational analyses are predominately concerned with measurement of organizations on the bureaucratic dimensions.

Organic Model of Organizations

By the early 1960s, Burns and Stalker (1961), Bennis (1993, originally published in 1966) and Argyris (1977) were predicting that radically new forms of organization would replace traditional hierarchical organizations. "Tomorrow's organizations will be federations, networks, clusters, cross-functional teams, lattices, modules, matrices, almost anything but pyramids," prophesied Bennis, in predicting the demise of the hierarchy. Burns and Stalker described the characteristics of the organic form of organization: team-based, flexible and less rule-bound than the mechanical hierarchy. In contrast to bureaucratic or mechanistic organizations, organizations which are oriented to change feature different organizational structures. Organic organizations reflect low levels of formalization, specialization, standardization, hierarchy and centralization. Generally, these organizations may be relatively small or relatively new, use new technologies, have multiple goals and be responsive or open to a volatile, changing external environment.

No consensus has developed on a name for the form of organization which is largely antithetical to bureaucracy – the organic or adaptive organization. This form of organization has been variously called a negotiated order or federation (Munch, 1986), loosely-coupled system (Pfeffer and Salancik, 1977; Orton and Weick, 1990), temporary systems, organic-adaptive organization (Bennis, 1993 originally published in 1966), coalition or external model (Pfeffer and Salancik, 1977), post-bureaucratic (Heckscher and Donnellon, 1994), colleague model (Argyris, 1973); interactive organization (Heckscher, 1994), network form (Powell, 1990), blended (Ouchi and Jaeger, 1978) and open organization (Mink et al, 1994) among other terms. Generally, these organic models are differentiated from market models, the latter which are usually formed deliberately within traditional hierarchies; "cleaned" bureaucracies which may feature empowerment of employees and flattening of organizational layers but do not change the basic nature of the organization; nor the "closed community" analogous to the Japanese approach to management with an emphasis on values and loyalty to a leader.

The absence of a consensus term for the organic-adaptive organization conforms with the general absence of this form of organization in the contemporary organizational population. Heckscher and Donnellson (1994) explain that, despite major advances toward this form of organization, there is not a single ideal example of a non-bureaucratic structure. Some organizations which come close to the non-bureaucratic form are Saturn automotive company and Apple Computer. And numerous organizations have moved in the direction of the non-bureaucratic organization, by flattening their hierarchy and developing a more interactive model of organization. Despite its scarcity in the existing population of organizations, the organic-adaptive organization is no idiosyncrasy; organizational forms simply do not spring forth in a mature or widespread form. The bureaucratic form of organization, for example, developed circa the Civil War, was generalized in the 1920s and only perfected in the 1950s. A similar pattern of development and expansion of the organic-adaptive organizational form may be anticipated over time.

The ideal form of the organic-adaptive organization is built around the concept that everyone takes responsibility for the success of the organization. Decision making occurs through informed consensus rather than a reliance on hierarchy and authority; decisions occur through the ability to influence and persuade rather than command. As such, these decisions are based on trust relationships rather than the authority and power relationships present within the hierarchy. Because influence-relationships are relatively fluid in the organization, the processes through which decisions are made must frequently be reconstructed (Heckscher, 1994).

Argyris (1973) adds that organizations of the future must reverse several properties of the modern pyramid of the bureaucracy – specialization of work, centralization of power and centralization of information, inherently increasing people's opportunity for self-control. As a consequence, the organic adaptive organization operates in accordance with an emphasis on mission, which is supplemented by guiding principles. In contrast to the impersonal rules of a hierarchy, the principles of the organic-adaptive organization are more abstract and can be considered as "consensual legitimation" (Heckscher, 1994) rather than canons or decrees.

The relative volatility or stability of the organizational environment in which organizations operate is probably the most important determinant of the resultant organizational form. There is widespread agreement among organizational theorists that organizations operating successfully in volatile environments are more likely to be adaptive – volatile environments typically select against a bureaucratic or hierarchical organization (Freeman, 1990; Hannan and Freeman, 1978: Meyer, 1978; Daft, 1986; Kimberly, Miles and Associates, 1980; Staw and Cummings, 1990; Lawrence and Lorsch, 1967; Heckscher, 1994; Powell, 1990).

Hannan and Freeman (1978) point out:

> When the certainty of a given environmental state is high, organizational operations should be routine, and coordination can be accomplished by formalized rules and the investment in training incumbents to follow those formalized procedures... When certainty is low, organizational operations are less routine...optimal organizational forms will allocate resources to less formalized systems capable of more innovative responses (154-155).

Since processes of natural selection increase the chances of survival for the form of organization most suited to the environment, an examination of the organization's environment provides important clues about the organization, including its structure and operations. Every organization has a different environment, consisting of all elements outside the organization. The environment includes all other organizations, including like-minded competitors and similarly-sized competitors. Other elements of an organization's environment include its field of operations or industry, customers, suppliers, resources, financial organizations and government organizations. Situations such as economic conditions, civil unrest, weather such as floods or drought constitute an important part of an organization's environment. Any element outside the organization that could affect the organization is considered the organizational environment.

Applying the principles of nature selection, organizations which are adaptive to their environment thrive, while maladaptive organizations that are not responsive to the external environment enter a period of decline (Kimberly, Miles and Associates, 1980; Staw and

Cummings, 1990). Blau and Scott (1962) note that "the concept of dilemma" enhances an understanding of adaptation or "internally generated processes of change in a social organization....Change does not occur unless new external conditions require adjustments" (p. 222). As an important element of the environment, competition (Hawley, 1950; Durkheim, 1933) is a significant determinant on patterns of organization. Hawley suggests that competitors become similar as competition brings forth a uniform response, selection eliminates weakest competitors, and deposed competitors differentiate territorially or functionally, often producing a more complex division of labor.

While adaptation to the external environment occurs to some extent in all organizations, Hannan and Freeman (1978, 1989) note that some of the relationship between structure and environment reflects adaptive learning. Different types of organizations operate in different types of environments; organizations can only adapt so much and so quickly. Organizations with investments in capital equipment and specialized personnel constrain their ability to adapt to environmental changes. Some populations of organizations are structured not to respond quickly to volatile environments, while others, which face long-term volatility, must necessarily be composed of generalist personnel who can adapt quickly. Specialization among personnel may sustain an organization facing short-term volatility, but will not be useful in a continuously volatile environment. Conventional wisdom suggests that in uncertain environments, processes of natural selection favor generalists over specialists (Katz and Kahn, 1966).

Thus, in a stable environment, bureaucracies are a common organizational form, implying highly standardized work or activity processes, with high levels of specialization and steep hierarchical structures. These features are suggestive of older and larger organizations (Daft, 1986). In a volatile or variable environment, adaptive organizations are favored. This form is suggestive of flexible organizational structures, few rules, little hierarchy – generally a more committee- or team-oriented organizational structure. Organizations that both emerge and survive in these variable environments are more likely to maintain multi-purpose and flexible organizational structures, with little differentiation between the roles of members and flexible leadership (Meyer, 1978).

Do Gangs Meet Definitional Requirements as Organizations?

In classic literature, gangs have been widely viewed as groups or informal organizations, variously described as play groups (Thrasher, 1963), groups (Goldstein, 1991), pseudo groups (Horowitz, 1983), near groups (Yablonsky, 1962), collectivities (Cohen, 1990), deviant peer groups (Fagan, 1990) and law-violating youth groups (Miller, 1980); occasionally as enterprise organizations (Padilla, 1993a; 1993b), moneymaking groups (Rosenbaum, 1983) or corporate entities (Taylor, 1990a, 1990b).

So, do gangs meet the basic definitional criteria as "organizations"? A reading of current gang literature suggests that most gang researchers would not consider gangs as organizations, primarily based upon two grounds. First, most gangs appear to lack or have a very weak orientation toward achieving goals and, secondly, most gangs appear to lack or have a very loose hierarchical structure, have unstable leadership, few rules and little role specialization.

Regarding goal orientation, Klein (1995) stated that gang members don't typically focus on group goals there are individual needs which take priority:

> Gangs are not committees, ball teams, task forces, production teams, or research teams. The members are drawn to one another to fulfil individual needs, many shared and some conflicting: they do not gather to achieve a common, agreed-upon end (Klein, 1995: 80).

Klein noted that group rewards are an important individual motivation for joining a gang. These group rewards include status, companionship, excitement and protection; among individual motivations, gang members routinely join for a sense of "belonging" or of family. And material rewards associated with group crime are also a factor in gang membership. "The excitement and loot that accompanies crime are certainly added incentives for many" (Klein, 1995: 79). Klein's "loot," however, may qualify the gang as goal-oriented. In fact, his description of the purposes of the gang – the group rewards – is similar to the description by Blau and Scott (1962) of the informal organizations which are omnipresent within formal organizations. As discussed previously, organizational theory suggests that individual and organizational goals are coexistent and, in adaptive organizations, these goals are integrated. Since we know, too, that groups comprise organizations, group members should be expected to have mutual interests and affiliation needs played out in the organization. And since groups may evolve into organizations – responding to pressures to organize as the group increases in size – the reasons of members for joining the gang may differ from the goals of the organization.

Gangs are also dismissed as failing to meet the definitional criteria for organizations because they are loosely organized (Decker, 1996; Klein and Maxson, 1994; Klein, 1995; Goldstein and Huff, 1993; and others). Such references to loose organization typically refer to measurements of gang hierarchy, leadership, rules and role specialization – organizational characteristics which are hallmarks of the bureaucratic form of organization. But bureaucratic forms of organization, despite being widespread and well known, are not the sole form of formal organization and, as discussed previously, have come into disrepute for their tendency to be inefficient and nonresponsive to the environment in which they operate. In fact, highly volatile environments appear to select against bureaucratic forms of organization, favoring organizations that are more adaptive or organic. Since evidence suggests that gangs are proliferating and have rising continuity in the midst of an apparently volatile environment – typified by numerous other gangs, and aggressive police and institutional responses – gangs must either be adapting to changing conditions or favorably selected because they have organizational characteristics which increase their chances of survival under prevailing conditions. Rules, labor specialization, and hierarchical leadership are organizational features that would limit such adaptation.

In contrast to most gang research, a few gang researchers suggest that some gangs are highly similar to bureaucratic organizations. Jankowski (1991) argues that contemporary gangs are organizations, largely conforming to the definitional requirements of Weber's ideal model of bureaucratic organization, except that gangs do not contain an administrative component (p. 29), a definitional requirement of a bureaucratic organization. Best and Luckinbill (1994) classify some sophisticated street gangs as formal organizations. Knox (1994) said gangs are social organizations and that at least some gangs are formal organizations, pointing out that the problem is that gangs "are more than a small group and less than a bureaucracy" (p. 233). In addition to

Jankowski, (1991), Taylor (1990a, 1990b) and Padilla (1993a, 1993b) make the strongest case for organization-gangs although the methods of each of these authors have been questioned by Klein (1995: 133-135).

In contrast to legitimate formal organizations, Best and Luckinbill (1994) describe deviant formal organizations – the most sophisticated form of deviant organization among a continuum of deviant organizations – noting that these organizations are intentionally organized to seek specific goals. However, these "deviant formal organizations are less elaborately organized than their respectable counterparts" (p. 53; and Miller, 1981) and are typically much smaller than legitimate formal organizations. Rather than sharing the formal organizational structure of legitimate organizations, deviant formal organizations share the "quality of being intentionally organized." Because these deviant formal organizations are larger than other social organizations of deviants – note again that size is a distinguishing feature – a "deliberately designed structure" is necessary. The authors categorize large street gangs, some drug networks and organized crime families as deviant formal organizations.

Consideration of gangs as organizations suggests comparisons to traditional organized crime. Discussion of the extent of organization present within contemporary gangs implicitly contrasts gangs with views of organized crime. In fact, classical sociologists viewed gangs as a stepping stone to organized crime, with organized crime groups recruiting youth from street gangs (Cloward and Ohlin, 1960). Thrasher (1927) recognized that the distinctions between gangs and organized crime were illusory: There is "no hard and fast dividing line between predatory gang boys and criminal groups of younger and older adults. They merge into each other by imperceptible gradations, and the later have their real explanations for the most part in the former" (p. 281).

But organized crime is not nearly so organized as is popularly believed. Almost every contemporary academic article about organized crime begins with a disclaimer about the mystique of the Mafia, refuting the popularized and exaggerated of highly organized and sophisticated crime network known as La Cosa Nostra (LCN) or the Mafia. Current thinking largely discredits the "Mafia myth," an image created by the work of Cressey (1969) and Salerno (1969), in favor of a view of organized crime as more diverse, less structured and more ethnically varied. This contemporary, broadened view of organized crime constitutes the prevailing organized crime paradigm. Notably, there is also some movement to further broaden the concept of organized crime to include what is often referred to as evolving (Kenney and Finckenauer, 1995), emerging (Lupsha, 1991), new gangs (Goldstein and Huff, 1993) or nontraditional (GAO, 1989; Huff, 1990) organized crime groups, such as Asian, Latin American and other groups, particularly those heavily involved in international drug trafficking.

Similar to the definitional quandary in defining gangs, there is no standardized definition of organized crime (Hagan, 1983; Lupsha, 1986, 1991; Reuter, 1983; Ianni, 1972; Albini, 1971; Maltz, 1985; Kenney and Finckenauer, 1995; Caiden and Alexander, 1985; Block, 1990, 1991; Potter, 1994; Abadinsky, 1987, 1990). Definitions range from the broad and tautological (organized crime is crime that is organized – Bynum, 1987) to narrow views as representing crime related to the 24 Italian-based families of the historic Mafia (Cressey, 1969). Hence, "social scientists have struggled for decades with the problem of defining organized crime, assessing its impact on society and determining the structure of individual organized crime groups" (Dombrink, 1988: 58)

Typically, definitions of organized crime incorporate views of the organizational structure of these criminal enterprises (i.e., hierarchical or decentralized), organizational features such as role specialization or versatility, goal orientation such as profit making through illegal activities, and evidence of durability such that the enterprise continues to operate regardless of changes in personnel (Hagan, 1983; Lupsha, 1986, 1991; Reuter, 1983; Ianni, 1972; Albini, 1971; Maltz, 1985; Kenney and Finckenauer, 1995; Caiden and Alexander, 1985; Block, 1990, 1991; Potter, 1994; Abadinsky, 1987, 1990; Goodson and Olson, 1995). Although the positions on the extent of these organizational dimensions vary considerably, since some researchers view organized crime as loosely organized (Potter, 1994) while others (Abadinsky, 1990; Lupsha, 1991; Reuter, 1983; Maltz, 1985; Kenney and Finckenauer, 1995) consider hierarchy as a defining characteristic of organized crime. The wide range of views of the extent of organization present within organized crime are very similar to the debate about organization within contemporary gangs.

As with organized crime, there are widespread differences of opinion about the extent of formal organization present within contemporary gangs. Most gang authors concur that gangs are widely varied along classification bases such as purpose, activity, and organization (Goldstein, 1991). These classification schemes typically array various gangs along some type of continuum, such that at least some gangs are more structured, more involved in criminal activity, more purposeful, more durable – hence more organized than other gangs. The proportion of contemporary gangs that may be considered as "more organized" is, of course, subject to discussion and may reflect only a small percentage of gangs. But these "more organized" gangs do exist; and organizational theory suggests that these gangs did not spring up overnight but evolved from smaller, less organized structures. Deductively, one can conclude that these "more organized" gangs – typically larger and gangs of greater longevity – have been subject to the effects of organizational dynamics and processes. Even Klein (1995) acknowledges that gangs which are more highly structured and organized are typically larger gangs. Actually, organizational theory suggests that the larger size of these gangs probably preceding and necessitated the resultant structure and organization. As Jankowski (1991) suggests – regardless of one's view of the extent of organization present within various gangs – gang researchers can rally around agreement that organizational dynamics affect gangs.

In research on gangs, preoccupation with measuring formal organizational characteristics common to bureaucratic organizations – and the finding that these characteristics are often minimal among certain and numerous types of gangs – has obscured the fact that at least some gangs do meet the definitional requirements of formal organizations and thus are clearly subject to organizational dynamics. And organizational theory literature – with extensive descriptions of nonbureaucratic forms of formal organizations – does not require that organizations contain hierarchy, rules and roles to be formally organized. Only bureaucracies have this requirement and, as discussed previously, a volatile environment selects against the bureaucratic form of organization.

Probably very few gangs can be considered bureaucratic because they would not fare well in an environment in which oppositional institutions – police, schools, families, other gangs among other institutions – are constantly adjusting tactics in order to control gangs. Since the apparent growth of gangs – in size, number and prevalence – is a generally consensual description of the contemporary gang phenomenon, agreement that organizational dynamics affect gangs is an important conclusion and a point of departure for further analysis.

If growth in gangs has occurred – and this is an issue that will be examined subsequently in this chapter – organizational theory suggests that this occurrence is related to the availability of resources; surplus resources in an environment contribute to an increase in the number of organizations in the population and/or an increase in the size of organizations in the population. Organizational theory also suggests that success of an organizational form contributes to more numerous organizations of that form; new organizations of that form are created, increasing the population of organizations. Since it is unclear exactly how organizational dynamics of growth has affected contemporary gangs, the phenomenon of gang growth is examined next, with an emphasis on the form and the processes through which such growth may have occurred.

THE GROWTH OF GANGS

Interest in the enumeration of gangs and gang members – a necessity for measuring the scope and prevalence of gangs – is not an altogether new phenomenon. Thrasher's (1963) study of Chicago gangs, first published in 1927, even included the number of gangs in the title – 1,313. Notably, he didn't indicate that this number was inclusive of all gangs in Chicago, just those gangs which he had studied! By contrast, Chicago police reported approximately 45 gangs in the city circa 1996 (Weisel, Decker and Bynum, 1997). Clearly, either major definitional differences have effectively "transformed" gangs during the intervening five decades or significant changes in the size and composition of gangs have occurred in the city during the last five decades. While Kornhauser (1978) stated that the "smallness of gangs is a basic feature of their organizational structure," Klein (1995) suggests that the average size of gangs has declined. It should be noted, however, that Thrasher's gangs consisted of 30 members on average while some of Chicago's gangs now number into the five figures. Spergel (1990) observed that there has been both growth in the number of gangs and gang members and declines – depending on the jurisdiction – in recent years although, "it is not clear what accounts for these shifts" (p. 185). Of course, differing definitions of the term gang and gang member complicate issues of counting the number of gangs and measuring the size of gangs – two procedures necessary for documenting growth. Thus perceptions of size and scope of gangs – and relative changes – are largely anecdotal and may be distorted by inconsistent or unreliable data.

Most gang researchers have not addressed the growth of gangs explicitly. Klein (1995) is probably the most specific on the issue of gang proliferation – a phenomenon closely related to some forms of gang growth. Klein suggests that gang proliferation in the 1980s was comprised primarily of small, autonomous gangs coming into being, contributing to smaller gang size on average. And Klein noted that without effective interventions, "there are a lot of acorns out there that could become stable, traditional oaks."(p. 104). Klein's remarks are suggestive that small, autonomous gangs — left to grow — become stable, traditional and larger gangs, the latter of which are countable and of concern to the public while the former are generally not.

Law enforcement agencies and the media have not been vague concerning perceptions of gang growth. The Bureau of Alcohol, Tobacco and Firearms (1992: 1) reported an "alarming growth of criminal gang membership in the last decade" despite the fact that definitions of gang and gang membership have not been explicit enough nor uniformly applied to permit reliable comparisons between cities and across time (Miller, 1975; Snyder and Sickmund, 1995) and that members of law enforcement agencies, tasked with the counting of gang members, are not uniformly trained in counting procedures such as criteria for gang recognition (Weisel and Painter, 1997). These issues have made counts of gangs and gang members questionable even within a single city (Jackson, 1989). Such limitations have not prevented claims of gang membership, such as Delattre (1990) who said there are more than 100,000 gangs in the United States with more than 1 million members (suggesting an average of 10 members per gang), including 750 gangs in Los Angeles with 70,000 members (suggesting an average of 93 members per gang) – a large difference in average gang membership.

Differing Notions of Gang Growth

There are different views of gang proliferation. It is widely presumed that gangs have proliferated – grown larger and more numerous or spread to new locations – in recent years, becoming much more prevalent. The use of terms related to the concept of gang proliferation suggest any or all of the following:

> Gangs have become more prevalent nationally, that is, they have been identified as occurring in a greater number of cities or jurisdictions than in the past;

> The organizational density of gangs has increased, that is, gangs have become more numerous because new gangs have started, older gangs have persisted and failed to disband or have splintered creating new gangs, and/or, because of organizational transformation processes, some groups, such as delinquent groups, have evolved into gangs; and/or,

> Individual gangs have become larger, representing a greater concentration of gang members or an increase in organizational mass. Organizational mass has increased via recruitment of new members, retention of older members, or through organizational dynamics such as merger and consolidation.

Each of these issues – rising gang prevalence, more numerous gangs or larger gangs via more numerous gang members – suggests a different but related phenomena related to the growth of gangs. Although gang growth is often mentioned in the mass media and gang literature, what is the evidence to document these trends? And how are issues of gang growth made more complex by issues of definition and source of information?

Complexities of Counting

To document the phenomenon of gang growth and accurately estimate the gang population requires a standardized procedure for counting both the number of gangs and the number of gang members within those gangs. This procedure must be consistent across time and space, ensuring that accurate comparisons can be made over time. Despite the straightforward nature of this need, operationalization of the terms gang and gang member are not standardized; there is no consensus definition of a gang or a gang member. Reliable counting also requires consistent and reliable sources of information about gangs and gang members over time, but these sources do not exist. And reliable counting also requires procedures for routinely updating enumerations of both gangs and gang members since new gangs come into being and old gangs may cease to exist; members of gangs also change, ceasing, commencing or even changing their gang affiliation at differing points in time. These complexities of counting must be addressed to document the nature of the growth of gangs.

Defining and Counting Gangs

The inability to adopt a consensual and standardized definition of the term gang, discussed earlier in this chapter, is perhaps most problematic for the issue of counting gangs. Decker and Kempf - Leonard (1991) point out the repercussions of a lack of consensus on definition: "The absence of an agreed-upon definition can lead to either minimizing the problem or overstating its incidence" (p. 21). The predominant source of information about the presence, number and size of gangs is usually law enforcement sources. Spergel (1990), Klein (1995) and Decker and Kempf-Leonard (1991) note that police estimates of gangs and gang membership are usually conservative, reflecting undercounting rather than inflated figures; such counts usually rely on narrow definitions of gangs and gang membership. In contrast, Yablonsky (1962) pointed out that gang members tend to inflate their numbers. In St. Louis, Decker and Kempf-Leonard (1991) found fundamental differences in counting the number of gangs (and gang members) by members of a school anti-gang task force, police, gang youth and non-gang youth, with the youthful groups counting more, and the adult groups counting far fewer gangs; estimates of gang membership made by youth were five times higher than estimates of gang membership made by police.

Part of the issue with making comparisons over time of gang counts is that even the locally-derived definition of gang may change over time. Knox (1994) points out that most of Thrasher's gangs studied in the 1920s wouldn't even be considered gangs today. Huff (1990:310-312), particularly describes the phenomenon of gang denial within cities, such that a city may report that it has no gangs one day, but a change in police leadership or political leaders or the occurrence of high-visibility gang-related events may suddenly result in the identification or declaration of a gang problem; such instantaneous recognition of gang problems occurred in Columbus, OH, following several violent gang attacks. Similarly, Hagedorn (1990) describes efforts in Indianapolis to deny the presence of any gang problem during a period in which the city was preparing to host the Pan Am games. Such reports of denial in a city often involve classification of what might otherwise be considered gang problems as delinquency or youth group problems. Since it is unlikely that the presence of gangs in these denial cities occurred instantaneously, the political realities of reporting gang problems contribute to reliability problems with estimates of gang numbers. Of course, denial can be considered a state of mind: if gangs are simply gradations of criminal organizations on a continuum, perceptions of these organizations changing over time must be locally defined. Simple denial that a city has a gang problem is not prima facie evidence that a city is "in denial" of a gang problem. Given the acknowledged wide variation in gangs and gang definitions, current reporting of gang problems must be taken at face value.

Another complication of counting the number of gangs is the presence of subsets or divisions which typically occur within larger gangs and may be present in gangs of all sizes. Gang membership is often subgraded into a set, chapter, faction, off-shoot or clique of a larger gang (Moore, 1978; Klein 1971; Spergel, 1990). These groupings – usually age-graded – may have a more specific name than the parent gang; and there are may be subgroupings within each of the suborganizations. Hagedorn (1988) described gangs in Milwaukee as a combination of age-graded groups, divided loosely into main groups and groups of wanna-bes. Spergel (1995 and Spergel et al, 1991) describe the small clique as the "building block" of the gang but the size of the clique has been a source of controversy. Klein (1971) said specialty cliques consist of 3-12 members; Koester and Schwartz (1993: 189) concur, describing a gang as comprised of sets for purposes of drug dealing: "A set is a more closely aligned group than an entire gang, and it is the level within which most day-to-day activities take place." Padilla (1993a) calls these groupings sections or subgroups;

Monti (1993b) refers to age-graded cliques and sets which can combine, dissolve and reassemble in different ways – a factor contributing to widely recognized impermanence of gangs.

In fact, the presence of cliques or subgroups within the gang may contribute to its impermanence. Spergel et al (1991: 64) report that "competition between cliques may be a central dynamic leading to the gang splitting into factions or separate gangs." Such organizational phenomena splintering and reorganizing of gangs – also contribute to what is perceived as relative impermanence or ephemeral nature of gangs. Subgroups of gangs are not always recognized. In fact, Knox (1994) reported that some people consider a gang chapter as a gang. An example of different counting procedures may be observed in Curry, Ball and Fox (1994). The authors report 503 gangs in Los Angeles while Chicago has 41 gangs, with 55,281 and 29,000 members respectively. It is difficult to believe that Los Angeles has more than 12 times the number of gangs as Chicago; instead, differences in the definition and counting of gangs in different ways probably account for part of the variation.

In addition to subgroups within gangs, other groupings of gangs may play a role in counting gangs. Decker (1996) grouped gangs by constellations or affiliations within larger gang networks. This is consistent with Delattre (1990) who noted that Crips and Bloods are associations of smaller gangs, the former consisting of 189 gangs, the latter of 72 gangs. Hagedorn (1988) describes the nations and supergangs of Chicago. Klein and Maxson (1989:210) describe the "rare but highly visible loose confederations" of gangs. Since these supra organizational structures may serve to mask changes in gang composition or facilitate cliques affiliating with a different gang, these confederations or alliances may further mask the enumeration of gangs.

Defining and Counting a Gang Member

Estimating and monitoring gang size is a necessary task for evaluating the growth of individual gangs. But if there are definitional problems in counting the number of gangs, these issues pale by comparison to the issue of counting the number of gang members. As with the counting of gangs, documentation of membership is usually done by law enforcement agencies and varies from one jurisdiction to another. Although some states (notably, California and Florida) have statutory definitions of gang members and minimum criteria for identification and counting of gang members, practices in other jurisdictions vary considerably.

Four issues confound the counting of gang members. First, in order to be counted initially, gang members must typically experience some formalized contact (such as an arrest or field interview) with a criminal justice agency. Since it is unlikely that all gang members have this kind of formalized contact, counting may be compromised and is likely to be underrepresentative of actual gang membership. Second, there are different kinds of gang members. In addition to role specialization or leadership rank, features which are common in some gangs, general membership types range from hard-core or core members, fringe, active and wannabes (Klein, 1995); adjunct, auxiliary (Taylor, 1990a, 1990b); marginal (Huff, 1990); verified or alleged gang members (Goldstein, 1991); leaders, veteranos, OGs or original gangsters (Padilla, 1993a; Huff, 1990); associates, peripheral or core members; known, suspected or associated members (Spergel, 1990); female auxiliary members (Monti, 1993b); peewees (Padilla, 1993b); peripheral or fringe, associates, wannabes or recruits, core members (leaders and regular members) (Spergel, 1995). If one were to count gang members, these differing levels or types of gang membership, often present within a single gang and variably present across differing gangs, confound the process of accurately counting and monitoring a count of gang members. Should these varying levels of membership all be counted as equivalent "members" across gangs? Given the relative transience of much gang membership, even members of the same gang may have difficulty answering these questions about other gang members.

Third, once counted, the names of gang members may be irregularly purged from records and such elimination may occur long after the individual's participation in the gang has ceased. Since the gang literature strongly suggests that gang membership is often shifting or transitory (see Thornberry et al, 1993; Spergel, 1990, 1995; Short and Strodtbeck, 1974; Esbensen and Huizinga, 1993; Yablonsky, 1962), even the best efforts to maintain accurate records of gang membership cannot accurately reflect the temporary nature which characterizes much membership in gangs. Although some law enforcement agencies purge gang membership files after periods of inactivity, it is unlikely that any database of gang members can maintain accurate and current information about membership status. Esbensen and Huizinga (1993) note: "[Gangs] are characterized by limited cohesion, impermanence, shifting membership, and diffuse role definition" (p. 72). Participation as a gang member in a gang is neither a permanent state of affairs nor a rigidly constructed role. The membership of individuals clearly waxes and wanes over time, with different members being more or less active in the gang at different times. Short and Strodtbeck (1965: 10) note that gangs are "shifting in membership and identity." Yablonsky (1962) observed that gang membership is shifting. Thornberry et al (1993) note that gang membership is more often a fleeting than a permanent condition.

Evidence of the Growth of Gangs

Empirical evidence of the growth of gangs is limited, primarily because the complexities of counting gangs and gang members have resulted in inconsistent information over time. Since the references to the growth of gangs typically suggest increases in the number of gang-involved cities, the total number of gangs or the gang population, the size of gangs, and/or number of gang members, evidence of growth typically comes from different sources.

City Prevalence

Perhaps the best evidence of the growth of gangs relates to the notion of gang prevalence or the emergence of gangs in previous non-gang areas. (See Spergel, 1990; Spergel, 1995; Curry, Ball and Fox, 1994; Klein, 1995.) Klein (1995) is concerned with the issue of gang proliferation, a term which he carefully distinguishes from the expansion or spreading of gangs; the latter terms suggest a systematic process of growth, such as migration or syndication of gangs; the previous term, more precise, refers only to a net increase. "Gangs have proliferated [not spread] from a few to many hundreds of American cities," reported Klein (1995: 31).

Klein documented the reach of gangs into numerous "new" cities, that is, cities which had previously not experienced gang problems. Prior to 1961, 54 cities reported gangs; from 1961 to 1979, 94 cities reported gangs; 1971-1980, 172; and up to 1992, 766 cities reported the presence of gangs (Klein, 1995: 91). At the time, Klein estimated that the number of gang-involved cities was at least 800 and might number up to 1,110; and he pointed out that the number of gang-involved cities was still rising. The growth in the number of gang-involved cities had been driven predominantly by the incursion of gangs into smaller cities and towns, including those with less than 10,000 population, changing what had been viewed as primarily an urban problem into a ubiquitous issue.

In contrast to Klein (1995), Needle and Stapleton (1983) conducted a survey of police in 60 cities to document the scope of gang problems at that time: 83 percent of cities over 1 million population reported the presence of gangs, while 50 percent of smaller cities (with population of 250,000-500,000) reported gangs and 39 percent of cities with population of 100,000-250,000 population reported the presence of gangs. Cities reporting gang problems were dominated by cities in the Western region of the nation, predominately occurring in California. (These authors distinguished between gangs and youth law-violating groups.)

Miller (1975) first raised the issue of gangs spreading to other cities, citing the identification of gangs in smaller cities. In a survey of 385 police agencies, Weisel, Decker and Bynum (1997) reported that larger cities continue to have more numerous gangs, larger gangs and "older" gangs which have been around for longer periods of time. In smaller cities, delinquent gangs were the most common "type" of gang;

and these gangs were much younger in terms of having originated in recent years.

Consistently, these studies had all documented the increasing onset of gang problems in American cities, documenting perhaps the most obvious indication of gang expansion or growth – the proliferation of gangs or increasing gang prevalence at the national level. The introduction of a periodic survey of law enforcement agencies – using consistent definitions of gang – in 1995 provided a new baseline of gang-involved jurisdictions. The National Youth Gang survey was administered in 1995, and replicated in 1996, 1997, and 1998. This survey, which counts only gangs defined as youth gangs, showed a decline in the number of gangs in the nation from 1996 to 1998. The decline was greatest among rural and suburban counties, and much less dramatic for urban jurisdictions.

Rising Numbers of Gangs

Despite definitional limitations, throughout the 1990s it was widely reported that the number of gangs in the nation was increasing (Bryant, 1992; Goldstein and Huff, 1993; Spergel and Curry, 1993; Miller, 1990). Numerous authors, such as Decker (1996), reported growth in the number of gangs within city. In a review of literature, Spergel (1990: 183-184; 1995) reported that the specific number of gangs within "gang cities" had waxed and waned over years and had not demonstrated a consistent pattern of uninterrupted growth. Steady growth of the number of gangs in its jurisdiction were reported in Dade County, FL, with four gangs in 1980 and 80 gangs in 1988; LA County, 239 gangs in 1985 and up to 800 in 1988; and San Diego County, three gangs in 1975 and up to 35 gangs in 1987. During a similar period, however, the number of gangs seesawed in Phoenix – 34 gangs in 1974, rising to 74 gangs in 1982, and declining to 31 in 1986. Some cities, such as New York, Fort Wayne, IN, and Louisville, KY, reported steady declines in the number of gangs from the mid-1970s to the mid-1980s. New York, for example, reported 315 gangs in 1974, 130 in 1982, dropping to 66 in 1987. Spergel did not report any variation in data sources for this longitudinal review of gang counts.

Although reports of gang growth were conflicting, more than three-fourths (78 percent) of large law enforcement agencies in the national study by Weisel, Decker and Bynum (1997) reported that gangs in their jurisdiction had grown larger during the previous three-year period. Establishment of the baseline gang survey by the National Youth Gang Center elaborated descriptive evidence of the growth of gangs. By 1998, the number of youth gangs reported had declined 7 percent in the preceding two years (National Youth Gang Center, 2000), showing the first evidence of a decline in the number of gangs.

Increasing Size of Gangs or Number of Gang Members

Have some contemporary gangs grown larger? According to a scheme used by Monti (1993a), a gang has four choices: it may be growing larger by gaining new members; losing members; neither gaining nor losing; or both gaining and losing members, with the latter two categories suggesting stable gang size. Among 24 gangs in St. Louis studied by Monti, more than half – 54 percent – reported that they were gaining members; one gang or 4 percent, losing membership; 17 percent, neither; and 25 percent, both gaining and losing members. Thus, 42 percent of the gangs in that city were of stable size, however, most of the gangs reported growing in membership.

There is no definitive source of information about gang size. Klein (1995: 104) stated that traditional gangs typically range in size from "less than one hundred to several hundred active members" while "autonomous gangs...probably range from ten to fifty members at a time, weighted toward the lower end. When these develop into linked branches, then numbers in the hundreds make sense...."

Spergel et al (1991) and Spergel (1990) reported that the size of gangs has long been a source of controversy, with estimates ranging from small (4-25 members); medium (25-75 members); medium to large (25-200 and 30-500 members); and very large (up to the 1000s of gang members). These groupings may apply differently to different cities. In St. Louis, for example, of 24 gangs studied by Monti (1993a), more than half (54 percent) had 25 or fewer members; only two gangs (8 percent) had more than 60 members. Thirty-eight percent or 9 gangs were reported to have membership of between 25 and 60 individuals. In another study of gangs in St. Louis, Decker and Kempf-Leonard (1991) reported that different sources of information provided different estimates of gang size: police estimated an average gang size of 17 members for 26 gangs, while gang members estimated an average gang size of 88 members for 29 gangs.

One rough measure of gang size is to make estimates of average gang size based upon estimates of the number of gangs and number of gang members.   Miller (1982) reported 97,940 gang members among 2,285 gangs in 286 cities – an average of 43 members per gang.   In their national estimates of gangs, Curry, Ball and Fox (1994) reported 4,881 gangs with 249,324 members in 110 cities, figures which suggest an average of 51 gang members per gang.   These authors updated national prevalence figures from 1988 which indicated that there were 1,439 gangs with 120,636 gang members in 35 cities – an average of 84 members per gang.   The contrast between average gang size from 1988 to 1994 suggests that average gang size has increased during that period.   However, it should be noted that the sample size of cities increased three-fold from the first to the latter study, which may have had some effect on average gang size since gang research generally suggests smaller gang size in smaller cities.   Indeed, averages derived from the Curry, Ball and Fox study indicate that average gang size varies significantly from one city to another.   For example, Chicago had an average of 707 members in 41 gangs while Los Angeles had an average of 110 members in 503 gangs.   In New York City, the Task Force on Juvenile Gangs (1993) reported 28 documented gangs, an average of 28 members per gang; fewer gang members were reported for an additional 51 gangs under investigation – 20 members on average.   Using 1991 data, Klein (1995) estimated that there were 9,000 gangs with 400,000 members (among 261 respondents), an average of 44 members per gang.   Klein, noted, however that smaller cities tend to have fewer gangs and alludes that smaller cities with fewer gangs may have fewer gang members in those gangs.   (The National Youth Gang Center survey (2000) confirmed this observation.)   In 52 cities with gang violence, Klein estimated 2,600 gangs with 200,000 gang members – an average of 77 members per gang.   Since these violent gang cities are likely larger cities in Klein's sample, the average size estimates appear to be consistent with the observation about the relationship of gang size to city size.

In comparison to these contemporary estimates of gang size, Thrasher's gang study of 1,313 gangs in Chicago had 50,000 members, an average of 38 members per gang.   While that gang size fits in with national estimates of average gang size, it is far different than most estimates of gang size in the city of Chicago. The relationship between the size of gangs and the number of gangs in a city is an issue also alluded to by Spergel et al (1991). In contrast to Klein (1995), Spergel implies that where gangs are more numerous, gang size is relatively smaller; when there are fewer gangs, gang size is relatively larger. This truism is apparently supported by the contrast between average gang size in Los Angeles (an average of 100 members in 505 gangs) and Chicago (707 members on average in 41 gangs), and discounted by the few number and small size of gangs in New York City. During a six-year period in Hawaii, Chesney-Lind et al (1994) enumerated the number of gangs as rising nearly nine-fold from 22 in 1988 to 45 in 1991; to 171 in 1993; and to 192 in 1994. During the same period, gang membership increased about four-fold, from 450 members to 1,900 members. Average size of the gangs declined from 20 to 10 members during the period of enumeration.

More recent data about average gang size showed a decline from 1996 to 1998 (National Youth Gang Center, 2000). In the baseline year, jurisdictions averaged 50 members in each of 15 gangs, dropping to 40 members in each of 40 gangs in the latter time period. Averaging gang size can be misleading if there is wide variation in gang size within jurisdictions, however, it provides a basis of comparison across quite different places.

Spergel (1966) and Goldstein (1991) state that the size of contemporary gangs varies, according to by the size of the youth population, amount of police pressure, recruiting efforts of gangs, season of the year and other factors. Spergel (1966) adds that size of gangs also varies as related to the nature of their activity. A study of chronic gang cities by Jackson (1991) indicates that the size of the youth population and the decline of jobs are causal factors for gang formation.

How Gangs Grow in Number and Size

National prevalence figures may mask changes within specific jurisdictions. Changes in gang prevalence or gang growth can occur in different ways. There may be increasing prevalence of gangs – that is, more numerous gangs – in some jurisdictions while other gangs are considered to be larger with more numerous gang members. Each of these processes contributes differently to the total population of gangs.

City Prevalence: Migration, Franchising and Emulation

We have discussed previously how gangsappeared in new or "emerging" gang cities, in contrast to "chronic" gang cities in which gangs had been historically present. Prior to the decline in gangs reported in 1997 and 1998 (National Youth Gang Center, 2000), the rising prevalence of gangs, particularly their formation in smaller cities, had been a well-documented phenomenon (Klein, 1995; Curry, Ball and Fox, 1994; Miller, 1982; and others). The explanations for the rising prevalence of gangs in cities varies.

In emerging gang cities, some have speculated that gang formation occurred because of efforts of big city gangs to formally expand their drug markets. Others ascribe the perception of formalized migration patterns to normal family relocation efforts and emulation of big city gangs. In chronic gang cities, gangs were widely assumed to have grown more numerous because of worsening economic conditions which restricted the economic opportunity available to young adults (Klein, 1995; Jackson, 1991).

Part of the presumed spread of gangs to other cities was related to the intentional expansion of drug markets by some ethnic gangs (Skolnick, Bluthenthal and Correl, 1993; Skolnick, n.d.; Bryant, 1989; Goldstein and Huff, 1993; Taylor, 1990a, 1990b). Goldstein and Huff (1993) described the myth of gang franchising occurring in the mid-to-late 1980s. Field research invalidated the myth at that time, but by 1989, gang member migration did exist, with gangs from Los Angeles and other chronic gang cities expanding drug dealing operations to emerging and smaller cities in an entrepreneurial spirit. Skolnick (n.d.) studied the penetration of Bloods and Crips gangs into other cities, concluding that their presence was not copycat or mimicry behavior of locals but related to the planned expansion of drug markets in pursuit of profits. Such a planned expansion into new markets occurred because of the saturation and competition for drug markets in Los Angeles, according to Skolnick. Consistent with Skolnick, the State of California (n.d.) classifies Crips and Bloods as "organized crime" and identified at least 45 cities across the nation in which the gangs had set up drug trafficking operations. Numerous federal and state law enforcement agencies concur with the market expansion theory of gang growth (Bureau of Alcohol, Tobacco and Firearms, 1992; State of California, n.d.; FBI, 1991; Mydans, 1992; GAO, 1989; U.S. Attorneys, 1989). As a result, the FBI broadened its investigations perspective to include street gangs, primarily those engaged in drug trafficking, and established a gang unit within the FBI, although gangs have traditionally been the purview of local law enforcement (Ferraro, 1992).

In contrast to a view of gangs as organized syndicates, other researchers argued that there was little planned, formal migration of gangs (Maxson, 1993; Klein, 1995; Hagedorn, 1988; Moore, 1993; Horowitz, 1990; Snyder and Sickmund, 1995). Snyder and Sickmund (1995) reported that evidence of planned gang migration from one city to another was minimal; rather, the appearance of such migration could usually be attributed to "normal residential relocation [of individuals] and local genesis" (p. 54). As such, these gangs in "emerging" gang cities were not typically extensions of gangs from "chronic" gang cities (Hagedorn, 1988; Horowitz, 1990), a finding endorsed by Huff's 1989 study of gangs in Columbus and Cleveland, Ohio. Instead, such apparent migration of gangs primarily reflected the migration or relocation of individual gang members rather than the systematic migration or expansion of the gang (Goldstein and Huff, 1993; Knox, 1994). Hagedorn (1988) concurred: the presence of gangs in Milwaukee with the names of Chicago gangs apparently reflected only some limited diffusion from Chicago, and generally reflected a pattern of emulation of the larger city's gangs.

A corollary to the notion of informal gang migration as a factor in gang proliferation is the description of popular media as the primary diffuser of gang culture. This notion is suggested by several contemporary gang researchers (Jankowski, 1991; Klein, 1995; Klein, Maxson and Miller, 1995) as an explanation for the expansion of gangs. Klein, Maxson and Miller (1995) suggest the "diffusion of gang culture" through the media – as an extension of underclass theory – is a reasonable explanation of gang proliferation. Since the presence of underclass conditions are not typical of most emergent gang cities, the cultural diffusion explanation provides an alternative explanation for how gang culture extended from inner and deindustrializing cities to other cities, suburbs and small towns across America.

More Gangs: Longevity, Splintering and Organizational Transformation

More numerous gangs may be occurring through several organizational processes. If contemporary gangs have increased longevity, new gangs may continue to form while old gangs continue to exist, creating a net increase in the population of gangs within a jurisdiction and in the aggregate. Of course, gangs may also splinter, with new gangs being formed as spinoffs of existing gangs. And, lastly, organizational transformation may effectively alter youth or delinquent groups into a gang.

Early gang researchers such as Thrasher discussed the life span of gangs as usually brief. Horowitz (1983) said many short-lived gangs developed quickly and disappeared from the urban landscape at a similar pace. In contrast to earlier years, there is an increasing recognition that some contemporary gangs are long-lived; indeed, gangs may fail to disband with the frequency of previous years. Jankowski (1991: 34), for example, suggests that linkages between the gang and other organizations – media, criminal justice system and media – reinforces and contributes to the longevity of the gang. Such longevity increases the likelihood that the gang will achieve its goals.

Gang researchers as early as Thrasher have recognized the effect of oppositional structures on increasing gang continuity. In the absence of opposition such as police and other gangs, said Thrasher, gangs disband. Contemporary oppositional structures – characteristics of a gang's external environment – include police, schools, correctional settings, anti-gang programs as well as other gangs. Competition with other gangs and crises, such as acts of retaliation against a gang or its members, also contribute to growth in the size of the gang (Klein, 1971; Spergel et al, 1991). One may infer that such crises increase the success of recruiting new members, improve retention of members, thus serving to increase gang longevity. Indeed, much of the gang literature focuses on the notion of cohesion (or lack thereof) within gangs, and the contribution of intergang rivalry to increasing cohesion, hence contributing to the continuity or longevity of gangs.

There is no source of information on the longevity of gangs. Of approximately 20 gangs studied by Jankowski (1991) over a period of ten years, one lasted 18 months while others were still in existence at the conclusion of the ten-year research period. By omission, Jankowski implies that at least some of the other gangs in the study also disbanded. Among 19 gangs on the northside of St. Louis studied by Monti (1993a) in 1990, most had not existed before 1984. Of 24 known gangs in 1988, nine had been disbanded or absorbed by other groups by 1990; one split into three groups. Hispanic gangs, as those in Jankowski's study, have a reputation for intergenerational endurance. Indeed, evidence which shows continuing participation in gangs by adult members who have failed to "mature out" of gangs (Hagedorn, 1990) suggests rising longevity of gangs; neither the gang has declined nor has the older gang member desisted participation. Of 19 major gangs and 260 founding members studied by Hagedorn, the "overwhelming majority" had not left the gang and the gangs had existed for more than a decade. Assuming that gang members typically join the gang in their youth (perhaps around 14-15 on average), adult members in a gang of age 25 or more suggest that the gang has existed for at least a decade. From the presence of older members, we can deduce that contemporary gangs are of greater duration than typically assumed. It seems unlikely that newly-formed gangs would have much success in recruiting or attracting older, adult gang members.

In the field of gang research, there has been little discussion of the splintering of gangs although there is recognition that cliques or subsets of gangs have a life of their own. Spergel (1991) reported that internal competition within the gang may lead to gangs splitting into factions or separate gangs. Spergel also suggested that gangs might splinter and dissolve if more criminal opportunities become available to members through drug trafficking gangs or other criminal groups.

Although Chinese gangs are not typical of most American gangs, Chin (1990) describes a process during the 1970s and 1980s where gang youth in New York's Chinatown had to protect themselves from intragang rivalry. In the Ghost Shadows gang, for example, a serious rivalry related to the distribution of money within the gang erupted between older and younger factions. The rivalry led to fights and shooting and resulted in the division of turf between separate factions of the gang.

Goldstein and Huff (1993) note that there is serious intragang rivalry between Blood and Crips sets in Los Angeles, especially when related to the profits of drug dealing. The authors note that there can be as much violence between different sets of the same gang as between rival gangs, a factor that may contribute to further splintering within the gang. Decker (1996) noted that the rise of violence within larger gangs can result in the emergence of splinter gangs. Monti (1993b) suggests that, at a certain size, gangs would split and become separate when friction occurred and remained unsettled between members. This splintering occurs because when the gang is small, the gang can exercise cohesion and control through face-to-face intimate interactions (Kornhauser, 1978). But large increases in the size of an individual gang often led to a breach in the gang, resulting in more numerous gangs in the population.

Terms related to organizational evolution have increasingly crept into the vernacular of gang research although these terms are seldom explained and have not been the focus of research. Generally, there is recognition that at least some gangs undergo organizational transformations which result in a change from one type of group or gang to another. Thus, a group of delinquent youth may become explicitly organized over time and grow larger so that it meets the definitional qualifications as a gang. Time is an essential dimension to such organizational transformation. Kornhauser (1978) described the general process of evolution:

> The gang naturally evolves from a diffuse, loosely organized to a more solidified group. Many gangs do not however, progress beyond the diffuse state...The solidified gang has developed over a longer period [of time] (p. 53).

In the transition from a diffuse gang to a solidified gang, a group process known as "institutionalization" of gangs occurs and elaborates the social structure of solidified gangs. Similarly, Cressey (1972) said informal organizations such as gangs can become formal organizations if they assume a rational and purposeful character; however, the structure of the formal structure need not be hierarchical.

Importantly, Kornhauser suggested that the degree of structure present within the gang is related to

> the average age of its member and duration of its life span. Even solidified gangs, however, are highly structured only in comparison with other gangs [emphasis in original], which may at any given time constitute a large though unspecified proportion of all gangs (Kornhauser, 1978: 55).

Cloward and Ohlin (1960), Thrasher (1963) and others, as discussed earlier, viewed gangs as a stepping stone to organized crime. Some contemporary researchers concur: Spergel et al (1991) noted: "One may speculate that a certain rough sequence of stages develops in the relation of law-violating youth groups, youth gangs, and criminal organizations" (p. 139). Spergel (1990: 181) noted "that delinquent groups in some cities can be converted or organized into youth gangs and that youth gangs in turn are changing into criminal organizations of various kinds" depending upon changes in population and recruitment activities of drug traffickers or prison groups. Spergel et al (1991) alluded to the movement of gangs move through development stages from deviant youths to youth groups to gangs to organized crime and stated:

It is also possible to argue that the gang is being transformed. The turf gang is being replaced by criminal organization, especially with the expansion of the street level drug market (p. 211).

Knox (1994) describes four developmental stages of a gang, proceeding from a pre-gang, to an emergent gang, a crystallized gang to a supergang, the latter characterized by the existence of chapters or sets, franchises and a formal organizational structure. "Most gangs must necessarily follow a developmental sequence and have a particular level of maturation," said Knox (p. 608). These stages of development can be distinguished on the basis of 12 characteristics, such as presence of written rules, organization size, leadership form and commitment of membership. Importantly, Knox (1994) points out that maturational processes for gangs are not unidirectional – a pre-gang may become an emergent gang, but then may go back to pre-gang status or dissolve or become more organized into another developmental stage.[e]

Knox's stages of gang development extend the idea described by Short (Jensen, 1994: 63): "I see the delinquent gang as a sort of phase of stage of development of street gangs in general." But Short points out that not all gangs evolve in this manner. Gangs heavily involved in drug trafficking run contra to the development perspective:

[The drug gang] is certainly not a typical street gang...They didn't even grow out of a street gang. These kids started out to make money by peddling crack and that is a very different phenomenon than street gangs (p. 66).

Knox's developmental stages of gangs are similar to those described by Chin (1990b), who describes Chinese gangs in New York as evolving through four stages over a 30-year period – emergence, transformation (characterized by violence), crystallization and diffusion. Unlike Knox, Chin used these terms to describe Chinese gangs in the aggregate – that is, periods of development of gangs rather than describing these as stages through which each individual gang must proceed. Nonetheless, he reported than Chinese gangs in New York were effectively transformed from self-help groups to predatory gangs.

Despite the increasingly vernacular use of terms related to evolution in the gang literature, little is known about the organizational evolution of any gangs. Only a few writers have described changes of specific gangs. Padilla (1993a, 1993b) and Taylor (1990a, 1990b) provide the best evidence of gang evolution. Padilla studied a gang known as the Diamonds which featured a major change in the thrust of its operations. This gang began as a musical group but reorganized in 1970 as a violent gang in response to the accidental shooting of one of its members. The Diamonds reorganized again in the late 1970s, formulating themselves as a "businesslike" gang, with retaliation and violence becoming subordinate to business operations.

Taylor (1990a, 1990b) suggests that gangs progress naturally from scavenger to territorial to corporate. In a case study of Detroit's Young Boys Incorporated, Taylor documented this change over time and the process of gangs copying successful and charismatic crime groups, claiming that territorial gangs made the transition into corporate gangs in Detroit in the 1980s, using violence in as equally a menacing way as did Al Capone in the 1920s. As gangs progress through these stages of types, leadership becomes more clearly defined and crime becomes more purposeful.

Hagedorn (1988) describes how Milwaukee gangs evolved from dance clubs and corner groups into gangs after participating in fights between groups. Short (1990) describes how the Nobles, a Chicago gang, developed from a neighborhood play group into a delinquent gang. And Short describes the Vice Lords of Chicago which began through a youth training school where leaders decided to affiliate and form a larger gang. Within a decade, the gang had expanded rapidly and became one of the city's "supergangs" of the 1960s.

There is some limited evidence that less serious gangs can and do evolve into more serious gangs under certain conditions (Short, 1990). Moore (1993) concurs that some "youth gangs develop into criminal organizations, but this is not the norm" (p. 41). Fagan suggests that "organization" gangs are at the highest risk of becoming more formal criminal organizations (1989). Rafferty and Bertcher (1963), in researching the formation of what they call a "primitive gang," conclude that a gang is an intermediate stage of a group in its evolution from no regular social interaction to well-defined social interaction. Such an intermediate group has two or more individuals, roles and hierarchy, distinguishes non-members, and develops norms to regulate relationships between individuals.

Spergel (1991) raises the possibility that delinquent groups can be converted into organized youth gangs based partially upon the entrepreneurial efforts of drug traffickers, citing cases of youths being routinely recruited into organized crime, particularly among Asian groups. Skolnick, Bluthenthal and Correl (1993) describe the progression of California gangs from the dominance of the historic cultural gang to the entrepreneurial gang organized around profitable criminal activity. There is some disagreement on the subject of gang evolution: Best and Luckinbill (1982) state that there is no evidence of progression to more sophisticated forms of deviant organizations, claiming that most juvenile gang members, if they commit crime, do mostly property crime and fighting.

Although organizational evolution or life cycles have not been used to describe or explain gangs, the notion of organizational life cycles has been used, albeit in a limited fashion, to describe other criminal groups, notably organized crime (Lupsha, 1991; O'Kane, 1992; and Salerno and Tomkins, 1969). Lupsha suggests that organized crime groups go through a "life cycle" including a predatory phase in which groups engage in defensive criminal acts which are primarily territorial. That territoriality may be to exclude others from an area, control a monopoly over use of force, or to eliminate rivals and competitors. With the opening of a "window of opportunity," the predatory phase segues into a parasitical phase in which a street gang has matured; its members are older, have more sophisticated criminal skills, the organization has more defined leadership and labor tasks are specialized. In a final stage, the organized crime group becomes symbiotic, with a mutual interdependence with the legitimate political and economic structure.

O'Kane (1992) asserts that criminal organizations pass through an evolution process consisting of six stages. The organization begins with individual criminality, in which individuals engage in predatory crime, occasionally collaborating with others in a "haphazard, opportunistic fashion" (p. 79). Individual criminality, however, gives way to intra-ethnic gang rivalry in which like-minded individuals with a common ethnic heritage join forces to achieve power and greater income. In stage three, competing ethnic gangs consolidate their organizations and challenge other groups in order to further their ambitions. O'Kane's fourth stage occurs when competing ethnic groups reach a truce in order to develop a healthier business environment, freed of violence. Such truces may be short-lived. In stage five, one ethnic organization emerges achieves dominance by effectively suppressing competitor groups. In a final stage, the ethnic group, once dominant, fades from power in the face of public opinion and criminal justice sanctions. The group gives way to competition from other organized groups in O'Kane's depiction of hegemony and subsequent decline.

In contrast to the more generalized life cycle model described by organizational theorists, the stages described by Lupsha and O'Kane focus primarily on the organizational behaviors of criminal groups and their changes over time. It is noteworthy that none of these models address the concept of organizational growth in terms of size, a concept which is of critical importance in the organizational literature. If the models are applied to gangs, these evolutionary cycles suggest that – under certain conditions – gangs or gang-like groups mature over time into highly structured, organized crime groups.

Larger Gangs, More Gang Members: Retention, Recruitment and Merger

Through most of the 1990s, gang membership in the nation and numerous cities appeared to have significantly expanded in terms of numbers (Hagedorn, 1988; Maxson and Klein, 1990; Miller, 1990, 2001). Part of this growth can be related to more numerous gangs in cities which previously had none. But there is some evidence that individual gangs have also grown larger. Growth of individual gangs typically occurs through three methods: retaining existing members who might have matured out of the gang; adding new members by recruiting or attracting young members to join the gang; or expanding gang membership through organizational processes, such as merging the gang with another gang.

Membership in contemporary gangs typically includes older non-juvenile members (Spergel, 1990; Hagedorn, 1988; Maxson and Klein, 1990; Fagan, 1990; Goldstein and Huff, 1993).   Indeed, evidence indicates that some individual gangs may be growing larger simply through retention of older members, or the decline in rates of attrition. Klein (1995: 21) reported that "[Gang members] are hanging on longer and longer [to their gang membership]."

Although there is widespread support for the finding that youthful members of gangs do not age out or mature out of contemporary gangs as in years past, instead retaining gang membership into early adulthood (Hagedorn, 1988, 1990; Spergel et al, 1991; Spergel, 1990; Goldstein and Huff, 1993; Klein and Maxson, 1989; Horowitz, 1983, 1990; Moore, 1978; Fagan, 1989, 1990; Goldstein, 1991), there is not total consensus on this issue. Lasley (1992), for example, found that adult gang membership was rare in a study of 445 active gang members in Los Angeles; gang membership in that study peaked around age 16-17 and then steadily declined. Lasley found that adult membership was rare despite variation in economic deprivation; this finding is contra to hypotheses that older gang members retain gang membership because of restricted economic opportunities.

In "emerging" gang cities — that is, those cities with relatively new gang problems — gang members are apparently more youthful. Snyder and Sickmund (1995) report that 90 percent of gang members in emerging gang cities are juvenile (less than 18 years old) while only one-fourth of gang members in "established" gang cities are juvenile. This observation supports the notion that older gangs, that is, those which have been around for longer periods of time, are more likely to include young adult or older members while newly-formed gangs draw from the ranks of juveniles.

Although there has been debate about the phenomenon of gang members leaving the gang, there is some evidence that quitting the gang may not be an easy process. Despite their interest in leaving the gang, some gang members may be coerced into remaining in the gang. Such coercion may occur through threats or beatings – and such tales are advanced by the mass media – but it is not known how widely such coercive measures are used to force members to retain their gang membership.   Knox (1994) said voluntary termination of gang membership is not an option in many gangs; in many gangs, members join for life, making numerous gangs the "no quit" variety (p. 30).

Spergel et al (1991) suggest that two complementary events contribute to the rising involvement of older youth and young adults in gangs – the loss of employment opportunities for unskilled youth and increased opportunity in the illegal economy.   Moore (1993) suggests that an illegal economic system develops in underclass communities where the legal economy is inadequate.   Since gang membership tends to take youth out of the mainstream of possible advancement, instead locking individuals into a pattern of low educational attainment, low job status and wages, over time, gang members probably become less attached to conventional society and have reduced access to legitimate economic opportunity.

Membership in contemporary gangs begins at an early age (Pennell, 1994; Goldstein and Huff, 1993) and numerous gang researchers believe that the age at which individuals join gangs has been decreasing (Goldstein, 1991; Goldstein and Huff, 1993).   It is unclear the extent to which gangs participate in overt or covert recruitment of new members.   Gang expansion has occurred at least partially through processes of both overt and subtle types of recruitment.   Based on her study of gangs in San Diego, Pennell (1994) reported that "recruitment into a gang occurs on an infrequent basis and is rarely coerced.   Most youths ask to join the gang and usually nothing happens to those that refuse to be part of the gang" (p. 99).   Spergel (1990) concurs: forcible recruitment is uncommon, although prison gangs and drug traffickers do induce individuals to join their organizations.   Most frequently, youths begin their process toward gang membership by hanging out with the gang; many have friends or relatives who are already members of the gang (Hagedorn, 1988; Pennell, 1994; Spergel, 1990; Padilla, 1993a).

Chin (1990a and 1990b) describes a process in which some, but not all, new members of Chinese gangs are coerced, sometimes in a subtle manner.   Gang members may recruit youths through buying meals or providing female companionship; or prospective gang members may be beaten to convince them "that their lives are more secure if they are gang members than if they are alone" (p. 134). Jankowski (1991) describes three types of recruiting used by gangs: fraternity-type, in which parties are given, prospective members are courted and then must undergo a trial period prior to acceptance during which the individual's fighting ability is assessed; obligation-type recruitment, in which gang members widely recruit by invoking the argument that individuals must serve the community; and coercive recruitment, in which physical or psychological intimidation is employed, the latter through threat of bodily harm to the individual or his family, the former involving infliction of physical pain or destruction of property. Jankowski claimed that coercive recruitment is used as a measure of last resort in order to build the numbers of a gang; its use, however, is not infrequent.

Hutchison and Kyle (1993) describe two avenues of recruitment for Hispanic gangs in Chicago. The first avenue is through friendship networks developed in the neighborhoods where adolescents lives. The second avenue involves "the active recruitment of gang members through intimidation and violence" (p. 118). These authors describe a process of gang members stopping prospective gang members in the school setting or on the street and "demanding [to know] their gang affiliation." Verbal harassment and physical intimidation often follows in an effort to entice individuals to join the gang. Although assertions of gang recruitment are common, youth or young adults may join gangs willingly, without overt coercion.

Rising membership of gangs through additional members may also be explained by a growing youth population. The juvenile population, comprised of individuals less than 18 years old, declined during the 1970s and early-1980s, but has been rising since 1984. Immigration to the United States from other counties contributes to a sizeable portion of the growth in the juvenile population (Snyder and Sickmund, 1995; Snyder, Sickmund and Poe-Yamagata, 1996).

The notion of gang mergers is occasionally mentioned in the gang literature but not has not been fully discussed. Although little is know about gang merger, this organizational phenomenon seems likely to occur under conditions of increased gang longevity and could contribute to gangs of larger size.

During a two-year period in which Huff (1989) studied gangs in two Ohio cities, the number of gangs declined from 50 separately named gangs in Cleveland to 15 or 20 gangs; in Columbus, 20 gangs were reduced to a count of 15 during the course of the study. Merger of some gangs accounted for the reduction in the number of gangs, according to Huff, although dissolution of gangs occurred and some groups originally identified as gangs may have actually been splinter groups rather than gangs. As mentioned previously, Monti (1993b) said cliques and sets can combine and reassemble in different ways; a portion of the gangs he studied in St. Louis were "absorbed" into other gangs during a two-year period. Sale (1971) described the growth of the Blackstone Rangers in Chicago as occurring through takeovers of existing gangs and "renovation" of cliques. The original street clique of the gang clashed with rival gangs, and then later combined with those gangs. The result after a ten-year period was a much larger version of the Blackstone Rangers. The observations that merger is an organizational feature of contemporary gangs and occurs over time is an accepted but poorly understood dimension of the organizational growth of gangs.

SUMMARY AND CONCLUSION

Although criminological theories generally enhance understanding of the formation of gangs, current theories have not been used to explain why gangs became more prevalent in the 1990s – a phenomenon characterized by more numerous gangs, larger gangs, and the emergence of gangs in "new" gang cities. The most compelling theory explaining the increase in gang prevalence is underclass theory, which suggests that gangs emerge – and endure – because of the absence of legitimate economic opportunity in poverty areas. The phenomenon of gang proliferation within deindustrializing cities can be explained by underclass theory but this theory is inadequate for explaining gang proliferation beyond those cities. An important feature of contemporary gangs and gang prevalence is that the membership of gangs was no longer drawn exclusively from minority groups and poverty conditions; gangs no longer existed only in inner city areas (Monti and Cummings, 1993: 307). Indeed, Klein, Maxson and Miller (1995) suggested that expansion of the underclass as a reason for gang proliferation may apply only to African Americans and "may be less pertinent to many smaller gang [emerging] cities where the factors [of minority segregation and deindustrialization] may be less severe" (p.

110).   The explanatory value of underclass theory, however, is enhanced by the hypothesis that inner city gang culture has been diffused through the mass media, resulting in widespread emulation of gangs and gang behavior.   This two-part theory augments an understanding of gang proliferation but has not been operationalized or tested.   Of course, an integrated theory, incorporating criminological theories with explanations of cultural diffusion and evidence of a rising youth population may inform much of the gang proliferation phenomenon (Elliot, Ageton and Cantor, 1979) but prevailing criminological theories offer no insight into the processes through which gangs progress to become larger, more numerous or more prevalent.

Organizational theory provides a mechanism for understanding the processes of rising gang prevalence.   Although there is no consensus that gangs are organizations, there are numerous indications that gangs are subject to organizational dynamics.   Like organizations, new gangs are formed frequently but are often subject to decline in the vulnerable early stages of their life cycles.   Other gangs persist, growing larger over time by attracting new members or retaining old members.   The large size of some gangs provides a buffer against unstable environmental conditions characterized by intensive criminal justice efforts and competition from other gangs.   Some gangs merge into larger gangs; through schism, others splinter into smaller gangs or decline because of environmental pressures and cease to exist. And more new gangs form to imitate gangs that are already successful. These and related organizational dynamics reveal a volatile process affecting the net population of gangs – a process likely driven by the death and birth of probably thousands of gangs and indicating rising adaptation of gangs which persist in a volatile environment.   Indeed, the rising prevalence of contemporary gangs suggests that gangs have some essential organizational features that make them uniquely suited for survival in the contemporary environment.   Since it is widely believed that the current population of gangs is not only surviving but is thriving, gangs exhibit either great adaptability to changing environmental conditions or unique organizational characteristics which facilitate their survival in this environment.   These processes of metamorphosis or natural selection ensure that gangs will be widely imitated or replicated, contributing to their viability as a form of social organization.

But how do these processes of organizational dynamics inform our understanding of rising gang prevalence? Various models of organizations provide a useful framework for understanding contemporary gangs. Despite its commonality and the widespread use of its organizational dimensions to analyze gangs, the bureaucratic or mechanistic view of organizations does not appear to be the most relevant model for understanding gangs. Bureaucracies, for example, emphasize specialization and standardization, while individual members of gangs appear generally to be versatile and may serve the organization in numerous roles. Indeed, gang members are not like cogs in a production chain; gangs in general just do not appear to be that highly structured, although increasingly, some criminal organization-gangs demonstrate evidence of hierarchy, having printed rules and policies and taking assertive measures to ensure compliance with group norms. Nonetheless, in contrast to highly-bureaucratic organizations, such as formal business enterprises, gangs appear fairly rudimentary on these measures (see Weisel, Decker and Bynum, 1997, and Decker, Bynum and Weisel, 1998, for a thorough analysis of these organizational measures related to gangs).

The organic model of organizations provides a promising framework to analyze the growth of contemporary gangs. The prevalence of gangs – hence, their success – in the current volatile environment is a key feature of the organic model and reflects the apparent adaptability of gangs. Gangs which fail in this changing environment are selected out for some reasons; while gangs which survive have features compatible with the mercurial environment. For example, since much law enforcement effort focuses on identifying and removing leadership from gangs (see Weisel and Painter, 1997; Spergel, 1995; and Goldstein and Huff, 1993), gangs with ephemeral or multiple leaders are probably more successful, ensuring the durability of the gang. Since the ephemeral-leadership gang is successful, its form becomes replicated through imitation and schism. Similarly, since law enforcement agencies are organized to investigate specific types of crime (e.g., auto theft, robbery, and so forth), criminal specialization by members rather than versatility would be selected against in a natural selection or adaptation model. Since the organic-adaptive model also integrates the objectives of individuals with those of the organization, this model does not feature hierarchy, role specialization and formal rules. Its simple prevalence of form suggests that contemporary gangs – or at least some of them – can be accurately described as organizations albeit highly adaptive to a volatile environment and nontraditional as compared to legitimate organizations.

The acknowledgment that gangs vary, supported by the various classification schemes for gangs, suggests that distinctly different types of gangs probably constitute differing gang populations. Organizational theory suggests that within a population, there is a pull toward standardization of size and structure of organizations. This approach to thinking about gangs can be applied to different classification schemes. For example, Huff (1989) classified gangs as either informal, instrumental or predatory. If each of these types constitutes a specific gang population, the size and structure of gangs within that type will tend to be similar. Gangs which grow larger than other gangs within that specific population will effectively become classified as a different type of gang or changed population group. In other words, for example, if the informal gang grows larger than most other informal gangs, it will probably become an instrumental or predatory gang. This evolutionary phenomenon is consistent with Klein's (1995) analogy, mentioned previously, that left to their own devices, lots of acorns (spontaneous gangs) will grow into oaks (traditional gangs).

The growth in size of individual gangs and the number of gang members are arguably the most important organizational phenomena occurring among contemporary gangs, although reliable evidence of such growth is absent. Data for counting and monitoring the number of gangs and gang members within an individual gang are of poor quality. As Spergel (1995) stated – the more organized the gang, the larger the gang. He stated this inversely; since organizational theory suggests that as the organization – the gang – becomes larger, there are increasing pressures for the organization to become explicitly organized. Knox (1994) is the only gang researcher who has specifically noted the linkage between gang size and sophistication. Organizational theory suggests that reliable information about organizational size over time and age provides important insight into the processes of organizational dynamics.

Concerns about the prevalence of gangs raise numerous questions about contemporary gangs. What is known about contemporary gangs is that they come in many different shapes and sizes. There is no uniform or accepted description of a gang across venues. Nor is there agreement about varying types of gangs. The resultant debates about the definition of gangs and gang members and descriptions of varying forms have dominated much of the discussion and research on gangs. Despite the definitional debate, there appears to be evidence that gangs are subject to processes of organizational dynamics – gangs form, grow and add members, or decline. Since gangs as a form of organization have been successful – as evidenced by their growth and rising prevalence, replication and persistence over time – organizational theory provides an untapped avenue for examining these phenomena.

Key questions related to the application of organizational theory for understanding processes of gang proliferation include:

Are gangs organizations? How central are goals to the functioning of the gang? How do formal organizational objectives compare to the goals of the informal organization and individual members of the gang?

How do organizational dynamics affect gangs? What happens to gangs after they are formed? How do gangs change over time? How large are different gangs? Have gangs grown? In what ways have gangs grown? Through what mechanisms and why have gangs grown?

What factors contribute to the organizational persistence of gangs? How adaptive are gangs to a volatile environment? How do gangs adapt? What features of gangs suggest that they can best be understood as organic-adaptive organizations rather than bureaucracies?

These questions can be addressed by examining large gangs which have been in existence for an extended period of time. Since, as Blau (1962: 224) noted, these organizations did "not spring into existence full-blown but develop[ed] out of simpler ones," an examination of these mature gangs may provide unique insight into the effect of organizational processes on contemporary gangs. Importantly, the answers to these questions may provide greater understanding of the evolutionary or life cycle processes through which gangs progress. Of course, there is no institutional memory of the organizational processes through which gangs have progressed. Insight into organizational dynamics must be gained through examining the knowledge of individual gang members to develop a composite view of the maturational process. The next chapter describes the research approach to gathering this information in a systematic way.

CHAPTER III:
RESEARCH DESIGN AND METHODOLOGICAL APPROACH

The study of youth gangs published by Frederic Thrasher (1963) in 1927 has alternately been characterized as seminal, landmark, pioneering, ambitious, richly detailed, classic and in other equally laudatory terms. (See, for example, Joe, 1993; Goldstein, 1991; Skolnick, Bluthenthal and Correl, 1993; Cummings and Monti, 1993.) Thrasher has been widely referred to as a "leading authority" on gangs (Taylor, 1990a), based on his study of some 1,300 youth gangs in Chicago. He is cited extensively in virtually every significant work on contemporary gangs. His comprehensive seven-year study incorporated official records but was primarily based upon observing behavior and conducting interviews with gang members in the natural setting of the gangs – the neighborhood. The study utilized the University of Chicago's naturalistic methodological approach to social science research of the 1920s which forced its students to go "from the library to the streets" (Kirk and Miller, 1986: 39).

Although Thrasher's work can be classified as a general survey of gangs in Chicago, the ethnographic approach produced rich data, yielding numerous theoretical trails which were widely pursued by successive researchers. Among these theoretical trails was the concept of gang as facilitator of delinquency, a trail pursued by Cloward and Ohlin (1960), Cohen (1955), and Bloch (1958). Empirically testing the impact of the gang on delinquent behavior were Yablonsky (1962),

Short and Strodtbeck (1974), Miller (1974) and Spergel (1966). Other theoretical trails identified by Thrasher were pursued by contemporary gang researchers: Joe (1993) picked up Thrasher's ethnic-specific focus; Jankowski (1991) pursued the idea of gangs as organizations; and other researchers widely replicated his finding that "...no two gangs are alike..." (p. 45) reflecting the wide variation in gangs both across and within cities and neighborhoods. As a methodological approach, the abundant material gathered by Thrasher about gangs offered numerous opportunities for additional research.

Although Thrasher's work has been widely lauded, there are numerous criticisms of the qualitative approach to social research. Like Thrasher's approach, the research design described in this study is qualitative or descriptive. The rationale for the use of a qualitative approach is described in this chapter as well as both the limitations and advantages of the design.

DEBATE ABOUT QUALITATIVE OR
QUANTITATIVE APPROACHES

After World War II, the social research approach employed by Thrasher and other Chicago School researchers of the era fell into disrepute because data were widely used in a "nonsystematic and nonrigorous way...[The] monographs based on qualitative data consisted of lengthy, detailed descriptions which resulted in very small amounts of theory, if any" (Glaser and Strauss, 1967:15; Joe, 1993; Smith, 1994). Thrasher's work specifically was criticized for the nonsystematic collection of data, inadequate analysis, inadequate relating of key factors such as age and organizational features to gang behavior, and the existence of significant data gaps (Cummings and Monti, 1993).

The rejection of qualitative social research such as Thrasher's followed advances in quantitative methods in the 1940s. During the period, quantitative researchers furthered their ability to establish causality, produce evidence and conduct empirical tests of theory. Quantitative studies, especially experimental or quasi-experimental designs, were developed for their capacity to reduce the uncertainty associated with making causal claims. In general, quantitative researchers use Popper's (1959) concept of falsification, "proceed[ing] less by seeking to confirm theoretical predictions about causal connections than by seeking to falsify them." In contrast, qualitative studies aim to develop "the very theoretical constructs which the quantitative research seeks to falsify" (Cook and Campbell, 1979). In other words, one method develops, one method disproves; the former by finding examples, the latter by finding the exceptions.

The rise in quantitative methods held little promise for gang research, since gang data have not been not widely available nor reliable. The focus on quantitative methods effectively insured that gangs were also out of fashion for social research – reliable samples could not be selected because population parameters were unknown and statistical methods were hampered by the small numbers typically associated with gangs. Only a few studies on gangs were conducted between 1930 and 1980; these were primarily deductive based on existing research or archival data such as arrest reports.

Its historical beginnings may have contributed to the stereotype that "anything goes" in qualitative research (Silverman, 1985: xi; Kirk and Miller, 1986; Smith, 1994; Marshall and Rossman (1995)), stereotyping the social science method as inferior and unscientific. This view of qualitative research continues today. There are five primary criticisms or limitations of qualitative methods – the method is often viewed as subjective or biased, lacking in sufficient rigor thus having little validity, inappropriate to establish causality, unsuitable for answering empirical questions, and have limited generalizability. Each of these limitations can be addressed through a strong design.

Qualitative research is often viewed as subjective, non-scientific research that is laden with the researcher's own values. Clearly, this charge was true in Thrasher's research. He took an activist role in the gang-ridden communities of Chicago in order to develop effective interventions.

All research methods are vulnerable to bias because there are judgement calls inherent in selecting issues to study, questions to include and subjects to study (Kuhn, 1962; Cook and Campbell, 1979).

It is widely accepted that qualitative methods cannot be used to establish causality. Qualitative studies, however, can be rigorous and rule out numerous threats to validity through a series of verification tactics. Internal validity can be increased by insuring data reliability through a triangulation process of repeated verification using different kinds of measures of the same phenomenon; corroborating or seeking contradiction of findings from informants; making comparisons between data sets; examining the meaning of outliers, searching for rival explanations and negative evidence; ruling out spurious relationships; and replicating findings (Miles and Huberman, 1984; Kirk and Miller, 1986).

Rigor of qualitative studies is enhanced through the use of systematic processes for data collection, recording and coding of data – generating categories, themes and patterns; data reduction and interpretation; testing the emerging hypotheses against the data; searching for alternative explanations; (Glaser and Straus, 1967; Marshall and Rossman, 1995; Johnson, 1975; Whyte, 1984; Silverman, 1985; and Bailey, 1994). Techniques such as pattern matching, comparative studies and cross-site case studies can be structured to collect quantitative data, and thus answer many empirical questions (Glaser and Straus, 1967; Miles and Huberman, 1984; Hedrick, 1994; Yin, 1984; Smith, 1994). Much of qualitative data can be converted into quantitative information through coding and counting, permitting the statistical testing of data gathered through qualitative methods. This analysis produces greater explanatory power and greater generalizability.

Qualitative studies are often criticized for their inability to generalize from a single case to larger populations. Although this criticism may be appropriate for some qualitative studies, particularly single shot case studies, some qualitative designs use probability sampling methods, avoiding drawing conclusions that are not representative or generalizable to other settings or groups (Miles and Huberman, 1984; Marshall and Rossman (1995), Glaser and Straus (1967). But theoretical sampling is sufficient to develop theory (Glaser and Straus, 1967).

Glaser and Straus claim random sampling is not necessary to discover relationships and is important only if the researcher wishes to describe "magnitude of relationship within a particular group." Indeed, random sampling is not always possible because of an inability to determine population parameters. Sampling limitations limit statistical validity but Glaser and Straus (1967: 228) point out that data can be verified through the "aggregation and comparison of evidence of different kinds and from different sources"). As early as 1932, qualitative researchers emphasized the importance of objectivity, continuous revisions of 'classification' schemes as additional data were collected, the use of 'provisional hypotheses' to suggest lines of investigation – all precursors of contemporary qualitative research issues (Webb and Webb, 1932: 202).

Studying Gangs: Advantages of Qualitative Methods

Once qualitative methods of social science research fell out of favor following World War II, field research took years to make a resurgence. As far as gangs and delinquency were concerned, the qualitative method remained out of favor in the 1970s and 1980s because of disinterest among funding agencies, an emphasis on the criminal dimension of gangs and law enforcement responses, and continued interest in quantitative techniques (Hagedorn, 1988; Joe, 1993). There were also perceived difficulties in accessing gang members, fears of safety, and the investment in lengthy periods of time necessary to conduct meaningful field research. During this lull of nearly 15 years, public officials and the media paid scant attention to gangs.

By the mid-1980s, police and city officials began to be concerned about gangs and rising violence. A new wave of research on gangs emerged in the 1980s, making great use of face-to-face methods such as in-depth interviews and observation of gang members. A growing number of researchers invested the time and effort to conduct field research on gangs, drawing on the legacy of Thrasher and other ethnographers such as Whyte (1981). Joe (1993) suggests that the application of qualitative approaches to studying HIV among intravenous drug users contributed to the resurgence of interest in ethnographic methods for studying gangs in the mid-1980s. The field research method, commonly used in anthropology, was also effective to "get behind...controversial aspects" of subjects (Ayella, 1993).

The distance between qualitative and quantitative design in the 1990s narrowed primarily because qualitative researchers – through systematizing many of their research processes – have been able to redress many of the concerns that condemned early qualitative studies. In the study of gangs, qualitative methods are recognized for their value in acknowledging the complexities of social life. The method does not attempt to oversimplify by reducing social constructs to a few pieces (Smith, 1994) while the process of operationalizing variables for quantitative research may not fully characterize the construct being sought.

The qualitative method provides access to information about gangs unavailable through other methods. Researchers, for example, can't reliably count gang members or gang events, intuit motivations for their behavior, or rely on official records or secondary sources of information. Field methods overcome data availability and bias issues related to quantitative data about gangs based primarily on official sources and records such as police field reports, gang unit documentation of gang members or arrest reports. Such sources are inherently flawed, noted Hagedorn (1988).

Qualitative studies about gangs continue to provide researchers with "richly" detailed descriptive information. Although the term "rich" is widely overused, often to account for other inadequacies in poorly designed qualitative research, "rich" data have empirical value in gang research. Such data provide a method for overcoming respondent duplicity by validating responses within and across multiple interviews; such data also serve to eliminate observer bias that may become evident during data collection (Becker, 1972: 52).

The availability of analytical software has improved the analysis of qualitative studies of gangs. Qualitative data can be rigorously analyzed using qualitative software, through coding, tagging of key words, word counts and groupings. Although there is no standard procedure for qualitative analysis, analysis aids the researchers in managing a large amount of information and systematically evaluating the information (Miles and Huberman, 1984).

Despite these general strengths of qualitative approaches, field methods contain weaknesses which the careful researcher must redress or accept as limitations. Field research is often expensive and time-consuming. The use of observation techniques, extended interviews with individuals and other ethnographic methods requires significant human resources. Jankowski (1991), for example, spent more than ten years in the field collecting information about gangs. Other contemporary gang researchers have also invested extensive amounts of time in the field collecting data. And the conduct of qualitative research continues to raise important concerns about the quality and consistency of the data, the risk of introducing bias, and other errors that may reduce the validity of the study.

Despite the willingness of a cadre of researchers to undertake qualitative studies, limitations of field research on gangs has troubled other contemporary gang researchers who have used the "up close" or "face-to-face" approach now common among contemporary gang researchers. Finding access to gang members has been emphasized as a key issue to successful data collection. Accessing gang members is difficult and successful researchers must find a way into gangs (Moore, 1991); "Successful entree is a precondition for doing the research. Put simply, no entree, no research" (Johnson, 1975: 50).

Contemporary researchers have used numerous methods to identify and get access to gang organizations. Some have used criminal justice contacts: Pennell (1994) used a county probation department to access juvenile gang members. Sanders (1994) used police informants to observe gang events and interviewed juveniles incarcerated in juvenile hall in San Diego. Campbell (1984) used police to help identify gang members and developed a series of biographies of female gang members. Skolnick, Bluthenthal and Correl (1993) interviewed gang members in five correctional institutions in California.

Other gang researchers have reached outside institutional settings to access gang members. Joan Moore (1978, 1991) used former gang members to help her locate other gang members. She involved these former gang members in every stage of research from formulation of interview guides to report preparation (p. 8). She developed a roster of members of two Latino gangs and drew a sample of cliques stratified by age of formation (early or recent) and prevalence of heroin use. Carl Taylor (1990a) used researchers from his security firm to interview gang members from his former neighborhood. Taylor used a six-month surveillance period, conducted extensive interviews with community members, and carried out individual and group interviews with gang members.

Felix Padilla (1993b) studied a Puerto Rican street gang in Chicago from 1989 to 1990. using contacts in social service agencies and probation officers to access gang members who served as informants and made referrals to other gang members. This "snowballing" or chain referral technique of accessing gang members has been used by other researchers, including Huff (1994) and Joe (1993). Short and Strodtbeck (1974) used youth workers, interviews with gang members and direct observation of gangs in their comprehensive study of 16 gangs and 600 gang members in Chicago. Hagedorn (1988) tracked the careers of 260 founding members of Milwaukee's major gangs, collaborating with a former gang member. That collaborator, Perry Macon, founded the Vicelords gang in 1982, and watched the origins of other gangs in Milwaukee as he built his criminal record. James Diego Vigil (1988) developed a life history of a gang, combining 'homeboys' and academicians to conduct the research. Like Whyte (1981), Vigil tried to become immersed within the culture of the gang community and its neighborhood context. Whyte lived with an Italian family and learned the language to gain access.

Jankowski (1991) studied 37 Latino, white, African American and mixed ethnicity gangs in three metropolitan areas (New York, Los Angeles and Boston) over a ten-year period. The population of gangs was developed through information from local police and "various people who worked in that area" as to names of active gangs, ethnic composition and estimated size of membership. Gangs were then randomly selected from a population stratified by ethnicity. He sought introduction through individuals or agencies which had worked with the targeted gangs.

With the exception of Fagan (1990), few of the studies about gangs have included a comparative component. Joe's (1993) study looked at Latino, Asian and African-American gangs, determining that "there are major differences in the development, activities and organization of varying ethnic gangs" (p. 20). Joe's work derives from Thrasher's original study in 1927 which referred to the wide variation between gangs and particularly ethnic variation. Jankowski's (1991) also represents comparisons between gangs of different ethnicity.

The approach of each of these gang studies is widely varied. Each sampling methodology was appropriately shaped by the researcher's access to gangs and the nature of the research proposition under study.

Have contemporary gang studies, making full use of ethnographic approaches to "get inside" gangs, been successful? Researchers were able to gain entree to these deviant groups, conduct interviews or observe gang activities, and gain insight into queries that have puzzled academicians, such as: What are the criminal activities of gangs? How are the groups organized? Why do gang members join gangs? How are the gangs structured? Answers to these and other questions have been answered but only within the narrow context of specific studies.

Each of these studies has contributed to a growing volume of knowledge about gangs but there is still insufficient information to develop a general theory of gangs (Horowitz, 1990; Hagedorn, 1990; Cohen, 1990; and Huff, 1990). "Despite all the research on gangs, there are many questions that have not been asked" (Horowitz, 1990:

53). Questions have not been asked and studies not conducted which address the widely acknowledged variability among gangs (Thrasher, 1963; Chin, Kelly and Fagan, 1993; Hagedorn, 1990; Spergel, 1990; and others) nor the changing nature of gangs (Goldstein, 1991; Hagedorn, 1990; Huff, 1990; Spergel, 1990; and others). In this context, case studies of single gangs, using the time- and labor-intensive participant observation method, will not produce accurate pictures of the gang situation in the nation.

Horowitz noted that comparisons across gang studies are limited because of the small sample sizes in most studies. Variations in definitions may contribute to this limitation. The use of non-probability samples has limited the ability to draw inferences across studies. Importantly, research which uses the gang member as a unit of analysis rather than the gang organization are flawed. Does this suggest that contemporary studies of gangs are failures? Clearly not, however, further research is needed to expand our understanding about gangs in a systematic way.

APPROACH TO RESEARCH

The research design for this study is a qualitative study using a semi-structured interview instrument to elicit detail about organizational dynamics from a sample of gangs and gang members. The research design, intended to gain an understanding about the development or evolution of successful or highly-organized criminal gangs, uses a non-random sampling process (see Tables 1 and 2) in a cross-site, multi-gang comparison study.

The sample of gangs and gang members is purposive and not intended to be representative. Two cities were selected for study which have numerous gangs and major gang problems – San Diego and Chicago. Because of perceived differences between gangs of different ethnicity, two gangs were selected in each city – one African American, one Latino gang. Although gangs are of widely varying ethnicity, particularly in San Diego, where there are numerous Asian gangs, Latino and African American gangs constitute the dominant membership of gangs in both cities.

Two specific gangs were selected in each city based upon informal discussions with local gang experts. These subject matter experts included police gang unit commanders, FBI officials, and District and

State's Attorneys heading gang prosecution units. These experts were asked to identify the most highly-organized gangs in their cities. Among the experts in Chicago, there was ready consensus on two gangs – the Gangster Disciples and Latin Kings. In San Diego, most of the experts agreed upon the Logan gangs (two subsets were Calle Treinte and Red Steps) and Syndo Mob. In contrast to Chicago, gang experts in San Diego do not typically use terms reflecting the degree of organization within gangs as descriptive indicators. These two gangs were recommended based upon perceived organization of drug dealing and high level criminal offenses rather than simply organizational structure.

Because an accurate sampling frame could not be developed for these four gangs, interviews were conducted with a purposive sample of knowledgeable gang members. The purposive sample is consistent with the notion of "focused sampling" (Glaser and Straus, 1967; Hakim, 1987); Hakim advises that qualitative studies focus on "the selective study of particular persons...that are expected to offer especially illuminating examples or to provide especially good tests for propositions of a broad nature" (pp. 141-42). Because of concerns that street-level interviews would generate interviews with numerous peripheral or wanna-be gang members rather than knowledgeable members, the study accessed gang members through two institutional sources – county probation departments and correctional facilities. Using police gang files, probation department records and prison files – all of which track gang membership for different purposes – members of each gang were identified in each of the two institutional settings.

Table 1: Basic sampling frame

	Chicago	San Diego
African American gangs	Gangster Disciples	Syndo Mob
Latino gangs	Latin Kings	Logan Heights

This dichotomous sampling frame for each gang generated a two-by-four matrix for guiding the conduct of interviews. The goal of the study was to obtain 15 interviews in each cell of Table 2, resulting in 30 interviews per individual gang or a total of 60 interviews with gang members in each city. Although there are three sampling frames (city, gang and gang members), the primary unit of analysis is the individual gang. Consistent with Mudrack (1969), the study examines individuals to gain insight into the group or organization to which the members belong.

Contacts were made with probation and correctional facilities in both cities. Gang workers in both institutional settings were provided a brief, standardized script for soliciting gang members for participation in semi-structured interviews. Efforts were made to minimize coercion by keeping the requests simple and straightforward. The interviews were estimated to take one hour to one and a half hours, with a modest honorarium paid to gang members for completion of the interview. Each respondent was provided with a statement of confidentiality, approved by the U.S. Department of Justice, consistent with its Human Subjects Research requirements. All interviews were conducted in the institutional setting and tape recorded for subsequent transcription.

The design of this study was intended to shed light about patterns of variations in highly organized gangs between ethnic groups and between different cities or regions of the country. Although the sample size in each cell was small (15) because of resource limitations, the total number of interviews is consistent with Hakim (1987):

> The more diverse and diffuse topics covered by social research usually require 30-50 depth interviews; but some will warrant over 100 depth interviews, at which point it becomes much easier to distinguish sub-groups and specific clusters or patterns of attitudes and related behavior (p. 27).

Each of the sampling methodologies in this design is purposive or opportunistic, based upon the knowledge of informed experts. There was no deference to selection of a probability sample of known gang members. The total population of the gang is unknown, a common problem in accessing illegitimate groups. Among offenders, there are no definitive lists of participants (Becker, 1970; Fagan, 1989; Short and Strodtbeck, 1974; Joe, 1993). In addition, many gang members are peripheral without substantive knowledge of organizational history or dynamics. A purposive sample of knowledgeable gang members, many of whom have held named positions of leadership, increases the likelihood that respondents will provide useful information. A single issue drove the sampling methodology: access to knowledgeable gang members. Since access is the single biggest issue facing qualitative researchers (see Johnson, 1975; Becker, 1973; Burgess, 1984), this sampling procedure is consistent with Glaser and Straus (1967):

Table 2: Sampling plan and location

	Source/ Setting	San Diego	Chicago
Latino gangs	Prison	Logan Calle Treinte/Red Steps Donovan Prison	Latin Kings — Joliet Correctional Center, Stateville Correctional Center
	Probation	Logan Calle Treinte/Red Steps San Diego Probation Dept.	Latin Kings — Cook County Probation
African American gangs	Prison	Lincoln Park Syndo Mob — Donovan Prison	Gangster Disciples — Joliet Correctional Center and Stateville Correctional Center
	Probation	Lincoln Park Syndo Mob — San Diego Probation Dept.	Gangster Disciples — Cook County Probation

> Research projects of this nature must sometimes be opportunistic ...[taking advantage of] access to some especially relevant social group...[The resultant focused sampling process thus reflects] the selective study of particular persons...that are expected to offer especially illuminating

examples, or to provide especially good tests for propositions of a broad nature (pp. 141-143).

Instrumentation, Data Management and Analysis

The instrument developed for the study was a 15-page questionnaire combining closed- and open-ended questions. The questionnaire consisted of 45 primary questions, some of which contained numerous follow-up questions. For purposes of this study, the questionnaire contained numerous questions about the history of the gang, membership composition, recruitment practices and estimates of size and growth. Gang members were also asked to define their gang, describe the purpose of the gang when the member joined and note any changes that occurred over time.

Two primary methods of analysis were used for this study. First, responses were quantified when possible. These questions included age, sex, educational level, and dichotomous responses to questions such as "How many members are there in the gang? How old is the youngest gang member and the oldest? When did the gang form?" These responses were coded and entered into SPSS-PC for analysis. There were more than 100 quantifiable questions in the instrument and these questions provide a mechanism for analyzing similarities and differences between the embedded samples in the study. Frequencies or counts, simple crosstabulations and t-tests were used to describe the samples and analyze differences between and within the various samples.

The second portion of the analysis was qualitative. The analysis of the descriptive data was carried out using FolioViews, a qualitative analysis software. Each interview was transcribed and portions of the text were tagged or coded according to the topic discussed by the respondent or key words used in the narrative. For example, a respondent's answer to "How does your gang get along with the police?" was tagged with the keyword "police." Additional references in the interview to police, including synonyms such as cops or the law, were also tagged with the "police" code. Such coding or data reduction techniques were used to "tame the data," a useful term suggested and described by Kleinman and Copp (1993). FolioViews was then used to search and sort the data set for relevant tags. Forty-six markers were inserted in the data set. Analytical procedures for these data also involved counting, classifying, testing emerging hypotheses against data, and searching for conflicting evidence including outliers, rival explanations and incongruous information. Although the analytical procedure was a time-consuming iterative process, the method proved reliable for building a corpus of evidence illuminating the basic research hypothesis. The relevant findings – both quantified and descriptive – are contained in the next chapter.

Strengths and Limitations of the Study

All research studies, of course, have strengths and limitations. This study is no exception. A randomized or representative sample of gangs and gang members was not part of this study's design and thus limits the generalizability of the findings. The objective of the study is to illuminate about how mature or highly-organized gangs evolve over time. In this context, the findings yield descriptive information about each of the gangs and provide insight into how four mature gangs have evolved. The use of comparison groups (four different gangs in two cities) provides an opportunity to generalize across these four gangs, and differences identified in the samples provide an opportunity to conceptualize quite different patterns of evolution, contributing to building a theory of how gangs grow and evolve over time. Analysis of the differences between gangs, however, was constrained because of a relatively small sample size caused by practical issue of resource limitations.

In addition to the small size and non-random sample, other factors may have affected the outcome of the study – the use of gatekeepers and institutional access may have biased the sample; the varying honesty and openness of gang members may have compromised the basis from which conclusions are developed; and interviewer effects may have adversely affected the quality of information collected. Each of these limitations is discussed subsequently.

The research design and issues of access required the use of "gatekeepers" in probation and correctional institutions in order to identify and solicit the participation of gang members. These gatekeepers consisted of gang workers and deputy wardens in the two prisons and probation officers in the probation agencies. Brewer (1992) noted that gatekeepers can impose significant limitations upon research. In this case, the "gatekeepers" were asked to play the role of both informants and collaborators to the research project, at the behest of their institutional supervisors. Thus, these individuals served as informants in identifying knowledgeable gang members and as collaborators in recruiting prospective respondents. There was a risk that these recruited collaborators would dissuade or coerce participants; either case could have affected the composition of the sample which participated in the interviews. An alternative method of "calling out" gang members to prison reception areas – to be invited by research interviewers to participate in the study – was rejected by prison officials concerned about coordinated gang actions. Direct contact of probationary gang members was rejected because of costs associated with contacting individuals and concern about safety of interviewers.

Use of criminal justice institutions as an access point to gang members created the possibility of systematic bias in the sample. Hagedorn (1990) especially criticizes this "surrogate sociology" or "courthouse criminology" approach which uses intermediaries to identify and control the interview process. Institutional bias may reflect only gang members who are "failed lawbreakers." Becker (1970), Hagedorn (1990), Wright et al. (1992) and Polsky (1967), among others, urge criminologists to study offenders in their "natural habitat." As Hagedorn noted, "Gangs will be portrayed differently when studied in their natural environment than when studied as homicide statistics, interviewed in prison, or described by public officials or other self-interested parties" (p. 244). Prison interviews also run the risk of confusing the street gang with the prison gang. Although a respondent's street gang and prison gang affiliation may be closely affiliated, gang members may join a new gang or become otherwise isolated from their former gang. Use of the probation interviews as validation of information collected in prisons may somewhat reduce the risk of this problem.

Conducting interviews in institutional settings, however, reduced risks related to interviewer safety – risks which Hagedorn (1990) and Horowitz (1990) say are overrated. Restrictions on time and funding to search and qualify gang members in neighborhoods or through other settings, such as recreational programs, also restricted the ability to conduct the interviews in a different neutral or neighborhood setting.

Were gang members honest? Letkemann (1973) and Wright et al (1992) note that criminals enjoy talking about their activities as there are few opportunities to talk to anyone about their work. Despite some rejections, numerous contemporary gang researchers have successfully enticed gang members to talk about their experiences; most have received monetary compensation. Taylor (1990a) and Joe (1993) both reported that younger respondents tended to exaggerate while older respondents minimized gang activity. Klein (1971) and Spergel (1984) report that gang members are unreliable sources of information about the gang. Members may exaggerate or hide information, or may not be privy to the scope of gang activities (Goldstein, 1991). Gang members may also suffer from failure to remember accurately. But recall problems for offenders are not usually not severe and "memory failures" – for example of offense history – typically occur with recalling participation in minor crimes (Gottfredson and Hindelang, 1981; Hagan and Palloni, 1988; Hindelang, Hirschi and Weis, 1981; and Farrington, 1973) . Hunt (1984) and Jackson (1986) suggested that female gender can be beneficial in interviewing. Female interviewers are often more successful in interviewing because they are less threatening – however, a female interviewer may inadvertently encourage male interviewees to put on a macho bravado and exaggerate some points. Hagedorn (1988) urges caution in accepting information provided by gang members. Information can be distorted because of fear of reprisal from other gang members, discomfort talking to middle-class whites and fear for the security of the gang. Hagedorn, an experienced field researcher, specifically warns:

> Be wary of your information. Gang members are quite adept at telling social workers and policemen self-serving lies. Glib misinformation is, in fact, a survival tool for many gang members (p. 4).

And Miller (1981) cautions that it "is folly to accept [gang member's] testimony at face value" (p. 306).

Specific steps were taken to address most of the limitations associated with the research design. To address the issue of misinformation by gang members, multiple interviews were conducted to validate claims by gang members. Respondent information was also validated through the dual contact points for gangs – prison and probation. Since the unit of analysis in this study was the gang and not the gang member – the individual member is used only to provide information about the gang – interviews from gang members are aggregated and multiple responses to a single question were used to insure the validity of responses. Thus, outlier responses – that is, those responses which appear inconsistent with the responses of other gang members – were scrutinized carefully.

To overcome concerns regarding secrecy of information, interviewees in the study were informed of the purpose of the study; they were promised confidentiality and signed a consent form (consistent with federal Human Subjects Research), which reinforced the verbal commitment of confidentiality. Good interviewers were used to obtain quality information. As Miller (1975) acknowledged, well-trained and competent interviewers can obtain "detailed, balanced, accurate information on gangs" (p. 307). Interviewers in Chicago were primarily female graduate students in sociology trained in the objectives of the study, and administration of the instrument, regarding probes and techniques for encouraging detailed descriptive information. The audio tapes of the interviews were reviewed to ascertain interviewer compliance with the research objectives. In San Diego, experienced interviewers were obtained from an experienced group of employees of the San Diego Association of Governments – employees who routinely conduct Drug Use Forecasting (DUF) interviews for the U.S. Justice Department with arrestees in a custodial setting.

Of course, gender, race, age and social status were not unimportant issues in conducting the research. The interviews were conducted primarily by young females (less than age 25) albeit experienced in interviewing subjects and well-trained in the administration of the survey instrument. Most of the interviewers were white and middle-class while the respondents were minority, lower-class males. The incongruity between interviewer and interviewee characteristics may have worked in favor of gathering greater insight. "Being an outsider can have value," noted Hagedorn (1990). Warren (1988), for example, said women can capitalize on the sexism of study participants who, not feeling threatened, may reveal greater detail. There is every evidence in this study that reliable information was gained rather uniformly across the respondent sample. Indeed, in the findings section, conflicting evidence is presented where this occurs.

Having addressed the limitations of the research design to the extent possible and practicable, the design produced a rich set of descriptive – albeit voluminous – data sufficient for articulating a theory about the evolution of successful or highly-organized gangs. By undertaking rigorous procedures to ensure the quality of the data and the reliability of the analytical procedures, strong evidence – in the form of classification and enumeration – is produced to support the theory; selective narrative comments illustrate key findings in the real-life language of gang members. The study also sheds light on the complexities of gang behavior – both from an organizational point of view, and from the point of view of the members within the organization. As such, the narrative findings illuminate the interwoven complexities of individual motivations, gang behavior, family and neighborhood influences, and other pulls toward the gang.

CHAPTER IV:
ORGANIZATIONAL FEATURES OF FOUR GANGS

The general consensus established in Chapter II is that most contemporary gangs can best be considered as groups or informal organizations. Hence, the bureaucratic measures typically used to describe and compare formal organizations appear to be largely absent from gangs. In divergence from this general viewpoint, we hypothesize that some contemporary gangs – despite their bureaucratic hallmarks of large size and organizational longevity – are formal organizations, but do not score high on other bureaucratic measures because they are a fundamentally different form of organization. To test this hypothesis, key concepts of organization theory are used to collect and analyze information from interviews conducted with gang members of four major criminal gangs. This approach is consistent with the methodology described in Chapter III.

INTRODUCTION

Evidence for the hypothesis is drawn from interviews and illustrative comments from respondents are cited in this chapter. Although a qualitative method of analysis was predominately used in this study, numerous data elements were quantified through grouping and counting similar responses (consistent with Weber, 1990) to systematically guide the analytic process and indicate the weight of evidence on particular points. Illustrative comments are reported directly and not edited for profanity or grammar. The use of direct quotes is intended only to illuminate findings and is included neither for shock value nor to embarrass or diminish respondents. Throughout this chapter, ellipses or brackets are used to indicate, respectively, deleted extraneous narrative or to suggest necessary verbiage for understanding the broader context in which the response may have been framed.

The importance of establishing the relevant boundaries of a "population" was discussed in the section on organizational theory in Chapter II. In general, a population is considered a set of organizations of a particular form and size, which may be defined by patterned activities, or a group of organizations which are in competition with one another and use a similar strategy (Starbuck, 1965; Boeker, 1991). This definitional test must be applied to the four gangs in this study as well. Since four gangs in two different cities were examined, population boundaries must be established to insure that similar types of organizations are being studied. Just as comparing a Mom and Pop store to Microsoft would be faulty logic, relevant population boundaries for these gangs must be established.

The original sampling strategy called for interviews with 15 members from each gang in Chicago and San Diego through probation contacts and in prison. This sampling plan would have resulted in 30 interviews with members of each gang, with a similar number of interviews drawn from either probation or prison. The results of subject recruitment efforts are displayed in Table III.

A total of 85 active gang members were interviewed for the project with approximately half (41) from San Diego and half (44) from Chicago. Among the gang member respondents, one-third (33) were contacted through prison or jail while the remainder (52) were accessed through probation departments of each jurisdiction.

The conduct of the interviews in both cities deviated from the sampling plan because fewer respondents were interviewed than planned. In Chicago, 26 interviews were conducted with the Gangster Disciples; 15 in prison and 11 on probation. Eighteen interviews were conducted with the Latin Kings gang in Chicago; four in prison, 14 on probation. In San Diego, 20 Logan gang members were interviewed from two sets – Red Steps and Calle Treinte. Half were from the prison setting and half from probation. From the Syndo Mob gang, 21 interviews were conducted; 17 from probation and four from prison. The total number of interviews obtained seems reasonable although less than originally planned. Combining some of the interview sources (sample cells as displayed in Table III), discussed subsequently, overcomes any problems related to small sample sizes.

TABLE III

Gang members interviewed by city and source

	Chicago		San Diego	
	Gangster Disciples	Latin Kings	Logan	Syndo Mob
Prison	15	4	10	4
Probation	11	14	10	17
Total	26	18	20	21

All the gang members interviewed for this study were male. There was some ethnic variation in the sample: half the respondents were African American; 38 percent were Latino; six percent Caucasian, and six percent missing and other. The respondents ranged from 15 to 48 years old while the average age of respondents was 25. Most (71 percent) of the respondents were single and 58 percent reported having children. The average age at which the respondent first heard of the gang was at 10 years of age; the average age at which respondents began hanging out with the gang was 12, while the average age at which respondents became gang members was 132.

Although there were some similarities in responses between the four gangs studied, the institutional access points and cities, there were also some important differences. These differences must be evaluated to determine if the entire gang sample can be analyzed as if it were one sample of 85 respondents — a population of gang members. To illustrate this point, consider an organizational examination of the Boy Scouts of America. Is a Cub Scout the same as a Boy Scout? Is a Boy Scout in Pasadena the same as a Boy Scout in Atlanta? And what about a Brownie Scout or an Eagle Scout? By examining differences in the Boy Scouts between cities (Pasadena and Atlanta), between levels (cubs and regular Boy Scouts), and between related groups (Boy Scouts and Eagle Scouts), the comparability of different scouting groups can be roughly determined. This evaluation of similar characteristics insures that a cub scout won't be asked to describe an Eagle Scout program and that other research missteps do not occur. In other words, consistent with organizational theory, this analysis is necessary to determine the relevant boundaries of the population for this study.

Since the study included at least three likely or possibly distinct populations – the samples by city, by gang, and by institutional source (probation or prison) – differences between each were analyzed to identify variations between the samples at each level.   This detailed analysis is included in Appendix A.   The analysis and discussion about the differences and similarities between the gangs and gang members in this study leads to a major assumption for the qualitative analysis and concomitant findings – differences between the gangs by city are more easily distinguished than are other differences. Differences between the two gangs within each city were minimal as were differences between the probation and prison sources for each gang, a likely surrogate for age and experience within the gang. Although variations between the cities may be explained by a host of factors, it is the differences discerned between the gangs of these two cities that provides a basis for organizational analysis.   Indeed, major factors such as age and size of the gang are variables which are examined in greater detail as part of the organizational analysis discussed subsequently. Since organizational theorists suggest that organizations of a similar size and formed at comparable periods of time are most likely to share a similar form, these variables are examined in greater detail.

ORGANIZATIONAL FEATURES

Gangs, like other social groups and organizations, exhibit organizational features. Although the gangs in this study scored low on characteristics of bureaucracy such as explicit rules and roles (Weisel, Decker and Bynum, 1997; Decker, Bynum and Weisel, 1998), these gangs demonstrate evidence of other basic organizational features.   At a minimum, groups and organizations have members, that is, there is an external boundary between those who are in the group and those who aren't in the group (often referred to as in-group out-group status). Since members can be counted, gang membership can be quantified and organizational size can be estimated. Since members constitute the organization, organizational longevity can be determined. And since organizations proceed through life cycles over time, being subject to pressures to become explicitly organized as they grow larger, organizational phenomena related to growth can be examined. Goal orientation or purposefulness, a defining feature of organizations as discussed in Chapter II, can be evaluated; the effects of the environment gangs can be assessed and the presence of informal organizations or groups within the gang can be determined. In the following sections, these important organizational issues are discussed and evidence from gang member interviews is presented to inform the extent to which these organizational features are present within the four gangs.

Membership

As discussed in Chapter II, both groups and organizations are composed of members. Without individuals as members, groups and organizations would not exist. This recognition of belonging – in-group or out-group status – is consistent with the definitional requirement that both groups and organizations must have external boundaries.

Most respondents in this study acknowledged current membership in a gang – 74 percent of respondents (62) said they are a member of a gang. Of those who did not acknowledge membership, many respondents claimed that they had "previously" belonged to a gang. Since many of the respondents were interviewed in either prison or probation settings, denial of gang membership was not used as a factor to exclude respondents from the study. (All respondents had been identified from reliable sources as members of a gang and virtually all respondents provided detailed information about one of the four gangs.)

Respondents in this study clearly differentiated between membership and non-membership in a gang. Respondents were asked to specify their age when they first started "hanging out" with the gang, and to specify their age when they became a member of the gang. A total of 65 percent of respondents (51) said a period of one year or more transpired between "hanging out" with the gang to joining the gang. These responses suggest that gang members believe membership status in the gang is quite distinct from "hanging out" with the gang. Similarly, gang members recognized termination of membership as well. Sixty-five percent (49) of respondents said they knew at least one person who had left the gang within the last year, effectively ending membership. Half of these respondents (51 percent) said four or more members had left the gang.

These conceptualizations of joining and terminating membership with the gang suggest that membership is a distinct role that can be differentiated from non-membership. Since membership in these gangs is a distinct organizational feature, information about the size of the gang can be collected by determining the number of members in the gang.

Size

Information about the size and age of organizations typically provides considerable insight into the structure of organizations. As discussed in Chapter II, organizational theory suggests that size and organizational age are distinguishing features of organizations and often determine relevant population boundaries. In addition, the characteristics of size and age are highly correlated and effectively determine the structure of organizations. Typically, as organizations grow larger over time, there is a shift towards bureaucracy, including more impersonal and formal interactions between members. As an important basis of organizational analysis, information on the size and longevity of the four gangs in this study was collected through interviews.

To estimate the size of the gangs in this study, gang members were asked, "How many members are there in your gang?" The responses revealed wide variation in size estimates for the relative gangs of respondents, making it difficult to get an accurate picture of the size of the four gangs.

The Gangster Disciple gang is generally acknowledged to be an extremely large gang. Rather consistently, GD prison respondents indicated that there were thousands of gang members in the gang. Respondent #15 said: "I can't put a number on it. There's 100,000 in Chicago alone – we've expanded worldwide." About two-thirds of the GD prison sample estimated their gang's membership at more than 10,000; 40,000-50,000 was the most common response. The remaining gang members said they were unable to estimate the size of their gang, or thousands, or simply "a lot."

The responses from the GD probation sample were consistent with the prison sample. Respondent #12 said: "I can't even say; [maybe] in the hundreds – we past the hundreds. I can't even count all that."

Similarly, respondent #17 said: "It's so many, I can't even count it." "In the world? This is the biggest gang in the world, so a million [gang members] I would guess." (#48)

The Latin Kings gang is also generally acknowledged to be a very large gang. Size of the gang was similarly an elusive concept to members of the Latin Kings, although the majority of respondents indicated that the gang was somewhat smaller than the GDs. About one-fourth of the sample said the gang consisted of thousands; a similar number reported the gang size consisted of "hundreds." Larger estimates of the size of the Latin Kings were reported by the prison respondents:

LKPRIS#14: [Gang membership is] 40,000 – considering everyone in Mexico, Hawaii, New York, Los Angeles and everything.

LKPRIS#50: Millions.

Estimates of gang size by the San Diego gangs were similarly varied but much more modest than those put forth by members of the Chicago gangs. For the Logan gangs, responses ranged from 60 - 70 members for the Red Steps to over 3,000.

LOGANPROB#57: I can't say [how big the gang is] – there is too many.

About half the Logan prison sample responded that the gang consisted of hundreds – from one hundred to a thousand, while the probation sample responses ranged from "hundreds" to 3,000.

Responses to estimations of gang membership were equally varied for the Lincoln Park Syndo Mob. Estimates of gang size ranged from "hundreds" to two thousand, by the prison sample; the probation sample responses were varied: nine respondents made estimates in the hundreds, while four respondents estimated in the thousands, with a high estimate of 2,000.

By city, Chicago gang members who provided specific responses to the question regarding gang size reported larger numbers than did members of the San Diego gangs. (See Table IV.) More than half – 57 percent – of Chicago gang members said their gang consisted of more than 1,000 members; while a third – 32 percent – of San Diego gang members made similar size estimates.

Table IV
Estimates of gang size by city

	Chicago gangs	San Diego gangs
35-100 members	17% (4)	19% (6)
101-1000	26% (6)	48% (15)
1001-10,000	22% (5)	13% (4)
10,000 or more	35% (8)	19% (6)

In summary, gang members appear to have widely divergent views of the size of their gangs and this variation did not seem consistent with greater knowledge of gang size by the generally older prison sample. Consistency in responses may have been confounded by a possible tendency of respondents to inflate the size of the gang to exaggerate its reputation.   Consistency may also have been complicated by different definitions of the term "gang," used by some gang members to refer to the respondent's group, set or clique – a sub-set of the gang – and by others to describe the entire parent gang.   Despite the variation in responses, the estimates suggest relative comparisons.   One is left with a general impression that the GDs are the largest of the gangs with the Latin Kings not far behind; the San Diego gangs appear to be much smaller.   Unambiguously, the size of all of the four gangs appears to be quite large, with each gang exceeding a size threshold in which face-to-face interactions between all members of the organization is possible. The large size of these gangs also suggests more impersonal and formal interactions between organizational participants as discussed in Chapter II.

Longevity

Organizational theorists assert that organizational size is typically related to organizational age – generally organizations begin small and become larger over time. Since the large-sized gangs in this study did not "spring into existence overnight," the length of their existence has implications for understanding their size and concomitant organizational structure.

To assess organizational longevity, all gang members in this study were asked "How long has your gang been around? What year did it get started?"

Gangster Disciple respondents were relatively consistent in their responses to the questions: Fifty-eight percent of the GDs responded that their gang originated in the 1960s (see Table V). Four respondents said the gang has been around since before the 1960s while six reported the gang was formed in the 1970s or 1980s. Latin King respondents were more varied in their estimates of the gang's age as an organization: Four estimated prior to 1960, four estimated during the 1960s; and four estimated 1970s or later. A clear majority of Syndo Mob respondents (12 of 17) reported that their gang started in the 1970s, while two reported the 1960s or earlier and a like number reported 1980s or later as the starting date for their gang.

Although the modal response to the question of when their gang started was 1950s for the Logan gang, the responses of these gang members were varied. Several members estimated gang age by recognizing that the gang has some members who are more than 60 years old. One Logan gang member said the gang had been around for more than 80 years. Of 17 Logan respondents to this question, ten said the gang started in the 1950s or earlier; three said the gang started in the 1960s and four responded that the gang started in the 1950s.

Table V
Year of gang formation

	GDs	Latin Kings	Syndo	Logan
1950s or earlier	17% (4)	33% (4)	6% (1)	59% (10)
1960s	58% (14)	33% (4)	12% (2)	18% (3)
1970s	25% (6)	17% (2)	65% (11)	24% (4)
1980s or later		17% (2)	18% (3)	

One explanation for the variation in responses about the date the gang started is evidence of the organizational birth and rebirth of these gangs over a period of years. Each of these gangs has been through periods of organizational transformation, including merger and consolidation or splintering of the gang. These important organizational events are discussed in the next section of this chapter. The occurrence of such historical events may make it difficult for the gang members to specify the founding date or beginning of their gang. Numerous youthful respondents had no firsthand or personal knowledge of the gang's formation, stating that the gang "started before my time." Typically, gang beginnings were differentially incorporated into the gang lore.

The age of the gang may be examined through an assessment of the age of its older members. Gangs with older members may have been founded earlier than other gangs. Although the sample of gang members is this study was not representative of the gang, an examination of the ages of respondents may provide some clues to the age of the gang (see Table VI). All the gangs included older members, but the median age of prison respondents for the Gangster Disciples and Latin Kings – 33 and 29 years old – appeared to reflect the inclusion of older members for these two gangs. In contrast, the smaller age range for the Syndo Mob – the median age of respondents was 22, the youngest median among the four gangs – seems to reflect the relative youthfulness of this gang. Three of the gangs included respondents in their forties.

To determine the age of gang members, especially older members, respondents were asked to estimate the age of the oldest member and the age of most members of the gang. In these estimates, there is a great deal of consistency across gangs as seen in Table VII. The mean age for "most members" in each of the four gangs was 20 or 21, with the age range consistently stated as 15 years of age for the low point. An examination of responses regarding the "oldest member" of the gang revealed that Logan respondents, on average, reported an age of 61 – nearly 20 years older than the means reported by the other three gangs. These responses confirm the long history of that gang in San Diego.

Table VI
Age of respondents

	Median age Prison sample	Median age Probation sample	Median age	Age range
Gangster Disciples	33	20	27	17 - 44
Latin Kings	29	23	24	15 - 41
Logan	23	25	24	18 - 48
Syndo Mob	25	21	22	18 - 32

On balance, the estimates of the oldest member's age and most members' ages proves inconclusive regarding the age or organizational longevity of the gang, however, it is noteworthy that the median age of most members (Table VII) is less than the median age of respondents (see Table VI). Respondents appear to indicate that most members of the gang are younger than the respondent, suggesting gang expansion at the entry level or among the younger ages of the gang's membership.

The lore and organizational history of each of the gangs in this study provided substantial descriptive evidence of the longevity and enduring nature of the gangs. Not all respondents were knowledgeable about the beginning of their gang, but numerous gang members – especially members of the Gangster Disciples – provided detailed descriptive information about the gang's origin.

Table VII
Age of oldest and most gang members

	Oldest member (range)	Oldest member (mean)	Most members (range)	Most members (mean)
Gangster Disciples	22 - 70	44	15 - 28	21
Latin Kings	26 - 75	45	15 - 32	20
Logan	38 - 82	61	15 - 38	21
Syndo Mob	23 - 93	42	15 - 30	20

Many gang members were able to describe the historical evolution of their gangs. Although it should not be overlooked that many gang members were either reticent or ignorant about their gang's beginnings, those who provided an answer to probes about the gang's beginnings were very consistent in the story they told. The most informed descriptions of gang history came from the GD prison sample. Again, this group of respondents was older than other respondent groups. These respondents were able to identify various leaders, prior gang names and a pattern of gang mergers which resulted in the large size of the GDs. Latin King members were much less forthcoming about their gang's history, a guardedness perhaps related to the oath of secrecy alleged to be a rule of the gang. The knowledge of San Diego gang respondents of their gang's history was weak and inconsistent.

The more detailed descriptions of the organizational history provided by members of the Gangster Disciples demonstrate clear evidence that the organization has survived despite changes in leadership such as death of leaders and fights over control of the gang. Continuation of the gang through these leadership changes, described by many respondents, is a key feature of formal organizations and a major factor contributing to organizational longevity.

GDPRIS#11: [I belong to the]Black Gangster Disciple Nation. Although the name changed technically in 1981. Ok, it's separate Gangster Disciples but in its inception it was the Black Gangster Disciple Nation and at that time when I was first inducted into it, I was inducted into the Black Gangster Disciples... The Black Gangster Disciple Nation started in 1979.

Before there was Black Gangster Disciple Nation, there was Black Gangsters and Disciples. Then you also had High Supreme Gangsters as well. The chief now, Larry Hoover, he was the chief when David Barksdale died in 1979. He started it, Larry Hoover completed it...It actually was all brought together in 1981.

It was commonly known that King David would have wanted Larry Hoover to be chief, that was commonly known. There was a lot of fights and things with the BD's, the Black Disciples. Their king, Shortie Freeman thought that he should be the overall king and they actually put a hit, along with the Black Gangsters, the Black Gangsters and the Black Disciples put a hit on Larry Hoover who is a GD but governs the whole thing Black Gangster, Black Disciples, and Black Gangster Disciples. They put a hit on him to try to put either one of them two in the spot. I forgot the one, Nissan, I think that's his name, the one from the Black Gangsters, I forget.

GDPRIS#15: In the beginning there was Devil Disciples which was headed by King David. When he died, before he died, he brought a few of those that was extremely close to him and told them how he would like them to carry on the organization. .... That's when it parted. That's when GD's became BD's and GD's became Black Gangster Disciples. That's how it split in the beginning. That was around 1971 or 1972 so therefore, that's how long the GD's have been in existence.

GDPRIS#16: If I'm not mistaken, 1978 [was when the gang started]. I think it was a little bit before then but it changed. It used to be Devil Disciples and then it changed to Disciples... When it changed from Devil Disciples to Gangster Disciples in 1978, Black Gangster Disciples. King David was the 5th founder. Once he passed away he left it with Larry Hoover.

GDPRIS#05: [The gang's] actual beginning was in like, it started, well this portion started like in the >60s but before then some of the leaders were leaders of other organizations.

GDPRIS#06: How long has it been around? You can go back to the '60's. It's been around since the '60's but it died out. Then in '79 when the prison system started releasing a lot of the guys that got locked up in the '50s and early '60s, they started it back.

GDPRIS#03: [The gang] started on the south side of Chicago, 1964 or 1965. A few guys got together as a protection thing, to protect the neighborhood from other guys coming into the neighborhood stealing... Guys who hung together made themselves into a gang. ...My father is a gang member also, and he said in the early >60s they gave Jeff Fort a government grant... Fort didn't do what he was supposed to do with that money. He didn't build no boy's clubs or do anything to help the community. So that started a big old rivalry between the Disciples, which was the newly founded group and the Black _____ that had been around earlier than the Disciples.

In contrast to the Gangster Disciple respondents, few Latin Kings were able or willing to provide any details of the beginning of the gang. A Latin King probationer was one of the few Latin King gang members to provide any specific information about the gang's beginnings.

LKPROB#54: Lord Gino, he is in prison, he is the one who created the Latin Kings...[He started the gang] because the Hispanics, the majority is more Puerto Ricans and they started

off first and then the Mexicans and then everybody started
following through like we got White Kings, Black Kings.

Among San Diego respondents, members of the Logan gang were
vaguely familiar with some of the early lore of the gang. This
information was often second-hand and the stories of the gang's origins
were somewhat varied.

LOGANPROB#67: [The gang started] back in the >70s. I'm
thinking for just my clique right there. The gang itself [has
been here] probably since the community of Logan Heights
has been there.... Yeah, cause like my grandpa, he is pretty
old, he used to hang around Logan... Before it was Logan, it
was Luckies.

LOGANPROB#29: [Logan's] an old gang. [It started] way
back. Because it used to have a different name before. They
used to call it Logan Heights Chariots, 33rd Road. That's way
back in I don't know when.

LOGANPROB#43: From what I understand, [Logan has] been
here since the 1930s... I know my clique, the Red Steps started
in 1970s. It was right around the same time that Chicano Park
started... The older homies, they used to live on the street, it's
called Newton Avenue. There used to be a lot of homies that
lived on that street. So there was a building on that corner and
they used to go over there and hang out and drink by the
building. So they just started calling it the Red Steps because
up around the building there was red steps so that's where the
name came from. So that's how it started and back then there
was only like a few of them. It was mainly just the people that
lived on that block.

LOGANPROB#66: ...Calle Treinta ...started in the early 80's.
It was just Logan Heights [before] then [in the 60's].

LOGANPROB#80: [Some Logan gang members are] 60 years
old, 70 years old, I'm not lying. But those 70 or 80 year olds
are from Logan Cherry Gang. There is some big ones

between 40 and 50 in Red Steps but the oldest gang was
Logan Cherry Gang. Then there was Luckies, Logan 26 but
they got taken out. There was a Logan Cherry gang.

Few Syndo Mob members could provide any details about the
origin of the gang. One member provided the following description –
among the most detailed and informative of any response provided by a
Syndo Mob respondent:

SYNDOPROB#37: The gang started in 1979 but we
originated from 5-9 Brim. The Brims been around since the
'60s and '50s; it's been around since the Black Panther days.

On balance, some gang members are extremely knowledgeable
about the formation of their gang. This institutional memory is
particularly clear for the Chicago gang of the Gangster Disciples.
Among the other three gangs, gang members' knowledge – or
willingness to share information – about their gang's beginnings is
uneven. Some of the information about gang lore is passed down
through older members or family members. Despite the inconsistency
of information, the weight of evidence collected through interviews
suggests that each of the gangs have been around for significant periods
of time. These gangs are not novices on the gang scene. In particular,
each of the gangs is rooted in history, with roots that extend to the
1940s or 1950s. The formation of the current gang configuration in
several cases raises questions about establishing the point in time of
organizational birth. Should predecessor gangs – that is, gangs from
which contemporary gangs emerged – be considered as the starting
point of the gang as currently configured? This issue is akin to parallel
questions about contemporary businesses in volatile industries such as
airlines or banking. When an organization is effectively transformed
by patterns of mergers, acquisitions and other actions – actions which
may result in a new name for the organization, larger (or smaller) size,
new leadership, and other visible changes – is the new organization
related to the old organization? Or does the emergence of the new
organization constitute a birth rather than a metamorphosis? This
pattern of thinking about gangs – a population ecology perspective – is
a necessity when evaluating evidence of the substantial organizational
dynamics and upheaval which have characterized these four gangs.

EVIDENCE OF ORGANIZATIONAL DYNAMICS

The evidence demonstrates that these four gangs have been in existence for many years. Over their organizational lives, each gang demonstrates significant evidence of organizational change affecting the gang. Changes in gang name and effects on gang size are the most noticeable evidence of organizational change, but organizational dynamics have likely also had effects upon leadership, structure, and other gang organizational features.

Growth: Consolidation and Splintering

Over the years of their history, Chicago gang members typically described a process in which the two gangs grew larger through the merger of street gangs or consolidation of smaller gangs into a larger gang. In contrast, San Diego gangs typically described a process in which larger gangs splintered into smaller gangs over time, typically dividing up geographic turf. It seems likely that these different organizational processes resulted in the much larger size of the Chicago gangs.

The processes of merger or consolidation were identified through descriptions offered by members of the Gangster Disciples of their organizational history:

GDPRIS#11:[Black Gangster Disciple Nation, Black Gangsters, Disciples and High Supreme Gangsters] actually was all brought together in 1981. Although you had the same members that came together, all these different gangs all came together under one name. It's like we'll take some of your doctrines, we'll take some of your doctrines to satiate everybody's upbringing, what they originally were and bring them all together under one thing....there was many different smaller organizations just in the process of being brought together. And then a couple of years later everybody was brought together under one law, under a one people concept, all of us being the same thing.

GDPRIS#15: At the time before I became a Black Disciple, I was a Rod; it was an extremely small organization and we converted over to GD's, to Black Gangster Disciples. ...Disciples been around for ages. Like I said, in the beginning there was Devil Disciples. But the GD organization has been in existence since 1971.

GDPRIS#05: They were attempting to form a conglomerate... it was three organizations that come together and formed one big organization. In the very beginning ...Larry Hoover ...got his authority from his brother. His brother actually ran the organization before he did. They were right next door to Jeff Fort too... They lived right next door to each other. They hung out together until philosophical differences split them up.

GDPRIS#6: [The Gangster Disciples and Black Gangster Disciples] all used to be one. Black Disciples, you got Shorty Freeman. He down here too. Shorty Freeman is king of the Black Disciples cause him and Larry Hoover don't see eye to eye cause particularly when they broke up, Short Freedman was supposed to become the king of the Black Disciple Nation but Larry Hoover got it so that's when they had they little thing.

[Hoover] took over an office that was the Supreme Gangsters. Everybody really called themselves Supreme Gangsters and Black Gangster Disciples. So he put that together, Black Gangster Disciples. He [is] the one that brought the mobs together. But then after the friction and all that happened, that's when they split up, BD's and Black Gangsters and GD's went they way. We used to be Black Gangster Disciples, now it's just GD, Gangster Disciples.

You would be surprised when the gang first started it was all about, when it first started you could stay like on the block you live on, you would have three or four blocks over, that might be another little block. You might live on Compton and be the Compton Destroyers. Then four streets down it might be another street and they something else. But really in the neighborhood you had eight to ten gangs in one little neighborhood. But then when the Black Gangster Disciples then all the neighborhoods came together and everybody became one mob. So it started out as really just a street thing.

GDPRIS#63: [Larry Hoover, David Barksdale and Jeff Fort]... are the people that basically originated the Gangster Disciples. But before the Gangster Disciples was formed it was Black Gangster Disciples. Both under the G. But Jeff Fort and Larry Hoover had got into it and David, he had cliqued with Larry Hoover. So it was the Gangster Disciples and then when Barksdale died, they still had what they called Black Disciples. So that's how you get the BD's and GD's. ... Now you don't have any Black Gangster Disciples but you do have some Black Gangster Disciples that are Renegades.

For the Latin Kings, the process of formation of the current gang appears to have occurred through the merger of neighborhood ethnic groups. Although Latin King members were extremely reticent to discuss the gang's formation and history, the name of a specific leader occurs in several interviews.

LKPRIS#49: Well, we were started right here around 25th and Christiana and our founder is named Don Juan and Sexy. Those were the original members and from there it got all the way to the north side and then there was always a conflict because the north side is Puerto Rican Latin Kings and we are the Mexican Latin Kings. I mean we are all Latin Kings but the majority, you know what I mean? We had personal rivals amongst ourselves, different backgrounds. But when it comes right down to it, we are all one under the sun.

LKPROB#21: ...When [the gang] started it was just a little street gang. It wasn't a gang – it was just party crews, just people that hang together. They made themselves Latin Kings. From there, they began fighting with other little clubs and they got to fighting with each other so then they didn't consider themselves a club they were a gang. They just started getting bigger and bigger. People started moving away from their neighborhoods. Someone started a section right here, started gathering people around that neighborhood, started calling themselves 19ths and that's how it all expanded.

LKPROB#83: I think it started in the 50's but they weren't Latin Kings really, they were called something else. Player Kings.... All I know is that when the Player Kings started it was just a neighborhood thing.

San Diego gang members, especially those belonging to Logan – the much older of the two San Diego gangs – often referred to second-hand information obtained from family members to describe the history of their gang. But many were able to describe a process in which their gang and other gangs began by splintering off from the parent gang. Even the parent gang, however, had metamorphosed through several name changes over the years. Gang members recalled that the gang had its roots in another gang known as the Luckies; because of highway construction dividing the neighborhood and territorial fights, Logan Heights eventually split into three affiliated gangs – Treinta, Red Steps and Trece Logan Heights.

LOGANPROB#69: Treinta started because we felt – I wasn't around back then but the older homeboys told me – that it started because Logan Heights, see, Logan Heights back in those days used to be all mainly Black Crips. So I guess older homeboys from Logan said we don't want that. We want Logan Heights to grow in the area. So they said, back then it was Chicano Park, Red Steps. So we are going to start hanging out right there and call it Logan Heights Treinta. So a lot of people started hanging out there and getting in fights with the Crips. So after due time, it was just Hispanic territory... They wanted to expand the territory of Logan Heights.

LOGANPROB#69: There is two more [gangs] in Logan Heights [in addition to Treinta]. There is Red Steps and Trece Logan Heights. But back in the old days, it used to just be Logan. But as time went by, they started separating because of freeways getting built and boundaries started separating them apart. But they are still united though. Except there is always family disputes between the different family cliques.

LOGANPROB#81: 30th Street was originally all of Logan. Then along came another hood called Logan Trece, another little gang. So they had to get permission from 30th to start their little gang. Give them a little part of Logan. So Red Steps came along and asked them too. So Red Steps and Logan Trece to gain some respect from other gangs, they had to start fighting and all that. So that's where it all started.

LOGANPROB#24: [The gang] started with Logan Heights, it was 33rd but then they got too old and they stopped.. From there the rest of us came out. Treinta was about, I think, they were [started] about the same time. But I think most of the older ones that aren't there no more, they were the Logan clique 33rd and the Luckies...It was started as Luckies. They were known as Luckies and from there they just went up. They went from Treinta to Red Steps to 33rd. It was probably a weak neighborhood when they started.

...It started out as Luckies [then] they all got older and they made their own little clique. It was a big area they were controlling but from there it's like different people control it now. They say well we are going to control this and then they separated and they started their own little gangs.

LOGANPROB#47: Logan Heights was strong in the beginning and it's still strong. It was so big, that's why it had to break up. That's why you got Shelltown now, that's why you got Sherman and Market. It was too big so people said we gonna call this neighborhood Shelltown, we are going to call this part Sherman, so they started Sherman.

Syndo Mob members described their gang's formation similarly as a pattern of splintering from a once-larger Lincoln Park gang. The Lincoln Park gang was preceded by Loews or 5-9 Brims; later, Lincoln Park split into Skyline Pirus and Lincoln Park Bloods, because of conflict between the gangs which may have been internal fighting.

Syndo Mob is a primary off-shoot of Lincoln Park.   The historical picture of this gang, however, is unclear because of inconsistencies in descriptions between various respondents.

> SYNDOPROB#34: Lincoln Park – a long time ago, they used to be Crips but it changed to Bloods. But they wasn't called Lincoln Park Bloods, they was called Lincoln Crips but then they changed. I forgot how it got changed but they changed it. It wasn't in Lincoln Park though, it was in a different area and then when they came here it was Lincoln Park Bloods. ...I just know that it was a Crip gang and then it got changed to a Blood gang.

> SYNDOPROB#37: We separated from the Nine's and started claiming our own, made our own gang...We split off from the 5-9 Brims [in 1979] and then formed our own gang. That's why we wear green rags instead of red rags. When I started it was Lincoln Park Blood already. Lincoln Park Bloods and Lincoln Park Pirus couldn't get along so we just killed the Piru and put the Blood.

> SYNDOPROB#39: [The gang originally] wasn't Lincoln Park, it was called something else.... and they changed it. It used to be called Loews...It went to Lincoln Park Pirus, like that ... because people had animosity.

> SYNDOPROB#42: First you got Lincoln Park and they [are] Bloods. Then you got Skyline which is Pirus. Then you got Lincoln Park Pirus. Which there is really no more of those because they are all separated. Lincoln Park right now is just Lincoln Park Bloods. Over here you got Skyline Pirus, East Side. Way back in the days it was Lincoln Park Pirus, the gangs was together as one.

> [At one time, the gangs] had they different names but they all were together so it was called Lincoln Park Pirus. But then, for whatever reasons, it might have been this person didn't like that person and they got into a fight and they broke up. Lincoln Park became Bloods and Skyline just became Pirus.

That's when they separated the colors out. They wear red, we wear green.

Descriptions of the organizational history of these four gangs show a clear pattern of change over time. Physical changes in the neighborhood (such as construction of major highways which created a physical divide), friction between leaders, and conflict over turf appear to be the primary reasons behind the changes. A power struggle between competing leaders, for example, characterized the establishment of the Gangster Disciples but the gang appears to have benefited in size by a series of mergers or takeovers of small street gangs. A merger of ethnic groups provided the basis for the founding of the Latin Kings. Divvying up a large geographic territory characterized the formation, resultant splintering and changes of the Logan sets, while the Syndo Mob apparently experienced so many organizational transformations that it is difficult to discern how the gang developed. Changing of gang names associated with the organizational transformations of these gangs marks the history of their evolution over time. Some gangs even changed alliances, for example, the Syndo Mob switched from an alliance with the Crips to an alliance with the Bloods. The dominant organizational processes of consolidation and its antithesis – splintering – appear to substantially explain and characterize patterns of growth in the size of gangs in Chicago and the number of gangs in San Diego.

Growth: Recruitment, Retention and Migration

All of the gangs in this study reported that their gang had grown larger in recent years. In addition to growing larger through merger or consolidation of neighborhood street gangs, gang respondents reported that their gangs had grown larger in several other ways. First, respondents reported that gang members move outside the neighborhood – to suburbs or other cities – but continue to claim the gang and come back to hang out in the original neighborhood. Only occasionally do these displaced members start a new gang chapter in their new community. Secondly, the gangs in this study grew larger as increasingly younger members joined the gang and, third, as older members have not left the gang but maintained an active or semi-active role in gang activities. Both of these processes effectively expand the available pool of candidates – human resources – for gang membership. In Chicago, the pool of gang-member candidates was also expanded through the broadening of ethnic composition of the gangs, according to some members. The Gangster Disciples dropped the label "Black" from their name to signal greater inclusiveness of races while the Latin Kings evolved from separate Latino heritages, such as Mexican and Puerto Rican, becoming a single multi-ethnic gang. These processes of gang growth appear responsible for at least a portion of the increasing size of the four gangs in this study.

Growth in terms of a larger geographic area also characterized increases in gang size. Overall, 61 percent of gang-member respondents said their gang had expanded to other cities within the last three years, while 69 percent said their gang had expanded to the suburbs during that period. These responses were more consistent for the Chicago gangs than for the San Diego gangs. Among the Gangster Disciples, 24 of 26 respondents said the gang had expanded to other cities and 25 of 26 respondents said the gang had expanded to suburbs. Among the Latin Kings, 13 of 14 respondents said the gang had expanded to other cities; a like number said the gang had expanded to suburbs. In San Diego, 16 of 20 members of the Syndo Mob said the gang had not expanded to other cities; eight of ten respondents said the gang had expanded to the suburbs. Among Logan, ten of 19 respondents said the gang had not expanded to other cities; and 8 of 19 said the gang had not expanded to the suburbs. Thus, the Chicago gangs appear to have been in an expansion mode in terms of geographic area – whether intentional or accidental – while the expansion of San Diego gangs has perhaps stabilized.

For the most part, the ways in which gangs grow by migrating to other areas appear to be ad hoc or accidental although one GD described a formal approach to "expanding" the gang:

GDPRIS#6: You might have a guy that live in Chicago and I might go and meet a couple of guys and they found out what I am and I tell them and then next thing you know, they what I am and then so on and so.

Q: So like you move somebody to a neighborhood and make friends?

#6: Right. Guy move to the neighborhood and he got a lot of money and collects a little following.

Q: Do you move, like, somebody who has made a little money at it?

#6: Right, got a shiny car, pretty woman with him, decent clothes, a lot of jewelry. Put that guy in an impoverished neighborhood, he gonna attract attention immediately. Then you have all the other little guys, the little brothers, they want to be just like him. That when they form it.

Alternatively, the start-up of new gang chapters appears to occur gradually over longer periods of time when individual gang members relocate to another area:

GDPRIS#9: [We've expanded through] actual members living there [in other cities] and individuals that's a firm part of the community joining. A member could move there, be there for three or four years and get to know certain people and then he can bring them a business proposition and then from there they gradually start pulling in guys that want to be in.

In contrast to the popular notion that traditional gangs are neighborhood-based – a description many of the respondents offered as the way in which they joined their gang – most respondents described their fellow gang members as not living in the neighborhood. Sixty-five percent of all respondents said not all members of the gang live in the neighborhood however many members stated that a neighborhood-connection – such as former residence in the neighborhood – "looks better" for the prospective gang member who wants to join the gang.

GDPRIS#2: [The gang is] spread out. You might have one faction on the west side, one on the north side, one on the south, one over in Gary, Indiana, some out in California...They are all over Illinois. East St. Louis, everywhere.

LKPROB#21: I don't live in my neighborhood. A lot of them live up there but a lot of them live somewhere else, out in the suburbs.

SYNDOPROB#35: Some [members live in the neighborhood], some don't. You can live in another neighborhood and still be from Lincoln Park...I can't live over here and go over there and say I'm from over there. You can live over here; you can't go over there and say I'm gonna be from you all set unless I used to live there. Like I can't be over here and say I'm gonna be in your set.

SYNDOPROB#38: [Members live] all over San Diego... They just move...You move in with your girlfriend or something or you get ready for your own house. It's not like you can't go where you want to go. It's not like that.

SYNDOPROB#27: It's like this. If you have a friend that you grew up with in the neighborhood and just because he moves away are you going to terminate that friendship? So you know.

SYNDOPROB#41: Most of them [gang members live in the neighborhood] or have before. ...It look better on you though. You down because you grew up with the people. You don't have to worry about them saying anything or doing anything because you grew up with them all your life. But if you an outsider you got to watch out for other people. It's different, I don't know.

SYNDOPROB#42: ...Like some of them might live way out or way over here, some even live in opposite sets but they come there every, back and forth and back and forth. So you don't necessarily have to live on that set to be from that set. Then some of them live in the set. It don't matter. Like me, I stayed [in part of Lincoln Park] there and we [my family] moved. It wasn't by choice, I wouldn't say. My parents moved. But when they moved I still caught the bus and went back after school got a ride down there and went back and forth. The majority of them do stay there and then they move and they come back.

Through this process of individual gang members moving away from their neighborhood but retaining their membership, the gang maintains its membership rolls and continues to expand. Alternatively, gang members who relocate may start new chapters or sets in their new neighborhood. In addition to retaining members who move away, these gangs have also grown larger by retaining older gang members in the gang. Asked whether the respondent's gang had grown during the past three years by keeping older gang members, most respondents (64 percent) said "yes." Among Latin King respondents, two-thirds (9 of 16) said yes; among Gangster Disciple respondents, 83 percent (20 of 24 respondents) said yes. Among the San Diego gangs, for Syndo Mob, 10 of 21 – almost half – respondents said yes; for Logan, 12 of 19 – about two thirds – respondents said yes.

Gangs may keep gang members among their ranks longer through the individual's volition, that is, the individual gains something through membership or has limited opportunities such as job possibilities outside of the gang. Earlier in this chapter, we discussed the differences between San Diego and Chicago respondents. In contrast to Chicago, San Diego gang members reported there were no consequences to leaving the gang. Although some Chicago gang members reported that there were no consequences to leaving the gang – GDPROB#17: "Ain't nobody forced to stay in it"– others reported that consequences, such as a violation or severe beating, were related to leaving the gang. Seventy-seven percent of all Chicago respondents said that consequences occur for members who leave the gang. These consequences can be severe:

LKPROB#21: [One member who left] gets his ass kicked every time they see him. That's about it. [And] they burnt his car...[They] put him backwards on the wall. [That means] they're gonna kill him.

LKPROB#53: [When you leave] you have to walk a line that is about a block long and people on both sides of the line are hitting you. Then if you fall you got to start back from the beginning of the line.

LKPROB#54: Right. If you go back or if say you left the gang without permission, we don't know where you are at, you just kind of get a smashed on sight no matter if it's just in the neighborhood or in public.

LKPROB#64: When I left I didn't have to get the five minutes head to toe because I did so much for the nation. I even got shot in a drive-by so that was my suffering right there.... They were disappointed [when I left]; they didn't want me to leave but I told them if they needed any help or anything from me I am always there for them. I ain't gonna go kill nobody for them, but if it takes another fist I'll go. I'll go stand up for my rights.

The pressures to remain in the gang are as much external to the gang as within. This phenomenon occurs at the institutional level, where gang members may continue to be labeled as gang members despite having left the gang. But fellow gang members and rival gangs also contribute to the labeling phenomenon. For example, former enemies from opposing gangs may carry a grudge against a gang member:

GDPRIS#3: But see you never really out [of the gang] because guys you done did stuff to back in the past know you as being who you are. I could tell you right now I'm gonna leave the gang right now this second I will leave the gang. Two years from now or an hour from now I could announce to the whole world I'm no longer with the gang but this guy is going to remember that I once shot him or shot his brother and he say, he a GD, let's kill him.

Some gang members suggested that the only way to leave the gang or terminate life membership is to physically leave or move away from the geographic area where the gang is active:

GDPROB#55: It be consequences [to leaving the gang]. It be like we don't want you to come back around. It all depends. Some people just don't say nothing and you still think they in the gang. They probably disappear, go out of town or whatever. To yourself, you know you ain't still in no gang but to the other people, they probably still go for a year or two and you go back to that place and they still know who you is. It goes on from there.

GDPRIS#03: And the reality is ...you don't really quit. You never really go out unless you just move out, just disappear, there is no out.... That's one of the laws you pledge, you pledge for life.

In contrast, some gang members describe a process wherein members can just retire from the gang or become inactive without formally leaving the gang.

GDPRIS#7: After about 30 or 35 [years of age] you can become inactive. You just don't have to do nothing but shell out some of that wisdom they got....You can leave at any given time, no strings attached, nothing.

LKPRIS#49: Sometimes we give [gang members] an open blessing [if they want to leave the gang]. If you want to do something productive either for religion purposes, you want to turn your life over to God or you want to be married, we will accept that with open arms. You never forget where you came from but once a king, always a king.

In sharp contrast to Chicago, San Diego gang members reported no consequences to leaving the gang. This difference probably contributes to the larger size of Chicago gangs. Failure of older gang members to leave the gang swells the membership rolls of these organizations.

Although criminological literature a strong nexus between age and crime – documenting the fact that delinquent or youthful criminals usually outgrow or mature out of crime as they grow older – few gang members in this study seem to leave the gangs. Asked whether anyone had left the respondent's gang during the last year, 65 percent of gang members in this study said "yes." But 75 percent of the respondents said that 10 or fewer members had left the gang during that time frame. Given the large size of these gangs, membership does not appear to turn over with great frequency. The following description of "maturing out" of the gang appears limited to a few members.

> LKPROB#64: About three or four [members left the gang while I was in it]. Some of them just grew up out of it and a couple of them just didn't have no more interest in it. Just too much problems from the police. [I] just grew up out of it. Just realize that it was wrong. My family was suffering and everything and I got caught up a lot of times by the police and everything. I just woke up and realized that, my girlfriend has something to do with it too.

Rather than describe a process of maturation and leaving the gang, numerous gang members referred to the intergenerational nature of the gang. For example, the upper age limit of gang membership mentioned by some respondents was 70 or 80 years old.

> GDPROB#17: Most of them [gang members are] in they 50s – old geezers out there wanting to be doing some of this shit. [They] should be in rocking they grandbabies to sleep or something [instead of] trying to hang with us young folks.

In addition to the gang growing larger through members migrating to new areas and retention of gang members, individual gangs also recruit new members. Recruiting new members is a necessity for a gang which is growing larger or even just maintaining membership by routinely replacing members lost through attrition. Individual gangs also grow larger through attracting new, often young, gang members: 94 percent of all gang members in this study said their gang had grown by adding new members during the last three years. All Latin Kings said yes; all but one Gangster Disciple said their gang had grown. In San Diego, only two Logan members said the gang had not grown while two Syndo Mob members – both of these incarcerated members – said the gang had not grown larger through adding more members.

Interviews with the gang members in this study turned up not a single incidence of active or coercive recruitment. Gang members made clear there is no shortage of youth who want to become gang members; hence, there is little need for active recruitment.

GDPRIS#72: [It's] just like join[ing] church – recruit and give people option to join and leave, no pressure.

LKPROB#74: [We just] tell them of the benefits.

SYNDOPROB#39: You don't [recruit]. It's on their behalf, their judgment, if it's what they want to do. I'm not gonna force somebody to join the gang. If they want to join they can join on their own.

LKPRIS#50: We let them ask us [to join the gang]..

GDPRIS#7: They come to us. We don't go looking for nobody.

LKPROB#19: [New members] they just come along.

LKPRIS#49: If we see a guy that got heart and he's a likable guy and we think that he could hold his own, we will ask him if he wants to be a member. We really don't need to ask. They be wanting to. We be trying to get rid of some sometimes.

LKPROB#32: We don't force nobody to join. If they want to join, they just come in. We are not out there forcing people because we have got too many people to go looking for new people.

Relationships and gang affiliation of family and friends apparently play a key role in introducing or exposing prospective members to the gang – much like providing a job referral. For the most part, this exposure appears to be an informal process to give new members a chance to evaluate the benefits of the gang.

GDPRIS#9: Most people grow into it, they have older brothers and uncles and stuff like that.

LOGANPROB#67: You got your little friends, your buddies and little brother and people bring their little brothers to the park and say they want to get jumped in.

GDPROB#48: Some of the shorties, the only reason why they turn gang bangers is because their older brothers are one and they want to do it while they are young because then by the time they get older they will have some rank and won't just be soldiers. That's another reason why they join. It depends on the history of your family if you want to or not.

GDPRIS#10: Like you on the streets and you hear about a certain type of gang and you might have a friend that is affiliated with that and he runs down to you what the gang is and the proceeds and the good things that happen in the organization and you get recruited like that.

The friend or family connection between the gang and the prospective member also serves to vouch for the prospective member. This process seems to work much like providing a character reference for a job. The friend or family member can vouch for the trustworthiness of the prospective member. In the vernacular of gang members, a prospective member who is trustworthy is "down."

LOGANPROB#57: Let's say one of my friends knows some guy and he say's he is pretty down and he kicks it with us for awhile. It's goes in a cycle. If you have a friend too that's down it goes in a cycle.

Growing up in a gang neighborhood provides numerous opportunities for prospective members to be exposed to the neighborhood gang. This kind of daily exposure to gang life appears to create a natural drift into gang membership in which joining the gang is not a conscious choice but reflects an ordinary and dominant way of life in the neighborhood.

LOGANPRIS#62: It's not like we got applications [to join the gang], we got an opening, it's not like that. People grow up there and people say I want to be there.

GDPRIS#2: It's not recruitment; it's a lot of it is growing up in those neighborhoods and they feel it's automatic that they become one. They are not forced, they are not told you have to be a part of this. A lot of young kids or teenagers feel that if they see the older guys with something.

SYNDO#78: New people, it's not hard getting new people. It's just young kids growing up...You just get the people in the neighborhood. You don't go to Skyline and get people from Skyline to be from Lincoln Park. That's not how it goes. You get people from Lincoln Park to be from Lincoln Park and people from Skyline be from Skyline. You get the people in the area.

Instead of an active recruitment process, gang members describe a two-staged procedure in which youth hang out around the gang over a period of time; following this period, the prospective members see the benefits of gang membership and ask to join. This process seems something like a trial membership or probationary period for current gang members to assess the prospective gang member and for the prospective gang member to assess the gang.

LKPROB#21: Yeah, we ain't forcing nobody to [join]. They got to be up to that if they want to be one of us. You got to know the people for awhile. You don't just hang out for one day, hey, I want to be one... They come to us, they start hanging around with us, they see what we do, how we treat each other. And then, if they want to be part of it, we take them to the side, we tell them about the situation, we tell them what they getting into and if they want to, they do if they don't, we don't force them.

LKPROB#56: It's like people that hang around. You got to hang around with them for awhile. They want to see if you can take care of yourself. If you can fight real good then they will let you in.

LOGANPROB#67: Well, you got to be around the neighborhood for awhile. People that just hang out for a minute and then that's when they finally say I want to get jumped in and then they get jumped in. People agree with them and then, alright, they do it.

During the trial membership or probationary period, gang members believe prospective members consciously assess the benefits of membership. Gang members believe that younger prospective members see them as role models and want the kind of financial resources or material belongings which gang members may possess.

GDPRIS#16: People see that we making fast money or driving fancy cars and just come and say they want to join.

SYNDOPROB#42: Like I said before, [prospective members] see what you doing and what you got and they want it. Like me. I knew this one guy in Spring Valley, I had three cars, I had a house, so he seen all this stuff I got and he was like, what's up man? So I took him to the set to meet all the homeboys.

Thus, the evidence from this study indicates that all four of these gangs are actively growing by retaining older members, attracting new and younger members, and expanding the geographic areas from which they draw beyond traditional neighborhood boundaries. These expansion processes suggest that gangs have found ways to increase their efficiency as organizations by becoming larger. While there is probably not an unlimited number of potential gang members available from which gangs may recruit, gang members have provided evidence of vast surplus of human resources in two cities in which gang membership is already high. The absence of active or coercive recruiting efforts confirms that there is a surplus of resources currently available for gang membership. The absence of active recruiting suggests that gangs in these cities will continue to grow larger in the foreseeable future, co-opting new members if necessary from non-traditional areas (for example, older persons, females and other ethnic groups) in order to maintain the growth trajectory of the gang.

PURPOSEFULNESS AND GOAL ORIENTATION

As discussed in Chapter II, centrality of goals is a key feature of organizations. Goals are the primary objective of formal organizations, and organizations are structured in order to maximize attainment of those objectives. It should be recalled, however, that goals may be "ambiguous, fluid, multiple, conflicting, and only loosely coupled with the action of the organization" (Popielarz and McPherson, 1995; Scott, 1993). And, as discussed in Chapter II, the goals of the informal organization (that is, groups within the organization) and the goals of individuals within the organization are often quite different from the goals of the organization. There may, however, be distinct linkages between the differing goals of these organizational levels and those of individuals comprising the organization.

Identifying the presence and nature of the goals of gangs examined in this study was a primary objective of the research. The absence of goals or purposefulness among the gangs in this study would increase uncertainty about classifying and thinking about these entities as "organizations." To detect the presence and nature of the gang's objectives, several qualitative probes were used in the structured interviews: "What is a gang? Why did you join the gang? What is good about being in a gang? What was the primary purpose of your gang when you joined? and How has that purpose changed over time?" These questions offer differing ways of detecting and examining the nature of the gang's goals since the queries examine perspectives at the formal organization, group and individual levels.

In this section, answers to these questions are examined – first separately, then together – to illuminate the purposefulness of the four gangs ranging from the individual's perceived benefits to perceptions of broader organizational objectives.

Although the questions about purposefulness appear to be straightforward, many respondents had difficulty articulating clear answers. Numerous gang members provided more than one answer to these questions; the answers of other respondents were difficult to interpret because of the rambling nature of the response. To clarify responses to these questions, all responses to these questions were analyzed for content based on key repeating words. (The quantified responses are arrayed in the following tables in this section which rank order categories by number of responses.)

The first of the related series of questions about purposefulness asked respondents to define a gang. Responses were classified based upon key words into 11 categories. These response categories are displayed in Table VIII. Responses are only loosely classified in order to reveal the nuances in descriptions offered by gang members.

Table VIII
What is a gang?
Responses in number of times mentioned

	GDs	Latin Kings	Logan	Syndo Mob	Total
A family, a brotherhood	5	8	8	3	24
Collective group of people, group with a common purpose	14	5		2	21
Homies, homeboys, folks you grew up with, friends			9	11	20
An organization, business	11	5			16
A group of people			7	8	15
People who come together to do crime, make money or sell drugs	8	4	2		14
Something to make life better, improve our lives	10	1			11
A neighborhood			5	4	9
People who look out for each other	1	2	1	4	8
A group governed by chain of command, rules	4	3			7
A group to protect turf	4		1		5

Almost every respondent incorporated the general concept or expression of the term "group" into the definition of gang. The two exceptions to the group-labeling phenomenon were those respondents who differentiated their gang as an organization or business rather than a gang; and respondents who identified the geographic area of their residence or neighborhood as the framework or foundation for the gang. (In the latter case, the gang is the neighborhood, hence the origin of local gang names – Logan for Logan Heights, and Syndo Mob is also known as Lincoln Park.) These sets of responses were specific to Chicago and San Diego gangs, respectively. That is, in their definition of gang, only gang members from Chicago incorporated the notion of gang as organization and only gang members from San Diego incorporated the notion of gang, or the set, as a geographic area. The following responses illuminate these two types of responses.

From Chicago:

GDPROB#51: ...My gang that I was in, we was really not a gang, we was an organization because we was coming together for a worthy cause to make things better for us in our community ...

GDPRIS#13: Personally, I don't consider [GDs] as being a gang. I consider it an organization... I look at it as being a growth and development organization.

LKPRIS#83: ... We don't consider ourselves gang bangers, we consider ourselves an organization.

And from San Diego:

LOGANPRIS#29: A gang is where you hang out. Your friends, you find a lot of love that you don't get at home, a lot of respect, they are always there for you. Friends, it's fun.... I don't call it a gang...It's just homeboys.

LOGANPRIS#69: [A gang is] a lot of people and you are all claiming where you live. So it's like a gang... Everybody is in it for the same reason, because they grew up in that neighborhood and they have love for the neighborhood they grew up in.

Overall, the responses to the question about defining a gang confirmed other differences between San Diego and Chicago gangs. Although respondents from both cities described the gang as a group, the use of the term "group" appeared sufficient to the definition of gangs by respondents in San Diego. In contrast, respondents from Chicago were much more likely to combine "group" references with specification of a common purpose, report the centrality of crime and/or moneymaking, or identify some other emphasis or characteristic attached to the group, such as adherence to rules. Thus, the Chicago respondents appeared to generally conceptualize the gang as a group with a function; San Diego respondents typically omit that sense of purposefulness from their definition, emphasizing a more informal, happenstance character.

From Chicago, the following responses represent this focus on purposefulness:

GDPRIS#5: A gang is a group of individuals bound together for a common purpose. [They are bound together] a lot of ways, socially, economically, emotionally sometimes.

GDPRIS#13: Basically [a gang is] a group of people with the same objectives, trying to reach for the same goals.

From San Diego, the following responses represent the absence of purposefulness, emphasizing the more informal character of the gang:

SYNDOPRIS#65: [A gang] is just friends that be together and hang out together.

SYNDOPROB#22: Well, to me ... just look at the word gang. It's a group. It's a variety of people or things or whatever the case may be. It would be two or more people and that's what I associate [gang] with.

SYNDOPROB#27: I don't really consider it a gang. It's just a group that grew up together.

Despite the limited evidence of purposefulness among San Diego gang members, a portion of San Diego respondents elaborated their definition of group with other characterizations. Most often, the description incorporated into the group definition was friendship or family. The notion of brotherhood was also incorporated as a description by San Diego respondents. The term "brotherhood" also appears frequently in the Chicago respondents' conceptualization of the gang. The common use of the term "brotherhood" across the two cities may reflect ambiguity of the term. Brotherhood may represent very different notions to gang members in Chicago and San Diego. In San Diego, brotherhood appears to reflect shared ethnic or neighborhood origins; in Chicago, the term brotherhood appears to reflect solidarity within the gang organization. Similarly, the concept of "family" may also suggest different things to different gangs and respondents. The context for the responses incorporating notions of family and brotherhood rarely illuminate the underlying meaning of these common terms although the typical use of the terms suggest that gang friends become surrogate family to the respondent. The emphasis of this relationship between friendship and family, however, varied between cities. The notion of friendship and family were often central to the definitions offered by Logan and Syndo Mob members, while family and neighborhood were secondary or subordinate concepts in the definition of the gang offered by Chicago respondents. The following responses reflect statements for gang members in each city.

From San Diego:

LOGANPRIS#62: [A gang is] a family [to me]....When I was growing up, I grew up on the streets and in juvenile hall. I never had nobody to tell me anything like stay home, go to school. [The gang was] there for me. I kind of fit in with them. If anything happens to them I feel hurt. We call ourselves like a real big family – especially inside the system.

LOGANPRIS#61: [A gang is] just my homeboys, the people that I hang around with, grew up with, family just like almost, friends. Most of them is family because I got family that is Logan too. I got homeboys that I grew up with from when we were little kids.

SYNDOPROB#26: It's just people that grew up in the same neighborhood that come together, that's a gang...I don't call them a gang. That's what everybody else calls them. They are just my homeboys really. Gang is just a name that they gave us. But basically to me, it's just my friends that I grew up with, like relatives that I grew up with cause I been knowing them for so long.

From Chicago:

LKPRIS#49: [A gang is] a group of brothers that agree to go by a set of rules or guidelines. To be something, a family within, outside of your own family, brotherly love. It's devotion, it's love, sacrifice, honor, obedience. If you can't go with that, then you have to take a ride.

GDPRIS#05: [The gang is] Money, support [for me]; I felt a sense of belonging, it was trust. There were people within the organization that I looked up to like father figures and big brothers and stuff. These were relationships that I never really experienced before. Something that I wanted.

GDPRIS# 03: Well, in my words, a gang ain't nothing but people come together to do crime and make money and be a family to each other. That's the original idea.

Any purposefulness associated with the gangs was rarely made explicit by gang members in their definition of the gang. To the extent that goals of gangs were incorporated when defining the gang, these were more specific in the definition of the gang by Chicago gang members. These explicit references most often involved money, particularly making money through drug sales. This elaboration of the group function – by attaching goals or objectives to the definition of a gang – is evident in the following comments from Chicago respondents:

GDPROB#85: A gang, nowadays, would be money making, make money.

GDPROB#48: [A gang] it's about the money for me.

GDPRIS#06: [A gang is] a bunch of brothers hooked up, trying to make money.

In summary, evidence of gang purposiveness as revealed through this examination of how gang members conceptualize the gang is typically absent or not clearly articulated at this level of inquiry. In other words, when gang members think about the gang as an organizational entity, group goals or objectives do not typically enter the picture.

The second of the related series of questions about purposefulness asked respondents: "Why did you join the gang?" This question is less general than the query about defining the gang. Indeed, this question is specific to the motivation underlying the individual's decision to join a particular gang, and was intended to examine or link individual motivations with the goals of the gang. For example, if the gang is a drug-dealing gang, the gang member may have joined as a means to get drugs or make money.

An analysis of responses to this query revealed that respondents rarely provided any reasons for joining the gang that related to a sense of purposefulness about the gang. Instead, fully two-thirds of responses (65) reflected a socialization experience, suggesting that either peer, family or neighborhood influence were primary factors or influences in the decision of the individual to join the gang (see Table IX). The social nature of joining the gang is consistent with findings from other studies, which show gang members typically "drift" into gang membership (Fagan, 1990: 210), rather than making conscious and rational choices about gang membership at discrete points in time. The following responses were typical:

LKPROB#32: I don't know [why I joined]. I just grew up with it. Might as well be in it. I be with them every day.

LOGANPRIS#61: Why did I join the gang? I don't know. I guess it was meant to be for me. I just grew up into it since I was small, since I got cousins and all that. I used to hang around with them and I used to go places with them and I just grew up into it.

GDPROB#12: It's something you shouldn't want to get into but you end up getting in it somehow, some way.

In addition to the socialization reasons for joining the gang, respondents offered a handful of other reasons for joining the gang: to socialize including partying, for fun, to get girls, because it's the "in" thing or it's cool; money; family-like support, love, or security; survival, protection or to protect the neighborhood; because of the gang's philosophy or positive aspects; or curiosity. Table IX arrays these reasons in rank order, with some limited grouping of similar terms.

However, there appears to be no clear consensus or obvious grouping among these other reasons offered for joining the gang. Perhaps the most noteworthy feature of the responses about why the individual joined the gang is the absence of consensus – different members join the gang for different reasons. Rarely did responses appear to reflect a reasoned, thoughtful approach to joining the gang.

Table IX
Reasons for joining the gang
Responses in number of times mentioned

	GDs	Latin Kings	Syndo Mob	Logan	Total
Friendship – friends were in, just happened	8	8	7	5	28
Neighborhood-based, fell into it, it was there	5	4	7	8	24
Grew up into it, inherited it from family members	3		5	5	13
Socialize, party, fun, girls, "in" thing, cool	3	3	2	2	10
Money	2		1	2	5
Family-like support, love, security	3			2	5
Survival, protection, to protect neighborhood	1	1	3		5
Philosophy, positive aspects	3	1			4
Curiosity	1		2		3

In examining differences between the reasons gang members in Chicago join gangs and the reasons of gang members in San Diego, there was only one distinction: more respondents in San Diego than Chicago mentioned the influence of their family members in their reason for joining the gang. This tendency to "grow up in" the gang because of older brothers, cousins or fathers belonging to the gang was expressed typically in the following statements from San Diego gang members:

LOGANPROB#28: I didn't join it, I was raised in it. [I] grew up in it.

SYNDOPROB#41: [I] grew up into it. Grow up over there and everybody else doing it, everybody I was hanging around with doing it, just grew up into it. Ain't no peer pressure or nothing like that. Got a couple of family members in there.

To follow up the question of why the respondent joined the gang, gang members were also asked about the advantages or benefits associated with gang membership: "What is good about being in the gang? What are the advantages to you?" Based on content analysis using key word counts, responses to questions were classified into a scheme that illuminates the nature of group or organizational benefits accruing to individuals. (Counts capture all responses offered during an interview; the number of responses was not limited.) These responses were classified into the following four categories:

Social interaction including party, socialize, fun, hang out, no purpose, women, girls, "in" thing, something to do, be cool, fighting/status, being tough, get attention;

Affiliation including family, support, help you out, brotherhood, love, belonging, being a part of something;

Economic opportunity including make money, sell drugs, jobs, clothes, steal together, productive, future-oriented with jobs, positive benefits, to protect neighborhood ; and,

Protection including survival, protection from rivals, respect, security, trust, learn to be a man.

These categories are listed in rank order in Table X, along with the key words comprising each category. Based on the key word count, one common response emerged which did not fit into the classification scheme. This response included "don't know, curiosity, nothing good" – 17 or 10 percent of respondents offered this answer.

Some responses were difficult to categorize because they are common hence somewhat ambiguous terms. Words such as "status, trust or survival" may be imbued with meaning for the individual respondent. But the meaning of "survival", for example, may be related to economic survival as in making money or physical protection from rival gang members. Similarly, "fighting" or "being tough" may be related to protecting the individual, one's friends, or economic markets, although the context for these responses typically suggested fighting and being tough as something which sounded like a social activity. When possible, context was used to place the response into the most appropriate category.

Table X

Benefits of gang membership

Responses in number of times mentioned

	GDs	Latin Kings	Syndo Mob	Logan	Total
Protection	15	10	13	13	29% 51
Economic opportunity	19	4	8	11	24% 42
Affiliation	10	5	9	14	22% 38
Social interaction	15	1	2	10	16% 28
Don't know, nothing good	3	0	10	4	10% 17

Most respondents offered multiple responses to the question about benefits or advantages of gang membership. On average, gang members offered two responses to this question. A respondent's multiple responses were occasionally classified into the same category, for example, a respondent might respond that the benefits of gang membership were selling drugs and making money. More often, however, multiple responses were categorized into different classifications; for example, a respondent might say the benefits or advantages of gang membership were making money and being loved.

Although a single response is assigned to only one category in the classification scheme (i.e., it is only counted once), the categories are not mutually exclusive. Indeed, the four primary categories appear to be closely related and complementary. The different categories provide a mechanism for quantifying the frequency with which differing responses were offered by gang members. In contrast to the previous questions about reasons for joining the gang, the question about benefits of gang membership elicited responses which clustered into a defensible classification scheme. Respondents articulated fewer reasons, and those reasons clustered logically. Reasons related to self-protection appear to be the most commonly perceived benefit from gang membership – 29 percent of respondents named this as a benefit of gang membership. Economic opportunity – that is, a chance to make money or sell drugs– were mentioned as a benefit of gang membership by 24 percent of respondents, while a similar number (22 percent) mentioned affective or affiliation reasons as a benefit of gang membership. Fewer respondents – 16 percent – mentioned purely social reasons, such as partying, as a benefit of gang membership.

Narrative responses reinforced the complementary nature of the classification scheme, indicating that gang members routinely integrate social interaction (such as partying) with affiliation (partying with friends) while pursuing economic opportunity. In describing activities of the gang, respondents provided numerous examples of these nested or complementary activities:

> GDPRIS#18: It's like everybody just be outside, hanging on the corner drinking beer, smoking bud and shit, messing with the girls, calling them all type of names. Everyday life down on that street....we stand on the corner, sell dope all day, mess with the honeys, just kick it with them.

> LKPROB#32: Really all we do is ride around, go places, go to stores, go with girls. When we are riding around, all we do is see people that are selling drugs. We'll see our friends and they will be out there selling drugs. We won't be there with them though; we will leave if they are selling drugs.

> SYNDOPROB#45: We kick it together, smoke marijuana, maybe jack something. If we think we can make some money selling it, we will take it.

Each of these descriptions suggests the routine integration of money-making activities, fulfillment of affiliation needs and participation in social activities. This integration seems to suggest that gang members move from one activity or role to another, seamlessly blending functions of family, friends, business, and social activities. Such an integration appears to generate the variation and complementary nature of the stated advantages or benefits of gang membership.

The responses of members about advantages of gang membership sheds some light on the purposefulness of the gang. The influence of "social interaction" factors in Table X diminished from the previous table – Table IX. The question about reasons for joining produced answers related to socialization experiences or drift; but the benefits of gang membership are much more clearly and specifically articulated. Gang members may have originally "drifted" into gang membership, but once a member, they are able to articulate one or more specific reasons for their continued involvement with the gang. With the exception of the 11 percent of respondents who see "nothing good" about gang membership, the rationale for staying in the gang is more explicit and non-social than the reason for joining.

Although one might assume that the benefits of gang membership to the individual are derived from the purposeful activities of the gang, this linkage is not evident in Table X. While a quarter of respondents believe they derive economic benefits from the gang – which would be prima facie evidence of purposefulness – most gang members did not mention economic benefits as a benefit of gang membership. However, the complementary nature of response categories does not invalidate the notion that the gang as an organization may be purposeful.

A final more direct question about the purpose of the gang was asked of gang members: "What was the primary purpose of your gang when you joined? How has that purpose changed over time?" Responses were classified based on content analysis and categorized consistent with the classification scheme in Table X. These responses are arrayed in Table XI, in rank order. Since the respondents typically were asked and answered these questions together, the responses for the questions are counted and coded together.

Table XI
Primary purpose of the gang
Responses in number of times mentioned

	GDs	Latin Kings	Syndo Mob	Logan	Total
Economic opportunity	24	15	15	16	53% 70
Social interaction	11	3	6	8	21% 28
Affiliation	5	1	4	4	11% 14
Protection	3	1	3	0	5% 7
Don't know, no purpose	1	0	10	1	9% 12

The theme of moneymaking and pursuing economic opportunity emerged much more strongly in this query than in the responses to any of the previous probes about gang purposefulness. More than half of respondents 53 percent – said the purpose of the gang was making money. The following responses were typical from gang members in both San Diego and Chicago:

LOGANPROB#29: Every gang, pretty sure you are going to find somebody with drugs. They are everywhere. That's where the money comes from.

LOGANPRIS#69: I got into it because there was a lot of money involved. That was my main concern, money. Dreams of having everything I wanted and pulling out that big old wad of money at school, buying clothes, buying my mom things, making her happy. So back when I started, I think money was the main thing.

GDPRIS#2: Standing on the street corner and talking and sitting there getting high all day, you make plenty of money, I'm not gonna lie about that but it gets tiresome always looking for the police too or looking for somebody that is gonna try to kill you for your money.

SYNDOPROB#39: We just a gang who have money. We have the money. We all about making money. [Making money by] selling drugs.

SYNDOPROB#42: It's this group of guys that are basically about making money.

In addition to making money, a large group of respondents mentioned other purposes for the gang: socializing, friendship and family, and protection were mentioned by 37 percent of respondents; 9 percent reported no purpose to the gang. Although a solid core of respondents indicate that their gang has at least one prominent goal or objective – money-making, these other expressed purposes of the gang cannot be ignored.

To summarize, the evidence from individual gang members suggests that economic gain is perceived as a central but not the only goal for the gang as a whole. In the absence of solid evidence about goal orientation towards a primary objective, one might conclude that these gangs are not particularly purposeful. However, there are substantial indications that the gang is a multi-functional unit in which individual needs, group goals and organizational objectives are blended and integrated. Indeed, the visibility of the organizational goals of gangs may be substantially obfuscated by the prominence of individual needs being played out in the gang. Much of the qualitative evidence suggests that the gang is a multi-functional entity for members, combining functions of family, friendship, and work into a single entity. These purposes and objectives become seamlessly integrated into a tangled web of complementary purposes and objectives. These purposes range from individual needs (self-protection) to small group functions (affiliation) to formal organizational objectives (economic enterprises) in one multi-purpose setting. Disentangling these complementary functions is a difficult task. Consider the following statements from gang members which indicate the ways in which different functions are combined.

Many gang members appear to seamlessly combine social interaction with making money:

LOGANPRIS#61: Throughout the whole time [I've been in the gang] I was a party cat. That was the one thing I did throughout the whole time was party. I always liked to party. Liked to have fun. If you are going to have fun you got to make your money. So you sell drugs or you do violent crimes to get money.

SYNDOPRIS#78: We get together and have little picnics and things with the community. Sometimes we get together and set up moves to make on other gangs. When you go to other neighborhoods and they selling certain things we go and take theirs, we make moves... We do more transactions, money transactions. We mainly making money. That is a main part of the gang, making the money. The riding on other neighborhoods and shooting and all that, that's part of the gang too but the main thing is getting our money.

SYNDOPRIS#46: [We] smoke weed, sell dope, I would say that's about it that I know of. [We] have parties and stuff... [We] Probably hang out, that's about it, make money.

Other gang members combine the concept of physically protecting the neighborhood (or drug markets) with making money:

SYNDOPRIS# 78: It was like you couldn't come over to Lincoln Park and try to set up shop, business, or organize anything in our area... The whole purpose of [the gang] was if you want to come to our neighborhood and set up business, you got to ask us. As far as you coming over there and trying to handle your own business, trying to make money or take things or violate us, that's what the purpose of the gang was, to keep us in our neighborhood and other people in their neighborhood.

One gang member astutely described how the goals of the gang (or of the individual member of the gang) change as the gang member matures in the gang. This view may explain why differing perspectives of organizational goals emerge from interviews – different gang members may be at different points in their career in the gang, and thus see the gang from a different perspective.

LKPROB#64: Well there is different stages of gangs really. They are out there to make money and they are out there to kill if they have to...The older you get it's really to make money but when you first start you got to show yourself by doing what you have to do...when you grow out of that [young] stage it's really [about] making money, it's holding your own neighborhood so nobody can come into your neighborhood and try to take the bread out of your mouth.

LOGANPRIS#66: ...Back a couple of years [ago], we used to fight but then we started changing – we started wanting to have money. So we started selling drugs because not too many people in their right minds will give people with tattoos a job. So we started selling drugs to make money and get things for ourselves if that's the only way we gonna get 'em.

GDPRIS#04: Taking care of the neighborhood [was our primary purpose]. To me, it's changed like the guys are basically out to get money for themselves. That's the way I see it now...as long as they get that drug money.

The sequence of evidence about purposefulness of gangs suggests that gang members originally drift into membership, predominately because of the dominant socialization influences of neighborhood, friends and family. Early and some extended careers in the gang continue the focus on social interaction (partying, drinking, fighting and girls) while some gang members clearly begin to focus on the economic benefits of gang membership. These economic benefits (from crimes such as theft and drug dealing) are dependent upon the ability of the gang as an organization to protect its turf or market from intrusion by other gang members. Thus, gang members may continue to derive affiliation benefits from the gang – benefits associated with small group membership – while sharing in the instrumental moneymaking goals of the gang – a benefit associated with membership in a formal organization. In this interpretation of goal orientation, the role or primacy of drugs and money becomes a more distinctive feature of the gang as an organization, achieving a primacy in the descriptions of gang members about the advantages, goals and activities of the gang.

While the findings about gang purposefulness – suggesting gangs are a multi-functional or blended organization – reflect an interpretation or concatenation of factual evidence, the interviews provide no contrary evidence. Indeed, conceptualizing the gang as a multi-functional organization seems a reasonable explanation to coherently blend the sometimes disparate evidence collected from gang members. The labeling of gangs as blended organizations is discussed in greater detail in the next chapter.

EVIDENCE OF GROUPS

Formal organizations, according to organizational theorists, contain groups or informal organizations. As described in Chapter II, these omnipresent groups – also known as peer or autonomous groups – exist within all formal organizations. Indeed, some organizational theorists conceptualize formal organizations as simply systems of overlapping groups; that is, organizations are comprised of subsystems of groups. It is these groups within an organization which actually carry out the day-to-day operations of the organization.

There is also consensus in the gang literature that most gangs do contain subsystems. These subsystems are variously labeled as sets, chapters or cliques, although there is no agreement on the relative size or the way in which these informal organizations are ordered or structured within a gang. Since many gangs – including those in this study – are too large for routine face-to-face interaction between members, smaller groups are necessary to facilitate interaction and activities between individuals.

To determine the presence of and relationship between subsystems within the four gangs in this study, gang members were asked to estimate the size of their set, chapter or clique; and asked to estimate the size of their smaller group in the gang. Estimates of gang size were reported previously in this chapter and are displayed in Table IV.

Results from queries about group and chapter size show that gang members make a measurable distinction between the size of the gang and these subsystems of the gang (see Table XII). To demonstrate the relative differences in size between these subsystems, the mean size for each was computed. On average, San Diego gang members said there are 1,081 members in the gang; 320 members in the set; and 12 members in the respondent's group. From Chicago, gang members reported a median of 10,920 members in the gang; 517 in the respondent's set or chapter; and eight in the respondent's group.

Table XII
Range and mean number of members in gang, set and group

	Number in gang	Number in set, chapter or clique	Number in group
San Diego	60 - 10,000 m=1,081 (n=23)	10 - 1,500 m=320 (n=23)	3 - 60 m=12 (n=24)
Chicago	35 - 55,000 m=10,920 (n=31)	4 - 10,000 m=517 (n=36)	1 - 40 m=8 (n=24)

These mean numbers provide some rough basis of comparison between the relative sizes of these different groupings, however, there was a wide range of responses offered by respondents for each subsystem, and outlier responses can distort medians. Variations in estimates by individuals may also reflect differences in the actual size of different sets or chapters, and groups to which different respondents belong since the sampling plan for the study did not attempt to select respondents from the same set or chapter, or group; indeed, it is likely if not probable that estimates refer to quite different subsystems.

Alternatively, variations in size estimates may be related to different interpretations of the terms by respondents. Indeed, gang members used various terms to express the concept of a "group" of gang members. These terms included: my guys, unit, clique, faction, buddies, group, section, roll dogs, homies, a little crowd, pack and bunch. These subsets occasionally bear a specific name or, conversely, may not even be recognized as a distinct grouping within the gang. Membership in these smallest units of aggregation ranged from one gang member to 60.

The important finding from these size estimates is that gang members perceive a set or chapter as smaller than the gang; while a group is viewed as smaller than a set or chapter.   As one gang member said:

> LOGANPROB#28: It's just too big to do everything with the gang. You have 2,000 or 1,000 people there so you do your little [thing].

Some gang members even described their group as a "set within a set."

> GDPROB#51: Well, when I was out there doing it, there was a particular group that I basically hung around with – GT....[that stands for] Gangstertown. It was a set within a set.

> SYNDOPROB#35: ...There is certain gang members that I run with and there is certain gang members that I don't. So it's like my own set. There is certain people in my set that I run with and there is certain people that is too wild for me.

San Diego respondents generally view a set or chapter as much larger than do gang members in Chicago (see Table XIII). Sixty-five percent of gang members in San Diego report that their set or chapter consists of 100 persons or more; 28 percent of respondents from Chicago report that their chapter is similarly sized.

The majority of respondents in this study reported belonging to a group within the gang. This level of membership was specified as "a group in the gang that you hung out with most." Three-quarters of all respondents (74 percent) said there is a group within the gang with which the respondent associates predominately. This finding was consistent across cities: 71 percent of gang members in Chicago and 77 percent of gang members in San Diego report hanging out with a specific group within the gang. There was greater consistency between gang members in each city in estimates of their small group size: 93 percent of Chicago respondents estimated their small group as 20 persons or fewer, while 88 percent of San Diego gang members made a similar size estimate.

Consistent with the literature on organizational theory, gang members report participating in different activities with members of the small group than with the larger gang. According to gang members, members in the small group routinely hang out, party, drink and use drugs together. Gang members in this study also reported participating in other activities with their group which are distinct or separate from the rest of the gang. These activities included gang banging, and specific types of crimes such as stealing cars, breaking into cars or other crimes.

The following comments reflect the range of activities associated with small groups:

GDPRIS#01: [In my group we do] robberies, burglaries, stealing cars. You name it, we did it – women, gamble, get high.

LKPROB#31: [We] whip people's asses.

SYNDOPROB#22: We would do stupid things. Go outside, just act crazy. Nothing serious to where we were looking at murder charges or nothing like that...

LOGANPROB#58: [We] go out and start trouble. [We] look for trouble, [go] to other hoods and write on their neighborhood. We did a couple of drive-bys together.

Table XIII
Size estimates for sets and groups

	Set		Group	
	San Diego	Chicago	San Diego	Chicago
Range of members	10 - 1,500	4 - 10,000	3 - 60	1 - 40
5 or fewer members		8.3% (3)	29% (7)	50% (13)
6 - 10	4.3% (1)	2.8% (1)	42% (10)	35% (9)
11 - 20	8.7% (2)	5.6% (2)	17% (4)	8% (2)
21 - 40	8.7% (2)	28% (10)	8% (2)	8% (2)
41 - 60	8.7% (2)	22.3% (8)	4.2% (1)	
61 - 100	4.3% (1)	5.6% (2)		
101 - 300	30% (7)	8.3% (3)		
301+	35% (8)	20% (7)		

GDPROB#48: [We] go party on Fullerton, on weekends we go drink. I don't sell drugs no more...During the week, one of the other sections come and do something to us; then on the weekend, we go take care of our business. We got to do what we got to do. So sometimes we drink, party, make a hit, drive-by, whatever is needed.

LKPROB#30: [We] take care of our neighborhood. We hang out on our specific set...We go cruising around.

LOGANPROB#25: [We] go gang banging and stuff like that [together] because I didn't really trust the rest.

LKPROB#70: [We're into] drinking, getting high; sometimes we would get into fights [with other gangs] and then other times we would sell drugs.

LKPROB#73: [We] make extra money.

SYNDOPROB#36: The group I hang around with, actually, drive-bys and stuff never was part of us... Basically most of the guys I be with never been through that [foolish] period. But you know at one time we were considered young fools, too [We] broke into people's houses; [we would] steal people's cars.

    In summary, gang members describe a wide range of activities – often very specific activities – associated with life as a group member in a set or chapter within the gang. The small groups within the gang were typically described as consisting of friends with whom the gang member had grown up; friends who had joined the gang with the respondent; gang members who lived close by; and gang members of a similar age and position, reflecting an age or rank gradation within the gang.

SYNDOPRIS#22: Well, I hung around with basically just, not the OG's, but the guys that I grew up with that were I guess in the same position that I was.

GDPRIS#02: Guys that was around in the area with me or most of the ones that I grew up with – those were the first ones that I started hanging with. Then as we got older, different things were seen and we started hanging with different people in the organization...I started hanging with the ones that I seen was in control of things.

GDPRIS#13: I hung out with basically everybody but I hung out with some people that was on the same level that I was.

SYNDOPRIS#78: There is some people that you hang out with more than the others. Like I'm 30. I will hang out with more people my age.

Thus, consistent with gang literature about the age- and rank-gradations of cliques within gangs, this study shows evidence that small groups comprise gang sets and chapters; these sets and chapters in turn comprise the gangs in this study. Overall, small groups of the gang appear to be constructed as friendship-networks in which paramount importance is attached to the ability of one group member to trust another. Since there is evidence that a wide range of legal and illegal activities are carried out in the small group context, the importance of trust between group members contributes to small group cohesion; is useful for establishing and maintaining group norms as standards of behavior; thus protecting the gang-group from institutional actions of police or other organizations including incursion by other gang sets or groups.

INFLUENCE OF THE ENVIRONMENT

Social organizations and groups exist and conduct their activities within a context or setting known as an environment. An organization's environment is typically considered to consist of everything outside the organization's boundaries – but particularly those elements with potential to affect the organization in some direct or indirect way. Some of the usual elements which comprise an organization's environment include human resources, markets, technology, economic conditions, government and competitors. For contemporary gangs, highly relevant elements of the environment include government institutions such as the police which attempt to regulate gangs, competition with other gangs, and economic conditions (such as availability of jobs). To determine the influence of the environment upon gangs, particularly to assess the relative stability or volatility of the gang environment, these three environmental domains were examined for the four gangs in this study.

As discussed in Chapter II, it is widely acknowledged by organizational theorists that the environment of an organization is closely related to the number and kind of organizations which emerge – that is, environmental conditions affect the form of organizations and the population of organizations. Typically, environmental conditions can be classified as stable and predictable or volatile and unstable, with the latter constituting an environmental threat contributing to organizational failure. Varying environmental conditions can constrain or encourage the development of more gangs or larger gangs or affect the way in which gangs are organized.

Police

The general objective of police and other law enforcement and government entities is to regulate gangs by controlling the activities of gangs and gang members. As such, police constitute a prevailing environmental threat affecting the day-to-day operations of gangs in these two cities and potentially constraining the growth of gangs. Regulatory actions can be minimal and mildly disruptive to gang operations or constitute a major interruption of gang activities. Almost all respondents in this study describe contact between police and gang members as frequent and highly acrimonious. Police contact with gang members is so frequent that it is omnipresent in the life of many gang members. Virtually every respondent in this study said members of his gang had daily or more frequent contact with police.

> GDPROB#18: [We're in contact] every day. Man, I can't even count the times those punks come.

> SYNDOPROB#37: [We're in contact] every day, 20 seconds out of the day, every 20 seconds, every 5 seconds...they [police are] all over the neighborhood. They like flies.

> SYNDOPROB#27: [Gang members are in contact with police] as we speak.... Probably every ten seconds a gang member is getting jacked by the police. I would say five and a half.

Acrimony typically characterizes the relationship between police and gang members in this study. The relationship appears to consist predominately of police efforts to disrupt gang activities through a variety of strategies. Gang members describe that police pick up or "come get" gang members; beat, shoot or kill gang members; "lock them up"; harass, hassle or "mess with" gang members; and take money and other things from gang members. The following comments are representative of descriptions offered by San Diego and Chicago respondents:

> GDPROB#17: I don't know how [the gang] gets along with [the police] but I hate them bastards. I ain't gonna lie, I hate them. ... Because, they think cause they got badges they just be trying to pick everybody up for stupid stuff when you got people out there doing wrong.

> SYNDOPROB#36: The police is there basically, it's a job to them and their job basically is like to keep you in check through confrontations.... They will always try and present a confrontation.

> LKPRIS#50: [We don't get along] good [with the police]. We feel like God didn't give them a job to shoot nobody or lock them up in no cage. They are more violent than we are.

> LKPROB#21: We don't like the cops. They kill us for no reason...We don't have no association with the police. To us they are like our worst enemy.

> GDPRIS#8: You can just be standing around, standing around in the front of a building and the police drive up and they got to mess with you, they got to bother you.

> LKPROB#32: We always get heat from the police. They be everywhere. Once they know your face, that's when they mess with you. That's what happened with me. They knew me, so they used to come get me all the time. As soon as they see me they come get me. They know my first name, last name, everything.

> SYNDOPROB#46: ... The cops harass us for really nothing. All you got to do is sit at the bus stop and the police gave me a ticket just for that. I was just standing there until a bus came.

GDPROB#18: [The police] don't care. They taking everything. They beating your butt and they taking your money, they taking whatever you got, they don't care. They shooting you for nothing. They don't care. So I guess that they feel that the problem is out of hand, to them.

LKPROB#56: It's always bad relationships [with police]. That's how come I moved because every time they see me out there they arrest me for like if I don't have my driver's license on me or no seatbelt. They always wanted me in the police station instead of driving my car around.

LOGANPRIS#66: Most of the time, [the police] harass us. Just from being in gangs, not necessarily Logan, but probably all gangs, they harass everybody.

LOGANPROB#24: The [police] want to beat you probably. They just want to harass you because they ain't got nothing better to do so they will pull anyone over.

Organizational theory suggests that organizations will make great efforts to control the environment in which they operate by reducing uncertainty. Efforts to control the domain of police enforcement were identified in responses from gang members in this study. In contrast to San Diego, numerous Chicago gang members made an effort to control the volatile environment by controlling the nature of their relationship with local police. More than half the Chicago gang members claimed that their gang bribed the police – either through cash payoffs or by providing police officers with weapons. (Only one San Diego gang member described a situation of bribing law enforcement officers.) The following descriptions are typical of this approach to controlling the law enforcement dimension of the gang's environment:

GDPRIS#72: Some police get paid, some out to get you. If police officer trouble them, [he is] "taken care of." As often as needed, enough to pay off.

LKPRIS#52: ...There is certain officers that can be bought. And yeah, we do pay a few off. [We come into contact with the police] every day. If you don't make your payment they will be sure to see you.

GDPRIS#6: Now the police got a little policy. I don't know what they get out of it, but say like if I'm selling drugs and I get a police a gun. He will leave me alone for that day or two. So I guess they got some kind of policy at the police department where if the police turn in a gun they get three or four days off with pay.

GDPROB#51: How the police make us pay them off is give them guns or tell them where they can find some drugs or a bigger load of guns.

GDPROB#12: ...We done had officers say things, like one of my boys got caught with two or three ounces of work and they just said, they just told us to give them two 9mm's and they let him go... So we got two 9mm's, give them to them, they even gave the work back.

LKPROB#53: [We pay off the police] with guns. Like there was one time that I got caught and they took it from me and said go home. So I guess they smoked it. I was petrified to be honest with you. Then they was like how much you got? I got five bags. [They said] get out of here.

LKPROB#71: [We] give them guns for peace and quiet.

In Chicago, some gang members appear to perceive police as more of a nuisance than as a major threat to the activities of the gang. The following response reflects this perception:

DPRIS#6: You get a lot of heat [from the police], but police really ain't nothing. They can't stop it. They can disrupt it, but they can't stop it cause the people they taking off the street ain't nothing but the lower level people no way. By the time they get the person that they really want to get, it be five or six years down the line. He have accumulated so much money in those five or six years that it's hard to lock a rich man up.

In contrast to Chicago, the omnipresence of police in San Diego and level of enforcement activity often serves to break up gang activity. The following comments were typical of gang members' perceptions in San Diego:

LOGANPRIS#62: The police, if there is more than five or ten people, you see about 20 police cars coming that way, [saying] get on the ground. And we were just talking, hi, how you been, long time no see

LOGANPROB#28: Nowadays you are stupid if you try to stand on the corner and sell drugs. Can't sell drugs like that no more [because of the] cops, because you will get caught. They sweat it more nowadays.

LOGANPROB#24: Back then the police would just pass by, shine the light and keep going but now, they stop, search you, probably beat you a little bit.

In summary, police constitute a major – if not the major – environmental threat to gangs. Through efforts to regulate or control gang activity, police make the environment in which gangs operate more difficult. The resultant volatility of the environment suggests that gangs must give some attention to their methods of operation. In an effort to stabilize environmental conditions, contemporary gangs adopt methods to avoid intrusion by police into gang activities – bribery, offering weapons or drugs are techniques to control police actions against the gang and individual members of the gang. By an apparent focus on controlling or removing individual members of the gang, police actions also suggest the need for the gang to maintain fungibility of gang members. To maintain gang activities over time, generalists rather than specialists would adapt more quickly to changing conditions. And generalist members of the gang are inherently easier to replace. Thus the constant volatility of the gang environment is likely to discourage specialization within and among gangs.

Competition

Another major element of the environment for gangs is other gangs. Competition between gangs, including intra-gang rivalry characterized by fighting over turf, has characterized gangs since the earliest documentation of these groups. Protection of gang turf or territory, in numerous early conceptualizations of gangs, was viewed as an expressive goal of the group. As discussed previously, gang members in this study still draw heavily upon a theme of neighborhood protection in terms of defining their gangs and its purpose. The research in this study, however, results in a description of turf that is more aptly characterized as an economic market and gang members invest significant efforts in protecting their market from incursion by other gangs. Although the market may be thought of as drug market, the gang's area, territory or turf also presents opportunities for monopolizing other illegitimate activities, such as robbery, burglary and auto theft. The geographic area may thus constitute the gang's market or territory for any type of criminal behavior.

Numerous gang members referred to the concept of turf as market and gang activities as protecting that market from incursion by other entrepreneurial gangs:

SYNDOPRIS#75: We were supposed to originally be a money-making gang. Supposed to be organized, that's what it was. Sell this stuff or do a robbery or some of them was getting jobs too. But mostly selling drugs [is] organized. This is our area, we are going to make money right here. [We] don't let nobody else come over here and make no money.

GDPRIS#2: Well, basically like any ethnic organization, [our gang] first started out trying to protect the neighborhood. Just wanted to keep other guys from coming over in our neighborhood and messing with women first off. After that we seen that money could be made in different ways. Then we started messing with selling weed and as the money came in the ideas changed. It wasn't so much keeping people out of the neighborhood and messing with the women, it was to keep them out of the neighborhood from selling drugs.

LOGANPROB#66: [30th and Oceanview by Memorial School and Chicano Park are] the [areas] that most of my homies hang out at... [They hang there] probably because they are well known, that's where everything happens most of the time. There is quick money to be made right there, people are busy, people going by all the time wanting to buy anything.

GDPRIS#15: [Gang members] are forced to do [things], like the violence, the drive-bys. They are forced to do this because of [inter-gang] rivalry. [The rivalry] comes about with the narcotics... they think the more narcotics they can sell the better off they will be.

The concept of drug market territory suggest that gangs are variously competitive with each other. Competition from other gangs is an important component of the environment in which gangs must operate. Chicago gang members report having good relationships with other gangs in their city: 21 of 26 GDs (81 percent) said their gang has good relationships with other gangs and 13 of 17 (76 percent) of Latin King respondents agreed. In San Diego, most Syndo Mob respondents reported a good relationship with other gangs, while Logan members reported the opposite; 15 of 20 Syndo Mob respondents (75 percent) reported good relations with other gangs while 14 of 19 respondents (74 percent) of the Logan gang said their gang does not have a good relationship with other gangs.

Cooperative relations between three of the four gangs suggest some level of collusion between gangs in terms of splitting up markets. The following responses are examples of this behavior:

GDPRIS#8: We could talk [with other gangs]. I'll put it like that, we could talk. You got to be able to communicate some kind of way because you don't want to be shooting all the time every time and somebody getting killed and all that. So you got to, see a lot of guys don't like to communicate with people anyway so you got to be able to communicate with guys in order to get an understanding. If not, it's gonna be the wild, wild west.

GDPRIS#3: If depends on if there is a problem [whether the gangs will meet together]. If it needs to be resolved and it's getting too violent and there is too much heat coming on the community, then we'll meet.

LOGANPRIS#69: [We don't have a relationship with other gangs] unless it's some money-making scheme. Like if we got drugs that they want to buy, we will deal with them just to make a profit but not for anything else...Only if money is involved. Money talks.

GDPRIS#6: [We meet together] on the street, if it got something to do with getting money or drugs and then in jail if it got something to do with killing a problem before it get bigger.

GDPROB#63: Yeah. Gangster Disciples get along with everybody, they clique with everybody under the six [pointed star]. So if somebody under the six came to our set and say they needed some help or whatever we would send them back to their set. We honor them but we don't clique with them like that.

LKPRIS#49:[We meet with other gangs] if something needs to be spoken about as far as boundaries or whatever.

Alliances between individual gangs most often appear to occur within a larger framework. Gangs in Chicago are associated with either the five-point or six-point star known, respectively, as People and Folks. In San Diego, gangs are affiliated with either the Crips or Bloods represented, respectively, by the colors red and blue. (Renegade or unaffiliated gangs, however, do exist in each city.)

LKPROB#32: We got our own cliques with different gangs. It's like Cobras and Gangsters and all them, they got their own clique together. We cliquing with the Unknowns and the LB's and the Vice Lords and the Stones.

We clique with all of those. It's just that we don't clique with, see we got in a fight with them from the start. The Cobras got the six point star so whoever is in the five point star, that's your clique. If you under the five point star that's who you are with. If somebody walked in here right now and he had a five point star, I would clique it with him.

LKPROB#64: There is two different cliques, they are called People and Folks. I will give you some example of People, there is Vice Lords, Kings, Black P Stones, they all cliquing together. There is more that I could name. Folks are Black Gangster Disciples, Royals, GDs, Latin Eagles, those are all Folks.... We didn't want to get too close even though we were cliquing together. You never trust none but your own...Even though they were cliquing, we would try to stay within our own.

This description of loose alliances and cliquing with other gangs suggests that Chicago gangs collude in a way that includes dividing up market territory and resolving inter-gang conflict. This pattern of cooperation with other gangs suggests an effort to reduce environmental volatility or uncertainty. Although California gangs also operate under a loose federation of alliances – Bloods and Chips – gang members in San Diego did not describe a similar pattern of cooperation as occurred in Chicago. This area of inquiry, however, was one of the few areas in which the Logan Heights gang differed from the Syndo Mob.

LOGANPROB#29: We don't get along with nobody. Logan doesn't. Other gangs get along with other gangs...There are gangs that unite together to fight us. We still win.

LOGANPRIS#61: Not my gang [we don't have a good relationship with other gangs. We are] too big for that... It's not that we only like Logan. It's just we are known to the point to where somebody from another gang might come and say what's up, how you doing and it's cool as long as he don't disrespect. He disrespect us then something starts up.

In contrast to the typically poor relations between Logan and other gangs, Syndo Mob appears to have neutral rather than cooperative or clique relations as described in Chicago.

> SYNDOPROB#34: We don't really do nothing together [with gangs we get along with]...You just don't shoot them but you don't do nothing with them. You might help each other fight every now and then.

> SYNDOPROB#36: At this time we have a good relationship with everyone. I can't really speak so much as far as Asian or Hispanics but as far as within the African-American community, we all have a hell of a relationship right now.

In summary, competition from other gangs – or intergang rivalry – appears to be a presence but not a focal point of the environment for the gangs in this study. Many gang members describe relations ranging from positive and cooperative for business purposes to a rather neutral state of affairs. This neutral situation, however, has a ring of impermanence: incidents of disrespect or market incursion could cause the relationship between gangs to change precipitously, reinforcing the notion that the current environment for gangs is unstable and volatile.

Economic conditions

The economic conditions in which the gang operates (and where gang members live) is an important element of the environmental domain for gangs. Economic conditions affect the availability of human resources, contributing to the organizational success of the gang through growth or decline in membership. Do opportunities exist which will deter prospective members from joining the gang or which will entice gang members to leave the gang? Poor economic conditions contribute to the availability of human resources for many types of gang activity. Numerous gang members described the gang as functioning as an economic enterprise in a crowded area with little access to legitimate economic opportunity. The following comments were typical:

> GDPRIS#3: [Our neighborhood is full of] unemployment, crime, drug activity, gang activity... Most of the buildings are

occupied. Just like a big cage almost. It's like 4,000 or 5,000 people living in a small cage almost, living right above each other.

GDPRIS#8: Well you got to look at it like guys that got no jobs so they got to survive so ...We got to eat too and we got to have somewhere to stay. So we don't have any jobs and we got the bills so we have to do something. It might hurt some people but I got to eat too just as well as they do. It's an economic thing anyway. You are already living in poverty level anyway, most of them are stacked on top of each other in the neighborhood. You got to make ends meet. You go to work and do what you got to do to make ends meet. Easy money, fast money they call it. So they got to take the risks and all that and whatever part of the risk, if you get killed, that's part of the risk too. So that's how it is. It's dangerous. I wish it didn't have to be that way but that's the way it is. I didn't make it that way.

SYNDOPROB#27:   It's like it's gonna be crime in a neighborhood, I don't care if it's white, black, Asian, Mexican, whatever, it's gonna be crime in any neighborhood as long as there is poverty there cause people want to get out of poverty. They are willing to do anything possible to get out of poverty. .. You want to do things to make life for your family better. So naturally you are going to tend toward a group of people that feel the same way. Some people call it crime, some people call it taking care of your family, I'm not gonna say what I call it.

SYNDOPROB#27: At poverty level, there is gonna be crime. There is gonna be a group of people that are gonna hang together, they are gonna bond, so there is always gonna be gangsters.

As part of the environment which influences gangs in these two cities, limited economic opportunity creates a ready pool of human resources. These resources eliminate the need for gangs to actively recruit new members or to force existing members to stay in the gang;

the absence of this coercion was described previously in this chapter. The surplus of human resources may also result in members who are an expendable commodity to gangs – one member is easily replaced by another. This limited economic opportunity probably also remedies some of the inherent volatility of the gang environment. With surplus human resources, gang members are influenced to remain generalists rather than specializing in a particular area. Regulatory activities (police enforcement) may result in the temporary or permanent removal of gang members, who are inherently fungible cogs in gang activities. Restricted economic opportunity also probably influences gangs as organizations to resist specialization and maintain a diversified approach to maintaining an income stream.

On balance, police enforcement, competition with other gangs, and bleak economic conditions appear to create an unstable or volatile environment which is highly conducive or favorable to the operations of contemporary gangs. Although the police routinely disrupt the gang environment, other gangs typically cooperate and economic conditions create a ready pool of prospective members who are highly fungible in the gang organization.

SUMMARY AND CONCLUSION

The four gangs in this study – gangs which are among the oldest and largest, hence most successful in the nation – exhibit little evidence of formal organizational characteristics (Decker, Bynum and Weisel, 1998; Weisel, Decker and Bynum, 1997). Although the dominant paradigm of organizational theory suggests that large size and organizational longevity stimulate – even necessitate – the emergence of bureaucratic features, these gangs demonstrate scant evidence of such organizational hallmarks. These gangs exhibit little evidence of formalization, such as rules and recordkeeping; there are few signs of role specialization or division of labor; and there appears to be little hierarchy – that is, leadership and roles – within the organization. In the absence of formalization, specialization and hierarchy – hallmarks of bureaucracy – these gangs bear a stronger resemblance to groups than formal organizations. As groups, they clearly fulfill the affiliation needs of individual members, and their members also share the common interests which typically characterize membership in groups.

Yet to classify these four gangs as groups – or to dismiss them as formal organizations – overlooks important organizational features. Indeed, substantial evidence of formal organizational characteristics for these gangs has been assembled in this chapter. These gangs exhibit the following features of formal organizations:

Membership and Large Size

The size of the gangs in this study was gauged by the number of its members, and gang members recognize membership in the gang as a distinctive role. Members express perceptions of joining the gang, belonging to it or ceasing to belong, and others as joining – all of which are descriptive of membership or in-group vs. out-group status.

Each of these gangs features a large number of members with hundreds or even thousands of members. The resultant large size of these gangs substantially exceeds the size threshold of groups. Groups, by definition, are delimited by a size in which members may maintain "face to face" interaction on a routine basis with one another. But gang members in this study did not even make consistent size estimates. These variations in estimates occur for valid reasons – gang members don't know all the members of the gang – a defining feature of groups; gang members do not all get together at one time; and there are no written records or lists of members.

Organizational Longevity

Each of these gangs has demonstrated substantial organizational persistence. Although gangs have a reputation as being short-lived entities, the roots of the gangs in this study extend from three to five or more decades, providing overwhelming evidence that the gang is, or certainly can be, an enduring form of organization. Evidence – in the form of growth – also suggests that these gangs have survived and thrived; in other words, these forms of organization are successful and efficient. Although leadership crises – such as the disposition of leaders in the GDs are common during early phases of organizational life cycles, these gangs have overcome major leadership changes and other internal organizational dynamics such as within-group conflict.

Organizational Dynamics.

During their organizational history, each of the gangs in this study has exhibited evidence of major organizational dynamics. The gangs have undergone organizational transformation through:

splintering and breaking up into smaller gangs – processes illustrated by the Logan gang;

replication and imitation by other new gangs – patterns described by gang members;

merger and consolidation of small street gangs into larger gangs – as demonstrated by the GDs and the Latin Kings in Chicago;

growing much larger through attracting new members – expanding membership to other ethnic groups, girls, older members; easing residence requirements; and offering trial membership to prospective members; and,

switching alliances with gang coalitions, such as the realignment of the Syndo Mob from the Crips to the Bloods

Although mortality is typically high for young or newly formed organizations – dissolution of organizations is a much more common process than is adaptation – over time, these gangs have managed to adapt, survive and even thrive. The gangs have exhibited evidence of organizational continuity through processes of continuous change and adaptation.

Evidence of intra-organizational groups

The gangs in this study show clear evidence that groups or subsystems exist and are operational within these gangs. These groups – whether they are referred to as sets, chapters, cliques or by other terms – are a dominant feature of the gang and appear to meet the strong needs of individuals for affiliation and function as socialization outlets. In addition to meeting needs for affiliation and socialization purposes, there are signs that these groups also function as teams or work-groups for carrying out the activities of the gang. Because of the dominance of these groups in gangs and the importance of the small group to individuals, the presence of groups has probably obscured formal organizational characteristics of the gang. For example, individual members of groups and gangs may have difficulty distinguishing between the purposes and characteristics of the gang and its subsystems since the gang structure – with the dominance of groups – appears to be organized in a way that meets both the needs of the organization and its members as individuals.

Goal orientation

The dominance of group needs being played out within the gang context almost certainly mutes or obfuscates the purposefulness of these gangs. Gang members articulate specific albeit multiple goals. Although many of the stated goals relate to socialization, the focus of the gang and gang members is economic opportunity. The notion of making money or acquiring material benefits is imputed – and often stated directly – throughout much of the narrative commentary. It should be noted that the moneymaking activities of gangs are predominately if not exclusively illegal. Thus, although the accumulated evidence about gang purposefulness is not fully convincing, the weight of evidence in descriptions about gang activities cannot be overlooked in assessing this issue. Indeed, evidence of gang involvement or focus on moneymaking is often embedded within other gang activities – common group functions of hanging out, riding around, drinking and partying. Many gang members appear to routinely integrate moneymaking functions of the organization into group interactions such as partying. In this way, gang members appear able to rather seamlessly merge their individual goals and the organization's purpose into one set of interconnected activities; moneymaking is not subordinate to other activities but either parallels or is incorporated into other activities.

Operate in unstable environment

Like other organizations, gangs function in an environmental domain. Based on extensive descriptions from gang members, the environment for gangs appears to be unstable and highly volatile. The environment is characterized by competition with rival gangs, efforts from police and others to regulate or control gangs, and generally limited economic opportunity in areas where gangs thrive. Despite this environmental volatility – indeed, probably because of this volatility – these gangs have thrived. Organizational theory suggests that the environment for particular organizations distinctively shapes both the form and number of organizations which emerge. The resultant number of organizations of similar form is considered the population of organizations. Within this population, organizations tend to be of similar size and structure and operate in a similar manner. Either through processes of adaptation or natural selection, the environment favors the form and size of organization uniquely suited to that particular environment. This finding explains why gangs within city in this study are more similar than gangs in different cities.

In conclusion, while there are many features of groups within gangs, the gangs in this study behave and look much like formal organizations. Key maxims of organization theory suggest that these large and long-lived gangs face increasing pressures to become formally organized – developing marked characteristics of formal or bureaucratic organizations. With few exceptions, the gangs in this study exhibit scant evidence of bureaucracy.

So if these gangs are large, long-lived and efficient, why aren't they more organized in terms of formal rules and roles? How can the inconsistency be resolved between theories and research about organizations and observations about these gangs? The most promising arena for resolving this inconsistency is an assessment of the environment for gangs. Little is known about organizational dynamics of gangs as a population form. The general consensus is that most gangs are relatively short-lived, an observation consistent with organizational theory documenting high rates of mortality for new organizations. The evidence in this study suggests that these four gangs have shown great facility to adapt to a turbulent environmental domain or that conditions of natural selection have selected for gangs as a form of organization. Through processes of natural selection or adaptation, these large gangs have developed as the form of organization uniquely suited to the unstable environment created by a quadrangle of available resources, intra-gang competition, economic conditions and regulatory pressures.

In the study of contemporary gangs, the organizational processes and dynamics which have contributed to the shaping the current population of gangs have been largely ignored. These issues are central to population ecology – the organizational phenomenon of adaptation and natural selection; organizational processes affecting the number and size of gangs in the population; and organizational dynamics such as merger or consolidation of gangs, splintering, and imitation or replication. These important organizational phenomenon – which contribute to the rising prevalence of gangs – have been overlooked as most gang research has instead focused on the formation of gangs. A focus on gang formation draws attention to descriptions of motivations of individual gang members and the generating milieu for gangs. Attention to gang formation takes attention away from assessing and monitoring changes in the composition of the population of contemporary gangs. Population ecology has rich potential for understanding the organizational dynamics of contemporary gangs, explaining growth, consolidation and other organizational processes including gang endurance. Population ecology offers answers to the conundrum raised in this study: If gangs are not groups yet they are not bureaucracies, what organizational form best describes and aids in understanding and comparing the persistence and increasing prevalence of this fundamentally different form of organization? This question is addressed in the final chapter.

Past studies of gangs have been largely stationary, offering a snapshot in time of a particular gang or set of gangs. Such studies have occurred within intact organizations, which remain relatively inert as members move into and out of the organization. Of course, it is difficult to conduct a longitudinal study of individual gangs because of attrition associated with individual gang members who are the source for information about individual gangs.

Future studies of gangs should also be undertaken to illuminate and document characteristics of the organic-adaptive structure of gangs. As long as the environment for gangs remains volatile, gangs will likely remain organic and such studies can determine the ways in which values and mission are communicated, examine processes of influence-relations, and detail the informal linkages within and between the subdivisions of the gang. Since post-bureaucratic or organic-adaptive organizations are not common, effort should be made to develop a method for recognition and study of this form. Such methods will illuminate comparisons between gangs and between different populations of gangs.

CHAPTER V:
SUMMARY AND CONCLUSION

In this study, four large and mature criminal gangs in Chicago and San Diego were examined to identify evidence of formal organizational features. An organizational assessment of the gangs was undertaken to illuminate the phenomenon of gangs becoming larger, more numerous and more persistent. In the context of an organizational analysis, these four gangs appear relatively disorganized – rules are present but not adhered to, meetings occur but irregularly and informally, leadership is ephemeral, and role specialization is minimal.

Despite these features, the four gangs in this study can be clearly characterized as formal organizations. Like other formal organizations, these gangs are large and demonstrate substantial organizational longevity; the environment for these organizations is volatile and affects their operations; the gangs are purposeful and goal-oriented, although these goals are multiple and not always clearly discernible; and, the gangs contain informal organizations or groups which carry out the day-to-day activities of the organization.

As organizations, these four gangs can be considered successful – an accomplishment made evident by their organizational continuity and expansion and growth in terms of members. Importantly, these four gangs have endured and thrived – and have been widely replicated – during periods in which environmental exigencies might have logically selected against such organizations. Their survival and growth has been punctuated by organizational changes – mergers, splintering, consolidation and other organizational dynamics. Although some theorists would consider the resultant altered organizations as "new" organizations and the organizational processes those of rebirth, these organizational changes have resulted in the large size as the gangs are currently configured.

Large-sized and mature organizations necessitate features of bureaucracy, according to organizational theory. Features such as formalization, centralization and specialization are necessary to maintain communication within the organization, as operations become more impersonal and formal due to the inability to maintain face-to face interaction among the sheer number of members. Yet these characteristics of bureaucracy are largely absent in these gangs. How then can large and long-lived gangs be so "disorganized" and continue to function? What has contributed to their survival hence their success?

Theories and observation of natural selection processes suggest that successful organizations get replicated. Expansion of a population of organizations – that is, replication and imitation – provide further evidence that contemporary gangs are successful and efficient. Since the four gangs in this study contain little evidence of bureaucracy, it is apparent that large-sized and non-bureaucratic gangs are the organizational form of gangs which are efficient and successful. (Although they were not examined directly in this study, small gangs are probably selected against or are not part of the population containing large-sized gangs.)

A bureaucratic structure would not be efficient for gangs because of the volatile environment in which gangs function; evidence presented in Chapter IV confirms that the environment for gangs – police, competition with other gangs, and bleak economic conditions – is unstable. A bureaucracy would hardly thrive in this volatile environment. Bureaucracies are well-known for their inability to respond or to adapt quickly to changing environmental conditions. The rules and required procedures typical in a bureaucracy are two constraints on rapid organizational adaptation. Bureaucracies also have difficulty adapting because of role specialization. Typically, specialists cannot adapt readily since they must learn a new set of complex skills while generalists are more well-suited to changing conditions.

The primacy of the environment in shaping the organization is a central tenet of organizational theory and natural selection. It is the environment which shapes organizations – including the population or number of organizations best-suited for the prevailing environment. As Stinchcombe noted, the forms of organizations which emerge – during periods of formation of the particular form of organization – are those which are uniquely suited to their environment. The concept of "waves of organizing," in which successful forms of organization are widely replicated during these founding periods, appears descriptive of the trend in the population of gangs, based on the literature about numbers of gangs. Founding patterns typically begin slowly, then increase so that there are lots of foundings. In time, the rate of foundings stabilize, and eventually slow. Organizational processes such as imitation and schism are common during spurts of growth of an organizational form – a phenomenon which characterizes recent changes in the population of gangs. Patterns of imitation and schism create numerous new gangs – gangs which are quite vulnerable in their infancy, thus subject to short life-span. Indeed, for most organizations, births and deaths typically far outnumber survival and adaptation. This pattern of frequent founding and frequent demise seems highly consistent with descriptions offered by gang members of organizational founding and dynamics over the gang's history. When integrated with counts of gangs and gang members from other sources, descriptions of these population dynamics for gangs provide insight into the rising prevalence of gangs.

The process of shaping the organizational population typically occurs either through natural selection – that is, organizations form and only those which are the best fit for the environment survive – or through the process of adaptation – that is, existing organizations change to adapt to environmental conditions. The organizational population may also be shaped by a combination of these processes – new organizations may imitate successful organizations, thus adapting by mimicry. Most theorists believe that natural selection is a much more common process than is adaptation simply because many organizations often having difficulty adapting. As discussed previously, bureaucratic organizations face the greatest difficulty in adapting to unstable environmental conditions. Thus, the processes of natural selection or adaptation appear to have unambiguously selected against gangs structured as bureaucracies.

Many gangs, and certainly the gangs in this study, can probably best be described as organic-adaptive rather than bureaucratic or hierarchal organizations. This conclusion is largely deductive and based upon compelling parallels or similarities with rather general descriptions of organic models and their context. As Daft (1986) points out,

Under conditions of rapid change, organizations are more
organic. When the organization must be free-flowing and
flexible, extensive bureaucracy is inappropriate...When an
organization must change frequently and rapidly, the absence
of bureaucracy will promote better performance. (p. 199).

Typically the internal structure of organic organizations is loose,
free flowing, and adaptive – rules and regulations are unwritten,
hierarchy of authority is unclear, and decision-making authority
decentralized. Burns and Stalker (1961) called this "organic"
management structure; Bennis (1993) calls these types of organizations
"federations, networks, clusters, cross-functional teams, lattices,
modules, matrices, almost anything but pyramids." To describe this
organizational form, other theorists use terms such as negotiated order,
federation, loosely-coupled system, temporary system, organic-
adaptive organization, coalition, external model, post-bureaucracy,
colleague model, interactive organization, network, blended or open
organization.

In stark contrast to the myriad works on bureaucracy, there have
been few studies of organic organizations – and thus there is a dearth of
descriptions of the form even among legitimate organizations such as
businesses. An examination of the recognized features of the organic-
adaptive model, however, suggests that the gangs in this study feature
the predominate attributes associated with this form of organization.
These features include: an emphasis on individual goals concurrent
with organizational goals, diffuse leadership, active role of groups,
generalist orientation, persistence in volatile environment, and
continuity despite absence of hierarchy. Each of these features is
discussed subsequently.

The goals or organizational objectives of bureaucracies are
typically clear and can be articulated. In contrast, a typical feature of
the organic-adaptive organization is the blending of organizational and
individual goals, so that the objectives of individuals are not
subordinate to those of the organization. Instead, goals of individuals
in organic organizations parallel and are typically compatible with the
goals of the organization; disparate goals are typically on equal footing
while many of the organization and individual goals are harmonious or
complementary. This blending of individual and group objectives often
results in the appearance of the organization having multiple goals as

there is usually no clear demarcation between the goals of the organization and those of individuals. Indeed, in the organic-adaptive model, elements of work and friendship become intertwined and carried out through the informal organization or subdivisions which comprise the organization. The gang members in this study demonstrate ample evidence that individual and organizational goals are mingled. This mingling occurs to such a degree in the gangs that it is difficult to disentangle individual objectives from those of the respective organizations. Since objectives of the gangs and individuals in the gangs appear to be highly complementary, conceptualizing the gangs as organic-adaptive suggests that the purposefulness of the gang provides a rather large and inclusive umbrella under which individual members can seek to meet their own goals.

Leadership is structured much differently in the organic-adaptive organization as contrasted with a bureaucracy. In organic-adaptive organizations, decision making is typically considered as "consensual legitimation" (Heckscher, 1994), rather than according to strict rules or by fiat. As such, decisions in the organic-adaptive model are often consensual, that is, so that decisions emphasize the empowerment or participation of employees or members. Rather than authoritative command from centralized leadership, decisions usually occur through processes of influence and persuasion. Decisions in the organic model are typically based on trust relationships between individuals rather than the authority and power relationships which are characteristic of a hierarchy. Because these influence-relationships are relatively fluid in the organic organization, decision-making processes are frequently reconstructed, necessitating flexible leadership and organizational structures.

Like the organic-adaptive model, the four gangs in this study exhibited little evidence of hierarchal leadership. For day-to-day activities of the gang, members indicate a reliance on subdivisions – the groups, cliques, sets and chapters which are the building blocks of the gang – and routinely emphasize the trust relationships between members by characterizing these relationships as brotherhood or family. There is an emphasis upon the conduct of joint activities – members do not appear to function in isolation; instead, gang members typically participate in collective activities. To the extent that continuous organizational structure is present, these gangs appear to feature flat age-graded layers rather than a vertical organizational structure. Within these flat layers, everyone appears to take some responsibility for the success of the organization or the small group in which the member is predominantly involved. Some clear leadership was identified in only one gang in this study – the BGDs. Much of that leadership appeared to relate to particularly charismatic leadership at only the top level of the gang. This leadership appears to be largely symbolic although there may also be more distinctive elements of functional leadership. The presence of charismatic leadership does not weaken the idea of shared, consensual leadership which appears to dominate decision making at most levels in this very large gang.

Every organization – even bureaucracies – contains informal organizations. These informal organizations – the teams, friendship-networks or work-groups within the formal organization – have an especially important role within an organic organization. In the absence of rules, procedures and formal leadership, informal organizations facilitate communication between members, generate cohesiveness by contributing to team spirit, and provide a form of support between members, enhancing their self-respect. These informal organizations also serve as outlets for affiliation needs and serve to build the self-esteem of individual members. The informal organization increases feelings of security for the individual, enhancing the individual's ability to cope with a threat that is common to all the members of the informal organization. All of these functions appear to be of critical importance to the workings of the gangs in this study. Members routinely and consistently emphasize the nature and importance of brotherhood and family associated with belonging to the gang. The gang members in this study routinely described their fellow members as "looking out for each other," frequently mentioning that fellow gang members can be counted on "to be there if you need them." These repeated statements emphasize the mutual love, trust, respect, and sense of security and belonging associated with belonging to the gang. There is also a recognition that fellow gang members seek to attain common goals. Much of the loyalty and kinship between gang members appears rooted in the bonds of growing up together and sharing of a set of common experiences in a neighborhood, hence the common use of terms such as "homies" to describe fellow gang members. Indeed, the strong cohesion of the informal organization within the gangs appears to be deeply grounded in the shared experiences of its members.

Since there are usually few rules within the organic-adaptive organization – instead there is an emphasis on a somewhat abstract mission and guiding principles – the informal organization is responsible for carrying out the day-to-day activities. This feature of organic organizations is typical of the gangs in this study. By establishing and maintaining group norms within the informal organization, functioning of the gang can continue over time in the absence of more formalized rules and procedures. Indeed, the presence of such strong group norms explains the general absence of restrictions on leaving the gang or terminating gang membership; strong cohesion within the small groups or informal organizations may act as a de facto barrier to formally leaving the gang.

The notion of informal organizations within formal organizations parallels the role of cliques or small groups identified within each of the gangs in this study. These groups appear to maintain the functioning of the gang over time despite changes in leadership. As organizational subdivisions – necessitated by the large size of these gangs – groups are so dominant in the four gangs studied that features of groups – size, age, activities, goals – probably tend to obscure features of the larger, formal organization. For example, goals of the small group become difficult to disentangle from goals of the formal organization. Since the goals of individuals are also blended into the organizational objectives of the organic organization, the articulation and assignment of goals becomes a difficult task of somewhat artificially separating and classifying these interwoven objectives.

Bureaucracies typically feature clear elements of role specialization. Organic-adaptive organizations typically feature little differentiation between the roles of members, partly because of diffuse leadership. Role differentiation, however, usually isn't necessary in organic-adaptive organizations because this form of organization is typically comprised of generalists who are able to quickly adapt to changing conditions. The generalist orientation necessitates an organizational structure which serves multiple purposes and is inherently flexible. This resultant flexibility contributes to the adaptability of the organization.

With a munificence of human resources, the gangs in this study are constructed so that members are generalists rather than specialists. Because of the volatility of the environment for gangs, gang members appear to be highly fungible – they are both interchangeable and expendable. If one member is lost or removed, then another gang member takes his place with no need for extensive training or development of skills that might be necessary for carrying out specialized tasks. Although this notion of fungibility is counter to the esprit de corps associated with the brotherhood of the gang, it accounts for the small but vocal cadre of gang members who claim there is "nothing good" about the gang. In addition to generalist gang members, the gangs in this study also appear to be configured as generalist rather than as specialty organizations. The absence of gang specialization is necessitated by the volatile environment. Changing conditions necessitate the ability to frequently change and reconfigure gang activities.

Bureaucracies typically do not perform well – are not efficient – in a volatile environment while organizational persistence under such conditions is prima facie evidence of the organic-adaptive form of organization. Since bureaucracies are typically unable to adapt to changing conditions – and thus prevail in stable conditions – organic-adaptive organizational forms dominate in volatile environments. All of the gangs in this study have thrived in an unstable environment characterized by hostile and highly frequent relations with police; even working alliances between gangs appear temporary and transitory. To maintain functioning and thrive, these gangs have by necessity changed and adapted.

In addition to organizational continuity in this study as prima facie evidence that the gangs are organic, the large size of these gangs is also evidence of organic organizations. Since the gangs in this study are very large, one might anticipate evidence of bureaucratic structure. These gangs show little evidence of formalization, specialization, standardization, hierarchy and centralization – characteristics associated with bureaucracy. Yet the gangs are much too large to be considered as groups and much too persistent to be considered as informal organizations. These gangs thus constitute a different form of organization. Although organic-adaptive forms of organization may be typical among new or small organizations, the volatile environment in the two cities in this study have exerted pressures for the gangs to remain organic despite their attainment of large size. This observation of gang size and structure provides compelling evidence that the current environment for gangs selects for large-sized gangs and probably penalizes – or selects against – small-sized gangs.

It is clear from this discussion that the four gangs in this study can best be considered as organic-adaptive organizations. These gangs are not ephemeral short-lived groups; nor should such gangs be evaluated and compared based on measures of bureaucracy. But what does the understanding of gangs as organic-adaptive suggest about the future of the population of gangs? Since there is widespread concern about the rising prevalence of gangs – that is, more numerous, larger or long-lived gangs – how does the organic conceptualization inform an understanding of features which have allowed these four gangs and thousands of other gangs to thrive in spite of volatile and threatening environment?

PREDICTING THE FUTURE OF GANGS

Population ecology enhances our understanding of rising gang prevalence. Since population form, size and environment are reciprocally related, as gangs grow larger, the number of gangs should decline if there are resource constraints in the environment. Similarly, as gangs grow more numerous, the relative size of gangs should decline.

Using the economists technique of *ceteris parabus* – that is, assuming all other things stay the same – a stable number of gangs should emerge within a given population of gangs; city or metropolitan area is probably the most relevant population boundary for contemporary gangs. Within a population, population ecologists suggest that competitors become similar as competition brings forth a uniform response and natural selection eliminates weakest competitors. Indeed, to develop an egalitarian bargaining position, organizations must be roughly equivalent in size.

Organizational density for gangs would typically be expected to stabilize following a period of rapid growth – that is, a rapid increase in the number of new gangs formed will typically be followed by a period in which the number of start-ups slows. During an escalated period of start-ups, the size of individual gangs may also be expected to stabilize and subsequently decline.

Given the prevailing unstable and malevolent environmental conditions for gangs, small gangs will be selected against, suggesting that larger gangs will be imitated and proliferate. The large-sized gangs are able to achieve some economies of scale, making them particularly efficient in an unstable environment. Since smaller gangs and newer organizations are more vulnerable to environmental exigencies and because they have fewer members to replace members lost through apprehension or other reasons, mortality rates for small gangs may be higher.

Removing the contingency of *ceteris parabus*, there is no evidence that gangs have reached limits of their growth in terms of resources. This idea that resources are limited and can be depleted is known as density-dependence. Since human resources are the primary resource necessary for gang growth, gangs have pushed and expanded resources in different ways and show no evidence of reaching a level of density dependence.[f]

The absence of identifiable resource constraints on the gangs in this study is one of the most important findings. Since the gangs have broadened their membership categories (to other or additional ethnic groups, gender, older and perhaps younger members and to broader geographical areas), human resources for membership appear unconstrained, as evidenced by absence of coercive recruitment and retention practices. Resources for Chicago gangs may be more numerous than those for San Diego. With 2.7 million population in 228 square miles, Chicago has a larger population and somewhat smaller geographic area than San Diego, which has 1.2 million people in 228 square miles. As compared to San Diego, Chicago has greater density of resources, a factor that may contribute to its larger-sized gangs. Of course, other factors also contribute to gang formation and continuity – including rates of poverty, low academic achievement, family and economic conditions.

Gangs may also be expected to become larger over time. Gangs with significant organizational longevity can be expected typically to be of larger size and to continue their pattern of growth. This study shows mixed results about the age-size connection. Indeed, one of the oldest gangs, Logan, is not one of the largest gangs. The nexus between size and age of gangs, however, is illuminated by the age of the gang population: gangs in Chicago date to the turn of the century; while gangs in San Diego are typically considered a much newer phenomenon, with the earliest gangs rooted in about the 1940s. And while there are no reliable counts of the numbers of gangs at these earliest points in time, Thrasher counted at least 1,313 gangs in Chicago in the second decade of the century! These gangs were much smaller than the city's contemporary gangs, confirming the pattern that over time, small gangs have either dissolved or merged into the larger contemporary gangs, as ecological processes have selected for larger gangs. Then, as gangs have gotten larger, organizational mortality has decreased as size has effectively buffered the gang against threats to its survival. Organizational mortality rates decline with age and size as organizations shield themselves against effects of environmental change.

As organizations continue to grow ever larger there are increasing pressures to become explicitly organized. Indeed, the Chicago gangs are somewhat more hierarchically-organized than in San Diego. Yet it is likely that the prevailing volatile environment will continue to exert pressure for gangs to remain in an organic organizational form in both San Diego and Chicago. These competing organizational pressures may eventually cause the large gangs to splinter into smaller, specialty groups rather than their current generalist orientation. Such a metamorphosis could occur if the large-sized organic gang is unable to carry out communication, coordinate activities, or exert general leadership to its members in the absence of a more formalized hierarchal, rule-driven structure.

In addition to the nexus between gang size and gang age, the reciprocal relationship between the size of individual organizations such as gangs and the number of organizations such as gangs in the population is also illuminated by population ecology. In practical terms, the size of gangs contributes to the number of gangs in the population. For example, in this study, gang members were asked to estimate the number of gangs in their city.[g] In Chicago, most gang members estimated 20-40 gangs, using qualifying terms such as "major gangs." The modal response for size of the gang population in San Diego was quite similar – most of the San Diego respondents reported about 30 gangs in the city. The similarity in gang number estimates is consistent with the different sizes of gangs in each city. Since there are a similar number of gangs in each city, one would anticipate that gangs – that is, the number of gang members in individual gangs and the total number – in San Diego would be smaller because of differences in resources between the cities.

There remain some inherent difficulties in counting gangs – and estimating the number of gangs in the population – because of variations in structure such as the presence of subdivisions within different gangs.   The branch structure within some gangs in Chicago confounded estimates

> GDPRIS#6: [How many gangs] in the city?   Gangster Disciples, Black Disciples, Black Gangsters, Vice Lords, Four Corner Hustlers, Stones, Latin Kings, Latin Disciples, Latin Lovers, [unintelligible] and Gents, Black Souls, Mad Black Souls, Gangster Black Souls. Cause the Vice Lords got about, Conservative Vice Lords, Insane Vice Lords, Double Eye Vice Lords, Undertaker Vice Lords, they got about five or six branches just within they mob. See the Vice Lords, they Vice Lords but they got about five or six different branches. They got about five or six different chiefs. It ain't like the GD's. We got one chief, Larry Hoover, that's it. They got five or six chiefs. I would say it got to be about 30 different gangs [total in the city].

The presence of new, emerging gangs in each city also presented difficulties in counting or estimating the number of gangs in the city. There is an element of ephemerality in the description of these new, often-unaligned gangs.

> SYNDOPROB#44:   There is a lot of gangs but as far as Bloods and Crips [African American gangs], there is two Crip sets and like five Blood sets. There is like off-brand gangs and stuff too.

> LKPROB#21: I would say there is a bunch of little gangs that you don't hear of, a bunch of little gangs coming up. You got all these different gangs. Sometimes we driving around, we see gangs we never saw before, they chasing the car or breaking it or whatever. So there is a bunch of different gangs.

Overall, respondents in both cities estimated a modest number of gangs, reinforcing the idea that the perceived growth in gangs may be limited primarily to expanding membership of existing gangs, rather than the start-up of new gangs or spin offs from older gangs.   Indeed, there is every likelihood that the "off-brand" gangs or "little gangs coming up" will be subsumed into the membership of larger gangs within the city. The pattern of larger gangs in Chicago appears to be related to these common organizational processes of merger and consolidation, while the pattern of smaller gangs in San Diego is rooted in organizational processes of splintering. These opposite organizational processes have affected the population of gangs as constructed in each city. This examination addresses the basic research question examined in this study: how and why gangs are becoming both larger and more numerous within the relevant population boundaries in which the counting of gangs and gang members must occur.

DIRECTIONS FOR FURTHER RESEARCH

Current theories of gang formation – focused on social and individual-level explanations – have been limited for explaining increases in the prevalence of gangs. Organizational theory explains the organizational transforming processes which have contributed to more numerous or larger gangs in the reciprocal relationship between the size, number and age of gangs – gangs organized as a quite different form of organization than typically examined. This population ecology explanation of the gang as organic-adaptive organization is not inconsistent with prevailing theories about the formation of gangs. In fact, the ecological perspective adds to theories of gang formation.

This findings in this study are consistent with theories of subculture, which emphasize the contribution of community conditions and norms to gang formation. Indeed, this study suggests that individuals do drift into gang membership, influenced predominately by the collective experience of growing up in the neighborhood in which family and friends belong to the gang. And the findings are consistent with theories of control, in which pulls toward the gang are enhanced by the prominence of family, friends and neighborhood in gang life. Indeed, the findings reveal that gang members have strong social bonds such as affective relationships with family and friends; these relationships, however, are counter to positive social bonds such as aspirations for jobs or academic success. The affective social bonds contribute to the cohesion found in the informal organization or subdivisions of the gang, which form the framework for the functioning of the gang as an organic-adaptive organization.

Findings from this study are also consistent with underclass/strain theory, which suggests the economic mismatch between individual aspirations and opportunity gives rise to gangs. Population ecology elaborates underclass and strain theories of gang formation by emphasizing the continuity or organizational persistence of successful gangs. Since large gangs are evidence of organizational success, processes of growth, imitation, replication and schism occur as part of organizational expansion. Successful gangs give rise to other gangs as the successful organizational form expands. Since the economic mismatch does not abate over time, and adverse economic conditions persist, most gang members in this study report little evidence of gang-leaving behavior. This finding is also consistent with theories of labeling, which suggests that members stay in the gang because their self-concept and oppositional institutional processes (such as a prison record or reputation with rival gangs) effectively restrict exit from the gang. Members think of themselves as gang members and this is a core part of their identity.

The findings in this study provide important guidance for future research. The study suggests that gang researchers need not be so preoccupied with documenting the presence or extent of hierarchy and bureaucracy within these gangs as these measures are essentially absent. Instead gang researchers may fruitfully examine population dynamics and document patterns of organizational change, further illuminating the conceptual model of gang evolution and growth described in this study. Recent gang literature has firmly established that gangs exacerbate individual criminality, suggesting that the gang as an organization is as important a level of analysis as the individual or social context which have dominated gang research. Indeed, much more study should be conducted of gangs at the social-organization level. Because of the absence of cross-sectional and longitudinal studies of gangs, little theory has been developed to explain the growth or predict the future of gangs. This study suggests that further research on the population of gangs and the organizational dynamics which affect gang prevalence, organizational density and mass is needed to further our understanding of change and evolution in gangs and to illuminate features of gangs which contribute to organizational longevity. Indeed, simply tracking or monitoring the number and size of different gangs within a population on a routine basis – perhaps semi-annually – may further illuminate our understanding of the organizational population of gangs and provide important insight into its changes over time.

Mature or successful gangs – those gangs of some longevity which have proceeded through organizational life cycles – provide useful case studies of organizational transformation processes. As with the organized crime model, gangs probably proceed through some distinct organizational patterns although these patterns cannot be detected from what were basically single-shot case studies of these four gangs. The formation of mature gangs – including changing organizational form and size, and environmental features – can be examined, documented and monitored to inform growth trajectories, size distribution, organizational density and mass within a population. Understanding these patterns of organizational dynamics can contribute to further understanding the growth and rising prevalence of contemporary gangs.

Studies of the population of gangs within cities (or within other relevant population boundaries such as similarly-sized gangs) show great promise for learning more about how these organizations rise and decline reciprocally.

As discussed previously, there is a great deal of variation between gangs. These variations are related to city and region; history, age and gang size; prevailing economic conditions; environmental characteristics; ethnicity; and probably a host of other factors. In this sense, gangs mirror the population of legitimate entrepreneurial enterprises – there is a vast array of different structures. Business organizations have largely been analyzed through in-depth case studies; and aggregations of business studies have largely been related to within-industry or similarly-sized organizations. One does not typically find business analysts comparing businesses across industry, for example, IBM with IGA, nor across sizes, for example, Food Lion chain with the corner grocery store. Organizational size and industry suggest constraints to organizational analyses of businesses that are probably appropriate to gangs as well. Determining the appropriate population boundaries is a necessary step to examining organizational dynamics within a population of gangs.

Gangs of different size and age may constitute distinctly different populations which are non-competing. These gangs may be more dissimilar than alike, explaining why differing classification schemes for gangs have emerged and why there is no clear and unifying description of a contemporary gang. Classifying gangs by size and/or age of gang may further illuminate differing types and features of gangs.

Understanding of contemporary gangs could also be enhanced by a large study documenting the organizational development of gangs within or across populations. Such an examination could illuminate the processes of growth and decline, detailing phenomena of gangs splintering and merging. Such a study could document the ways in which populations of gangs emerge within or across cities. Rising gang prevalence – with expansion to emerging-gang cities – provides fodder for examining this type of organizational process over time rather than relying on institutional memories of gang workers or gang members.

APPENDIX

Population boundaries were established for the samples of gangs and within gangs in this study. At the smallest population level – within gangs – variations between the prison and probation samples of each gang were evaluated. (This sample characteristic may be a surrogate variable reflecting the respondent's age or years of experience within the gang. Generally, respondents in the prison sample were older than those in the probation sample.) At the next aggregation of population, probation and prison responses for each gang were combined and analyzed to determine if gangs within each city could be considered as the same population. At the largest population level, all four cells for each city were combined and analyzed.

Once grouped into these three possible population size groups, variations within the three populations were then analyzed for a range of quantifiable questions which were embedded throughout the longer qualitative interview. These quantifiable questions were primarily dichotomous "yes" or "no" responses regarding gang form, size and activities – those characteristics useful for establishing population boundaries; there were approximately 170 of these questions.

At the smallest population level – within gang – establishing the population boundary means determining whether all gang members constitute the relevant population of the gang. A great deal of variation within a single gang would suggest that there are different and relevant populations within the gang – such as pee wee or veterano or age-graded cliques, as discussed in the review of gang literature. These different levels would then serve as distinctive population boundaries. The absence of variation, or minimal variation within gang, would suggest that the gang itself is the relevant population.

Among the quantifiable questions, only three questions were statistically significant within the Gangster Disciples gang:

"Do people take turns as leaders?" Probation respondents said "yes" to that question while prison respondents said "no"$(p>.002)$;

"Do [different] gangs meet together?" Prison respondents reported "no" $(p>.002)$; and,

"Is the gang involved in legitimate business?" Prison respondents reported "yes" (p>.001).

Qualitatively, Gangster Disciples prison respondents appeared to be more knowledgeable about their gang than probationers, offering greater detail and more definitive answers regarding history, number of members, activities and related issues. This qualitative observation is supported by differences between the median age of the Gang Disciple respondents; within-gang age differences were larger for the Gangster Disciples than for the other three gangs in this study. (See Table VI.) The average age of the Gangster Disciple prison respondent was 33 while the average age for the Gangster Disciple probation respondent was 20 years.

The Latin Kings were also examined in a manner similar to the Gangster Disciples. To examine within-gang population boundaries for the Latin Kings gang, three questions achieved significance:

"Are there leaders in the gang?" Probation respondents answered "yes" (p>.05);

"Do gang members do legal things together [in addition to illegal]?" Probation respondents responded "no" (p>.04); and,

"Has the gang become more organized in the last three years?" Probation respondents answered "yes" (p>.007).

Within the Logan gang in San Diego, two questions achieved significance:

"Are there rules in the gang?" Prison respondents responded "yes" (p>.009); and

Within the Syndo Mob gang in San Diego, only one question achieved significance:

"Is the gang involved in legitimate business?" Prison respondents answered "yes" (p>.03).

This examination of the variation in responses within gang revealed very few significant differences. Thus, the distinction between prison and probation samples – sources which are a likely surrogate for age and experience in the gang – is not a useful population boundary for the purposes of this study.

In addition to the variations within individual gangs, differences between gangs within city – between the Latin Kings and the Gangster Disciples in Chicago; between Syndo Mob and Logan in San Diego – were also evaluated to determine if both gangs in each city could be considered a relevant population. In Chicago, only two questions achieved significance in evaluating differences between the Gangster Disciples and Latin Kings:

"Are there consequences to leaving the gang?" Latin King respondents answered "no" (p.> .02); and

"Is the gang involved in political activities?" Gangster Disciple respondents answered "yes" (p> .0002)

In San Diego, five questions achieved significance in evaluating distinctions between the Syndo Mob and Logan gangs:

"Are there levels of membership?" Syndo Mob respondents reported "no" (p>.0001);

"Does the gang have good relationships with other gangs?" Syndo Mob respondents said "yes" (p>.002);

"Do gangs meet together?" Syndo Mob respondents said "yes" (p>.013); and,

"Do gangs do legal things together?" Syndo Mob respondents said "yes" (p>.05).

"Is the gang more involved or less involved in drug sales since you joined the gang? Syndo Mob respondents reported less gang involvement in drug sales (p> .02).

This examination of the variation between gangs within city also revealed few significant differences. Thus, we conclude that the distinction between gangs within city is not a useful population boundary for the purposes of this study.

In contrast to the previous examination within and across gangs in the same city in which minimal differences were identified, there were numerous differences which were statistically significant between the San Diego sample of gang members and the Chicago sample. (The following discussion thus aggregates the Latin Kings and Gangster Disciples into a nomenclature of "Chicago gangs" while Logan and Syndo Mob are referred to as the "San Diego gangs."

Responses varied distinctly between these two samples or populations. In contrast to San Diego respondents, Chicago gang members reported that their gang is more organized than when the respondent joined ($p>.000$). Chicago gang members said that levels of membership exist in their organization ($p>.03$); there are identifiable leaders in the gang ($p>.000$); the gang has regular meetings ($p>.000$); there are rules in the gang ($p>.03$) and the rules are written down ($p>.000$); and members pay dues ($p>.000$). In contrast to San Diego, Chicago gangs reported that there are consequences to leaving the gang ($p>.002$).

There were other significant differences on organizational issues between the cities and gangs in this study. Related to its primary organizational objective, Chicago gangs described a picture of fairly organized narcotic sales, reporting more drug sales since the respondent joined the gang ($p>.03$), expectations that each gang member sell a certain amount of drugs ($p>.000$), indicating that the main drug suppliers in gangs are its leaders ($p>.03$), and reinvestment in the gang occurs with drug money being used for gang activity ($p>.02$).

Respondents from Chicago gangs also reported a higher level of interorganizational collaboration. Chicago gangs reported having good relationships with other gangs ($p>.008$), meeting with other gangs ($p>.011$); and going on wars with other gangs ($p>.033$). Chicago gangs reported a greater level of sophistication as an organization including gang involvement in political activities ($p>.000$); gang involvement in legitimate business ($p>.08$); and greater use of guns since the respondent joined the gang ($p>.01$).

Despite the important differences between Chicago and San Diego gangs described above, the gangs in the two cities did share common responses, that is, instances in which there were no significant distinctions between the combined responses of the gang members in each city. Notably, 100 percent of respondents reported that their gang members sell drugs; 52.3 percent said their gang sells drugs together with other gangs. Some 72 percent of respondents indicated that the gang organizes drug sales rather than individuals. Among all gangs, 90 percent said their gang has relationships with gangs in prison while 75 percent said their gang had relationships with gangs in other cities.

Despite these similarities, the weight of evidence in an examination of differences between gangs in the two cities appears distinctive. Since none of the samples are random, it is a judgment call to use the distinction of gangs between cities as a population boundary. However, the weight of evidence suggests that city-level distinctions are the strongest parameter defining the population among between these four gangs and their institution-access points.

NOTES

[a]Attributed by Klein (1995: 203) to Covey, Menard and Franzese (1992: 178), however, the quotation could not be located in that book.

[b]And although much of the organizational ecology literature, as with organizational theory literature in general, deals with business organizations – sharing a bias because of data availability and access there are numerous ecological studies that have examined other types of organizations. Tucker et al (1988) and McPherson and Smith-Lovin (1988) examined voluntary social service organizations; Aldrich and Staber (1988) and Hannan and Freeman (1987) examined trade associations and labor unions. Other ecological studies have examined social movement organizations, bar associations, religious denominations and life insurance mutual societies (Halliday, Powell and Granfors, 1987; McCarthy et al, 1988; and Hannan and Freeman, 1989).

[c]Other criminologists, such as Cloward and Ohlin, 1960; Spergel, 1966; Wolfgang, Figlio and Sellin, 1972; Short and Strodtbeck, 1974; Bursik, 1980; and Rojek and Erikson, 1982, suggested that gangs do specialize in specific types of crimes.

[d]The use of the term >organic' should not be confused with the biological model of organizational evolution discussed previously. Although organic processes such as natural selection affect organizations, the term >organic organization= is used specifically to refer to a particular form of organization.

[e]Although Knox makes an important argument for organizational analysis of gangs, his dimensions of analysis are not consistent with organizational theory and show no evidence of being grounded in theory; he does not apply these dimensions to any gang, providing no case studies and only a few truncated examples. Nonetheless, his work makes an important contribution to thinking about the organizational transformation of contemporary gangs.

[f] Of course, resources are not unlimited and such a state of density dependence will be reached at some point in time.

[g]Estimates of gang numbers appear fairly modest given perceptions about the proliferation of gangs in these cities but the estimates of the number of gangs, however, were consistent with those of law enforcement in both cities.

BIBLIOGRAPHY

Abadinsky, Howard (1987). "The McDonald's-ization of the Mafia" in Timothy S. Bynum, Ed., *Organized Crime in America: Concepts and Controversies*, Monsey, NY: Willow Tree Press, Inc.

Abadinsky, Howard (1990). *Organized Crime*, 3rd edition, Chicago: Nelson Hall.

Albini, Joseph (1971). *The American Mafia: Genesis of a Legend*, New York: Appleton-Century-Crofts.

Aldrich, Howard and Ellen R. Auster (1990). "Even Dwarfs Started Small: Liabilities of Age and Size and Their Strategic Implications," in Barry M. Staw and L.L. Cummings, Eds., *The Evolution and Adaptation of Organizations*, Greenwich, CN: JAI Press.

Aldrich, Harold E. and Udo Staber (1988). "Organizing Business Interest: Patterns of Trade Association Foundings, Transformation and Death," in Glenn R. Carroll, Ed., *Ecological Models of Organizations*, Cambridge, MA: Ballinger Publishing Co.

Alexander, Herbert E. and Gerald E. Caiden, Eds. (1985). *The Politics and Economics of Organized Crime*, Lexington, MA: D.C. Heath and Company.

Argyris, Chris (1973). *On Organizations of the Future*, Beverly Hills: Sage Publications.

Asbury, Herbert (1970). *The Gangs of New York: An Informal History of the Underworld*, New York: Knopf. (Originally published 1928.)

Ayella, Marybeth (1993). "'They Must Be Crazy': Some of the Difficulties in Researching Cults," in Claire M. Renzetti and Raymond M. Lee, Eds. *Researching Sensitive Topics*, Newbury Park, CA: Sage Publications.

Bailey, Kenneth D. (1994). *Methods of Social Research*, 4th edition, New York: Macmillan.

Ball, Richard A. and G. David Curry (1995). "The Logic of Definition in Criminology: Purposes and Methods for Defining 'Gangs,'" *Criminology*, 33 (2): 225-245.

Baron, Robert S., Norbert L. Kerr and Norman Miller (1992). *Group Process, Group Decision, Group Action*, Pacific Grove, CA: Brooks/Cole.

Baum, Joel A.C. and Walter W. Powell (1995). "Cultivating an Institutional Ecology of Organizations: Comment on Hannan, Carroll, Dundon and Torres," *American Sociological Review*, Vol. 60, August, 529-538.

Becker, Howard S. (1963). *The Outsiders: Studies in the Sociology of Deviance*, New York: Free Press.

Becker, Howard S. (1970). "Practitioners of Vice and Crime," in Robert W. Habenstein, Ed., *Pathways to Data*, Chicago: Aldine.

Becker, Howard S. (1972). *Sociological Work: Method and Substance*, Chicago: Aldine Publishing Co.

Bell, Daniel J. (1961). *The End of Ideology*, New York: Collier.

Bennis, Warren G. (1966). *Changing Organizations*, New York: McGraw Hill.

Bennis, Warren G. (1993). *Beyond Bureaucracy: Essays on the Development and Evolution of Human Organization*, San Francisco: Jossey-Bass.

Berger, Ronald J. (1995). *The Sociology of Juvenile Delinquency*, 2nd edition, Chicago: Nelson-Hall.

Berne, Eric (1966). *The Structure and Dynamics of Organizations and Groups*, New York: Grove Press.

Best, Joel and David F. Luckinbill (1994). *Organizing Deviance*, 2nd edition, Englewood Clifts, NJ: Prentice Hall.

Bidwell, Charles E. and John D. Kasarda (1987). *Structuring in Organizations: Ecosystem Theory Evaluated*, Greenwich, CN: JAI Press Inc.

Blau, Peter M. And Richard A. Schoenherr (1971). *The Structure of Organizations*, New York: Basic Books.

Blau, Peter M. and W. Richard Scott (1962). *Formal Organizations: A Comparative Approach*, Scranton, PA: Chandler Publishing Co.

Bloch, Herbert A. (1958). *The Gang: A Study in Adolescent Behavior*, New York: Philosophical Library.

Block, Alan A. (1990). *Perspectives on Organizing Crime: Essays in Opposition*, Boston: Kluwer Academic Publishers.

Block, Alan A., Ed. (1991). *The Business of Crime:* A Documentary Study of Organized Crime in the American Economy, Boulder, CO: Westview Press.

Block, Alan A. (1994). *Space, Time & Organized Crime*, 2nd edition, New Brunswick, NJ: Transaction Publishers.

Blumberg, Abraham S. (1981). *Current Perspectives on Criminal Behavior*, 2nd edition, New York: Alfred A. Knopf.

Blumstein, Alfred, Jacqueline Cohen and David P. Farrington (1988). "Criminal Career Research: Its Value for Criminology," *Criminology*, Vol. 26, No. 1, pp. 1-35.

Boeker, Warren (1991). "Organizational Strategy: An Ecological Perspective," *Academy of Management Journal* 34 (3): 613-635.

Brenner, Michael, Jennifer Brown and David Canter, Eds. (1985). *The Research Interview: Uses and Approaches*, Orlando: Academic Press.

Brewer, John D. (1992). "A Study of Routine Policing in Northern Ireland" in
Claire M. Renzetti and Raymond M. Lee, Eds., *Researching Sensitive
Topics*, Newbury Park, CA: Sage Publications.

Brittain, Jack and John Freeman (1980). "Organizational Proliferation and
Density Dependence Selection," in John R. Kimberly, Robert H. Miles
and Associates, Eds., *The Organizational Life Cycle: Issues in the
Creation, Transformation and Decline of Organizations*, San Francisco:
Jossey Bass.

Brittain, Jack and Douglas R. Wholey (1989). "Assessing Organization
Psychology As Sociological Theory," *American Journal of Sociology* 95
(2): 49-444.

Bryant, Dan (1989). "Communitywide Response Crucial for Dealing with
Youth Gangs," Washington, D.C.: Office of Justice Programs, Office of
Juvenile Justice and Delinquency Prevention.

Bureau of Alcohol, Tobacco and Firearms (1992). National Gang Strategy, FY
92, Washington, DC: BATF.

Burgess, Robert G. (1984). *In the Field: An Introduction to Field Research*,
Boston: George Allen and Unwin.

Burns, Tom and G.M. Stalker (1961). *The Management of Innovation*,
London: Tavistock.

Bursik, Robert J., Jr. (1980). "The Dynamics of Specialization in Juvenile
Offenses," *Social Forces*, 58: 851-864.

Bursik, Robert J. and Harold G. Grasmick (1993). "The Neighborhood Context
of Gang Behavior" in *Neighborhoods and Crime: The Dimensions of
Effective Community Control*, New York: Lexington Books.

Bursik, Robert J. and Harold G. Grasmick (1996). "The Use of Contextual
Analysis in Models of Criminal Behavior," in J. David Hawkins, Ed.,
Delinquency and Crime: Current Theories, New York: Cambridge
University Press.

Bynum, Timothy S., Ed. (1987). *Organized Crime in America: Concepts and
Controversies*, Monsey, NY: Willow Tree Press, Inc.

Caiden, Gerald E. and Herbert E. Alexander (1985). "Introduction:
Perspectives on Organized Crime" in Herbert E. Alexander, and Gerald E.
Caiden, Eds., *The Politics and Economics of Organized Crime*,
Lexington, MA: D.C. Heath and Company.

Camp, George M. and Camille Graham Camp (1988). "Prison Gangs: Their
Extent, Nature and Impact on Prisons," Washington, D.C.: U.S.
Government Printing Office.

Campbell, Ann (1984). *The Girls in the Gang*, New York: Basil Blackwell.

Carroll, Glenn R. (1988). *Ecological Models of Organizations*, Cambridge, MA: Ballinger Publishing Co.

Chandler, David L. (1975). *Brothers in Blood: Rise of the Criminal Brotherhoods*, New York: Dutton.

Chesney-Lind, Meda et al (1994). "Gangs and Delinquency: Exploring Police Estimates of Gang Membership," *Crime, Law and Social Change*, 21: 201-228.

Chin, Ko-Lin (1990a). "Chinese Gangs and Extortion," in C. Ronald Huff, Ed., *Gangs in America*, Newbury Park, CA: Sage Publications.

Chin, Ko-lin (1990b). *Chinese Subculture and Criminality: Non-traditional Crime Groups in America*, Westport, CN: Greenwood Press.

Chin, Ko-lin, Robert J. Kelly and Jeffrey A. Fagan (1993). "Methodological Issues in Studying Chinese Gang Extortion," *The Gang Journal* 1 (2): 25-36.

Cloward, Richard A. and Lloyd E. Ohlin (1960). *Delinquency and Opportunity: A Theory of Delinquent Gangs*, New York: Free Press.

Cohen, Albert K. (1955). *Delinquent Boys: The Culture of the Gang*, Glencoe, IL: Free Press.

Cohen, Albert K. (1966). "Delinquent Subculture" in Rose Giallombardo, Ed., *Juvenile Delinquency*, New York: Wiley.

Cohen, Albert K. (1990). "Foreword and Overview," in C. Ronald Huff, Ed., *Gangs in America*, Newbury Park, CA: Sage.

Conly, Catherine (1994). "Gangs: What We Know," Washington, DC: Office of Justice Programs, National Institute of Justice.

Cook, Thomas D. and Donald T. Campbell (1979). *Quasi-Experimentation: Design and Analysis Issues for Field Settings*, Boston: Houghton Mifflin Company.

Covey, Herbert C., Scott Menard and Robert J. Franzese (1992). *Juvenile Gangs*, Chicago: Thomas.

Cressey, Donald R. (1969) *Theft of the Nation: The Structure and Operations of Organized Crime in America*, New York: Harper & Row.

Cressey, Donald R. (1972). *Criminal Organization: Its Elementary Forms*, New York: Harper and Row, Publishers.

Cummings, Scott and Daniel J. Monti, Eds. (1993). *Gangs: The origins and impact of contemporary youth gangs in the United States*, Albany: State University of New York Press.

Curry, G. David, Richard A. Ball and Robert J. Fox (1994). "Gang Crime and Law Enforcement Recordkeeping," Research in Brief, Washington, DC: National Institute of Justice (June).

Curry, G. David, Richard A. Ball and Scott H. Decker (1995). "Update on
    Gang Crime and Law Enforcement Record Keeping: Report of the 1994
    NIJ Extended National Assessment Survey of Law Enforcement Anti-
    Gang Information Resources," Washington DC: National Institute of
    Justice.

Daft, Richard L. (1986). *Organization Theory and Design*, New York: West
    Publishing Co.

Decker, Scott (1996). "Collective and Normative Features of Gang Violence,"
    Justice Quarterly, Vol. 13, No. 2: 243-264.

Decker, Scott H, Tim Bynum and Deborah Weisel (1998). "A Tale of Two
    Cities: Gangs as Organized Crime Groups," *Justice Quarterly*, Vol. 15,
    No. 3: 395-425.

Decker, Scott and Barrik Van Winkle (1996). *Life in the Gang: Family,
    Friends and Violence*, New York: Cambridge University Press.

Decker, Scott and Kimberly Kempf-Leonard (1991). "Constructing Gangs:
    The Social Definition of Youth Activities," *Criminal Justice Policy
    Review*, Vol 5, No. 4: 271-91.

Delattre, Edwin (1990). "New Faces of Organized Crime," *The American
    Enterprise*, pp. 38-45 (May/June).

Dombrink, John (1988). "Organized Crime: Gangsters and Godfathers," in
    Joseph E. Scott and Travis Hirschi, Eds., *Controversial Issues in Crime
    and Justice*, Newbury Park, CA: Sage Publications.

Dunn, L. (1991). "Research Alert! Qualitative Research May be Hazardous to
    your Health," *Qualitative Health Research*, 1, 388-392.

Durkheim, Emile (1933). *The Division of Labor in Society*, New York: Free
    Press.

Elliott, Delbert S., Suzanne S. Ageton and Rachelle J. Cantor (1979).
    "Integrated Theoretical Perspective on Delinquent Behavior," *Journal of
    Research on Crime and Delinquency*, Vol. 16, 3-21.

Esbensen, Finn-Age, L. Thomoas Winfree Jr., Ni He, and Terrance J. Taylor
    (2001). "Youth Gangs and Definitional Issues: When Is a Gang a Gang,
    and Why Does It Matter?" *Crime and Delinquency* 47 (1): 105-130.

Esbensen, Finn-Aage and David Huizinga (1993). "Gangs, Drugs, and
    Delinquency in a Survey of Urban Youth," *Criminology*, 4 (31).

Fagan, Jeffrey (1989). "The Social Organization of Drug Use and Drug Dealing
    Among Urban Gangs," *Criminology*, Vol. 27, No. 4.

Fagan, Jeffrey (1990). "Social Processes of Delinquency and Drug Use Among
    Urban Gangs" in C. Ronald Huff, Ed., *Gangs in America*, Newbury Park,
    CA: Sage Publications.

Farrington, David P. (1973). "Self-reports of deviant behavior: Predictive and Stable?" *Journal of Law and Criminology*, 64: 99-110.

Farrington, David P. et al (1988). "Specialization in Juvenile Court Careers," *Criminology*, 26: 461-485.

Fayol, Henri (1987). "General Principles of Management," in Jay M. Shafritz and J. Steven Ott, *Classics of Organization Theory*, 2nd edition, Chicago,IL: Dorsey Press.

Federal Bureau of Investigation (1991). Major Gang Initiative, memorandum from the director, Sept. 11.

Ferraro, Thomas (1992). "The FBI Takes Aim At Gangs," *Insight* (October 5).

Freeman, John (1978). "The Unit of Analysis in Organizational Research," in Marshall W. Meyer and Associates, Eds., *Environments and Organizations*, San Francisco: Jossey-Bass.

Freeman, John (1990). "Organizational Life Cycles and Natural Selection Processes," in Barry M. Staw and L.L. Cummings, Eds., *The Evolution and Adaptation of Organizations*, Greenwich, CN: JAI Press.

Freeman, John and Michael T. Hannan (1989). "Setting the Record Straight on Organizational Ecology," *American Journal of Sociology*, Vol. 95, No. 2, 425-438.

Fry, Charles L. (1934). *The technique of social investigation*, New York: Harper.

Gardner, John W. (1912). "How to Prevent Organizational Dry Rot," *Harper's Magazine*, October.

General Accounting Office (GAO) (1989). "Nontraditional Organized Crime: Law Enforcement Officials' Perspectives on Five Criminal Groups," Report to the Chairman, Permanent Subcommittee on Investigations, Washington, DC: Author (September).

Glaser, Barney and Anselm L. Strauss (1965). "The discovery of substantive theory: A basic strategy underlying qualitative research," *American Behavioral Scientist*, 8: 5-12.

Glaser, Barney and Anselm L. Strauss (1967). *The Discovery of Grounded Theory: Strategies for Qualitative Research*, New York: Aldine.

Glueck, Sheldon and Eleanor Glueck (1950). *Unraveling Juvenile Delinquency*, New York: Commonwealth Fund.

Goffman, E. (1989). "On Fieldwork," *Journal of Contemporary Ethnography*, 18, 123-132.

Goldstein, Arnold P. (1991). *Delinquent Gangs: A Psychological Perspective*, Champaign, IL: Research Press.

Goldstein, Arnold P. and C. Ronald Huff, Eds. (1993). *The Gang Intervention Handbook*, Champaign, IL: Research Press.

Goodson, Roy and William J. Olson (1995). "International Organized Crime," *Society*, Vol. 32, No. 2 (January/February), pp. 18-29.

Gottfredson, Michael and Michael Hindelang (1981). "Sociological aspects of criminal victimization," *Annual Review of Sociology*, 7: 107-128.

Gottfredson, Michael and Travis Hirschi (1986). "Career Criminals," *Criminology*, Vol. 24, No. 2, pp. 213-234.

Gottfredson, Michael and Travis Hirschi (1988). "Criminal Career Paradigm," *Criminology*, Vol. 26, No. 1.

Gottfredson, Michael and Travis Hirschi (1990). *A General Theory of Crime*, Stanford, CA: Stanford University Press.

Greiner, Larry E. (1972). "Evolution and Revolution as Organizations Grow," *Harvard Business Review*, 50, (July-August).

Hagan, Frank E. (1983). "The Organized Crime Continuum: A Further Specification of a New Conceptual Model," *Criminal Justice Review*, 8: 52-57.

Hagan, John and Alberto Palloni (1988). "Crimes as Social Events in the Life Course: Reconceiving a Criminological Controversy," *Criminology*, Vol. 26, No. 1.

Hagedorn, John M. (1988). *People and Folks: Gangs and Crime in a Rustbelt City*, Chicago: Lakeview Press.

Hagedorn, John M. (1990). "Back in the Field Again: Gang Research in the Nineties," in C. Ronald Huff, *Gangs in America*, Newbury Park: Sage Publications.

Hagedorn, John M. (1995). "Neighborhoods, Markets and Gang Drug Organization," *Journal of Research in Crime and Delinquency*, Vol. 31, No. 3 (August): 264-294.

Hakim, Catherine (1987). *Research Design: Strategies and Choices in the Design of Social Research*, Boston: Allen and Unwin.

Halliday, Terence C., Michael J. Powell and Mark Granfors (1987). "Minimalist Organizations: Vital Events in State Bar Associations, 1870-1930," *American Sociological Review*, Vol. 52, pp. 456-71.

Hannan, Michael T. and Glenn R. Carroll (1992). *Dynamics of Organizational Populations: Density, Legitimation and Competition*, New York: Oxford University Press.

Hannan, Michael T. and Glenn R. Carroll (1995). "Theory Building and Cheap Talk about Legitimation: Reply to Baum and Powell," *American Sociological Review*, Vol. 60, August, 529-538.

Hannan, Michael T. and John H. Freeman (1978). "The Population Ecology of Organizations," Marshall W. Meyer and Associates, Eds., *Environments and Organizations*, San Francisco: Jossey-Bass.

Hannan, Michael T. and John Freeman (1987). "The Ecology of Organizational Founding: American Labor Unions, 1836-1985," *American Journal of Sociology*, Vol. 92, pp. 910-943.

Hannan, Michael T. and John Freeman (1988). "Density Dependence in Populations," in Glenn R. Carroll, Ed., *Ecological Models of Organizations*, Cambridge, MA: Ballinger Publishing Co.

Hannan, Michael T. and John Freeman (1989*). Organizational Ecology*, Cambridge, MA: Harvard University Press.

Hawkins, J. David, Ed. (1996). *Delinquency and Crime: Current Theories*, New York: Cambridge University Press.

Hawley, Amos H. (1950). *Human Ecology: A Theory of Community Structure*, New York: Ronald Press.

Hawley, Amos H. (1968). "Human Ecology," in David L. Sills, Ed., *International Encyclopedia of the Social Sciences*, New York: Macmillan.

Hechter, Michael (1987). *Principles of Group Solidarity*, Berkeley: University of California Press.

Heckscher, Charles (1994). "Defining the Post-Bureaucratic Organization," in Charles Heckscher and Anne Donnellon, Eds., *The Post-Bureaucratic Organization: New Perspectives on Organizational Change*, Thousand Oaks, CA: Sage Publications.

Heckscher, Charles and Anne Donnellon, Eds. (1994). *The Post-Bureaucratic Organization: New Perspectives on Organizational Change*, Thousand Oaks, CA: Sage Publications.

Hedrick, Terry (1994). "Possibilities for Integration" in Charles S. Reichardt and Sharon F. Rallis, Eds., *The Qualitative-Quantitative Debate: New Perspectives*, No. 61 (Spring), San Francisco: Jossey-Bass Publishers.

Hindelang, Michael, Travis Hirschi and Joseph Weis (1981). *Measuring Delinquency*, Beverly Hills: Sage Publications.

Hirschi, Travis (1969). *Causes of Delinquency*, Berkeley: University of California Press.

Hirschi, Travis (1979). "Separate and Unequal is Better," *Journal of Research in Crime and Delinquency*, 16: 34-38.

Hirschi, Travis and Michael Gottfredson (1983). "Age and the Explanation of Crime," *American Journal of Sociology*, 89: 552-584.

Hirschi, Travis and Hanan C. Selvin (1996*). Delinquency Research: An Appraisal of Analytic Techniques*, New Brunswick: Transaction Publishers.

Horowitz, Ruth (1983). *Honor and the American Dream*, New Brunswick: Rutgers University Press.

Horowitz, Ruth (1990). "Sociological Perspectives on Gangs: Conflicting Definitions and Concepts" in C. Ronald Huff, Ed., *Gangs in America*, Newbury Park, CA: Sage Publications Inc.

Howell, J.C. and S.H. Decker (2000). "The Youth Gang, Drugs, and Violence Connection," *Bulletin*, Washington DC: Office of Juvenile Justice and Delinquency Prevention.

Huff, C. Ronald (1989). "Youth Gangs and Public Policy," *Crime and Delinquency*, Vol. 35, No. 4 (October).

Huff, C. Ronald, Ed. (1990*). Gangs in America*, Newbury Park, CA: Sage Publications.

Huff, C. Ronald (1994). Presentation at the American Society of Criminology, Miami (November).

Hunt, Jennifer (1984). "The Development of Rapport through the Negotiation of Gender in Field Work among Police," *Human Organization*, 43 (283-296).

Hutchison, Ray and Charles Kyle (1993). "Hispanic Street Gangs in Chicago's Public Schools" in Scott Cummings and Daniel J. Monti, Eds., *Gangs: The origins and impact of contemporary youth gangs in the United States*, Albany: State University of New York Press.

Ianni, Francis A.J. (1969). *The crime society – organized crime and corruption in America*, New York: Times-Mirror.

Ianni, Francis A.J. (1972). *A Family Business: Kinship and Social Control in Organized Crime*, New York: Russell Sage Foundation.

Jackson, Jean (1986). "On Trying to be an Amazon," in Tony L. Whitehead and Mary Ellen Conaway, Eds., *Self, Sex and Gender in Cross-Cultural Fieldwork*, Urbana: University of Illinois Press, pp. 263-274.

Jackson, John H., Cyril P. Morgan and Joseph G.P. Paolillo (1986). *Organization Theory: A Macro Perspective for Management*, 3rd edition, Englewood Clifts, NJ: Prentice-Hall.

Jackson, Pamela Irving (1991). "Crime, Youth Gangs and Urban Transition: The Social Dislocation of Postindustrial Economic Development," *Justice Quarterly*, 8 (3): 379-397.

Jackson, Patrick (1989). "Theories and Findings About Youth Gangs," *Criminal Justice Abstracts*, Vol. 21, No. 2 (June).

Jankowski, Martin Sanchez (1991). *Islands in the Street: Gangs and American Urban Society*, Berkeley: University of California Press.

Jensen, Gary F. and Dean G. Rojek (1980). *Delinquency*, Lexington, MA: Heath.

Jensen, Eric L. (1994). "An Interview with James F. Short, Jr.," *Journal of Gang Research*, Vol. 2, No. 2 (Winter).

Joe, Karen (1993). "Issues in accessing and studying ethnic youth gangs," *Gang Journal* 1 (2): 25-36.

Johnson, John M. (1975). *Doing Field Research*, New York: Free Press.

Kasarda, John D. (1974). "The Structural Implications of Social System Size: A Three-Level Analysis," *American Sociological Review*, Vol. 39 (February): 19-28.

Katz, Daniel and Robert L. Kahn (1966*). The Social Psychology of Organizations*, New York: John Wiley and Sons Inc.

Kelly, Robert J., Ed. (1986). *Organized Crime: A Global Perspective*, Totowa, NJ: Rowman and Littlefield.

Kenney, Dennis J. and James O. Finckenauer (1995*). Organized Crime in America*, Belmont, CA: Wadsworth Publishing Co.

Kimberly, John R., Robert H. Miles and Associates, Eds. (1980). *The Organizational Life Cycle: Issues in the Creation, Transformation and Decline of Organizations*, San Francisco: Jossey Bass.

Kirk, Jerome and Marc L. Miller (1986). *Reliability and Validity in Qualitative Research*, Beverly Hills: Sage Publications.

Klein, Malcolm (1971). *Street Gangs and Street Workers*, Englewood Clifts, NJ: Prentice-Hall.

Klein, Malcolm (1995). *The American Street Gang: Its Nature, Prevalence and Control*, New York: Oxford University Press

Klein, Malcolm and Cheryl Maxson (1989). "Street Gang Violence" in Marvin E. Wolfgang and Neil Weiner, Eds., *Violent Crime, Violent Criminals*, Newbury Park, CA: Sage Publications.

Klein, Malcolm and Cheryl Maxson (1994). "Gangs and Crack Cocaine Dealing," in Craig Uchida and Doris L. MacKenzie, Eds., *Drugs and Crime: Evaluating Public Policy Initiatives*, Thousand Oaks, CA: Sage Publications.

Klein, Malcolm W., Cheryl L. Maxson and Jody Miller (1995). *The Modern Gang Reader*, Los Angeles: Roxbury Publishing Company.

Kleinman, Sherryl and Martha A. Copp (1993*). Emotions and Field Work*, Newbury Park, CA; Sage Publications.

Knox, George (1994). *An Introduction to Gangs*, Bristol, IN: Wyndham Hall Press.

Koester, Stephen and Judith Schwartz (1993). "Crack, Gangs, Sex and Powerlessness: A View from Denver," in Mitchell S. Ratner, Ed., *Crack Pipe as Pimp*, New York: Lexington Books.

Kornhauser, Ruth Rosner (1978*). Social Sources of Delinquency: An Appraisal of Analytic Models*, Chicago: University of Chicago Press.

Kuhn, Thomas S. (1962). *The Structure of Scientific Revolutions*, Chicago: University of Chicago Press.

Lasley, James R. (1992). "Age, Social Context, and Street Gang Membership: Are 'Youth' Gangs Becoming 'Adult' Gangs?" *Youth and Society*, Vol. 23, No. 4.

Lawrence, Paul and Jay W. Lorsch (1967). *Organization and Environment*, Boston: Graduate School of Business Administration, Harvard University.

Lemert, Edwin M. (1951). *Social Pathology*, New York: McGraw Hill.

Letkemann, Peter (1973). *Crime as Work*, Englewood Cliffs, NJ: Prentice-Hall.

Lilly, J. Robert, Francis T. Cullen and Richard A. Ball (1995). *Criminological Theory: Context and Consequences*, 2nd edition, Thousand Oaks, CA: Sage Publications.

Lippitt, Gordon L. (1982). *Organizational Renewal*, 2nd Edition, New York: Appleton-Century-Crofts.

Lofland, John and Lyn H. Lofland (1995). *Analyzing Social Settings: A Guide to Qualitative Observation and Analysis*, Belmont, CA: Wadsworth.

Lupsha, Peter A. (1986). "Organized Crime in the United States" in Robert J. Kelly, Ed., *Organized Crime: A Global Perspective*, Totowa, NJ: Rowman and Littlefield.

Lupsha, Peter A. (1991). "Organized Crime" in William A. Geller, Ed., *Local Government Police Manag*ement, 3rd edition, Washington, DC: International City Management Association.

Maltz, Michael (1985). "Towards Defining Organized Crime" in Herbert E. Alexander, and Gerald E. Caiden, Eds., *The Politics and Economics of Organized Crime*, Lexington, MA:

Marshall, Catherine and Gretchen B. Rossman (1995). *Designing Qualitative Research*, Newbury Park, CA: Sage Publications.

Maxson, Cheryl (1993). "Investigating gang migration: Contextual issues for intervention," *The Gang Journal* 1 (2): 1-8.

Maxson, Cheryl, M.A. Gordon and Malcolm Klein (1985). "Differences between gang and non-gang homicides," *Criminology*, 23: 209-222.

Maxson, Cheryl and Malcolm Klein (1990). "Street Gang Violence: Twice as Great, or Half as Great" in C. Ronald Huff, Ed., *Gangs in America*, Newbury Park, CA: Sage Publications.

McCarthy, John D. et al (1988). "The Founding of Social Movement Organizations," in Glenn R. Carroll, Ed., *Ecological Models of Organizations*, Cambridge, MA: Ballinger Publishing Co.

McPherson, J. Miller and Lynn Smith-Lovin (1988). "A Comparative Ecology of Five Nations: Testing a Model of Competition among Voluntary Organizations," in Glenn R. Carroll, Ed., *Ecological Models of Organizations*, Cambridge, MA: Ballinger Publishing Co.

Merton, Robert K. (1938). "Social Structure and Anomie," American *Sociological Review*, 3, 672-682.

Meyer, John W. (1978). "Strategies for Further Research: Varieties of Environmental Variation" in Marshall W. Meyer and Associates, Eds., Environments and Organizations, San Francisco: Jossey-Bass.

Meyer, John W. and Brian Rowan (1992). "Institutionalized Organizations: Formal Structure as Myth and Ceremony" in John W. Meyer and W. Richard Scott, Eds. *Organizational Environments; Ritual and Rationality*, Newbury Park, CA: Sage Publications.

Meyer, John W. and W. Richard Scott, Eds. (1992*). Organizational Environments; Ritual and Rationality*, Newbury Park, CA: Sage Publications.

Meyer, Marshall W. and Associates, Eds. (1978*). Environments and Organizations*, San Francisco: Jossey-Bass.

Miles, Matthew B. and A. Michael Huberman (1984). *Qualitative Data Analysis: A Sourcebook of New Methods*, Newbury Park, CA: Sage Publications. D.C. Heath and Company.

Miles, Robert H. and W. Alan Randolph (1980). "Influence of Organizational Learning Styles on Early Development," in John R. Kimberly, Robert H. Miles and Associates, Eds., *The Organizational Life Cycle: Issues in the Creation, Transformation and Decline of Organizations*, San Francisco: Jossey Bass.

Miller, Walter (1958). "Lower class culture as a generating milieu of gang delinquency," *Journal of Social Issues*, 14 (3), 5-19.

Miller, Walter B. (1972). "Youth Gangs in the Urban Crisis Era," in James F. Short, Ed., *Delinquency, Crime and So*ciety, Chicago: University of Chicago Press.

Miller, Walter B. (1975). "Violence by Youth Gangs and Youth Groups as a Crime Problem in Major American Cities," Washington, D.C.: U.S. Government Printing Office.

Miller, Walter B. (1980). "Gangs, Groups, and Serious Youth Crime," in David Shichor and Delos H. Kelly, Eds., *Critical Issues in Juvenile Delinquency*, Lexington, MA: D.C. Heath and Co.

Miller, Walter (1981). "American Youth Gangs: Past and Present" in Abraham Blumberg, Ed., *Current Perspectives on Criminal Behavior*, New York: Alfred A. Knopf.

Miller, Walter B. (1982). "Crime by Youth Gangs and Groups in the United States," Washington, D.C.: National Institute of Juvenile Justice and Delinquency Prevention.

Miller, Walter B. (1990). "Why the United States Has Failed to Solve Its Youth Gang Problem" in C. Ronald Huff, Ed., *Gangs in America*, Newbury Park, CA: Sage Publications.

Miller, Walter B. (2001). "The Growth of Youth Gang Problems in the United States: 1970-1998," Report. Washington DC: Office of Juvenile Justice and Delinquency Prevention (April).

Mink, Oscar et al (1994). *Open Organizations*, San Francisco: Jossey-Bass.

Mintzberg, Henry (1979). *The Structuring of Organizations*, Englewood Clifts, NJ: Prentice Hall.

Mintzberg, Henry (1983). "An Emerging Strategy of 'Direct' Research" in John Van Maanen, Ed., *Qualitative Methodology*, Beverly Hills: Sage Publications.

Mishler, Elliot G. (1986). *Research Interviewing: Context and Narrative*, Cambridge: Harvard University Press.

Monti, Daniel J. (1993a). "Gangs in More- and Less-Settled Communities," in Scott Cummings and Daniel J. Monti, Eds., *Gangs: The origins and impact of contemporary youth gangs in the United States*, Albany: State University of New York Press.

Monti, Daniel J. (1993b). "Origins and Problems of Gang Research in the United States" in Scott Cummings and Daniel J. Monti, Eds. *Gangs: The origins and impact of contemporary youth gangs in the United States*, Albany: State University of New York Press.

Moore, Joan (1978). *Homeboys: Gangs, Drugs and Prison in the Barrios of Los Angeles*, Philadelphia: Temple University Press.

Moore, Joan (1991). *Going Down to the Barrio: Homeboys and Homegirls in Change*, Philadelphia: Temple.

Moore, Joan (1993). "Gangs, Drugs and Violence" in Scott Cummings and
     Daniel J. Monti, Eds., *Gangs: The origins and impact of contemporary
     youth gangs in the United States*, Albany: State University of New York
     Press.

Morash, Merry (1983). "Gangs, Groups and Delinquency," *The British Journal
     of Criminology*, 23: 4 (309-335.

Mudrack, Peter E. (1989). "Defining Group Cohesiveness: A Legacy of
     Confusion?" *Small Group Behavior*, Vol. 20, No. 1 (February); 37-49.

Mueller, Robert S. III (1991). Testimony before the U.S. Senate Permanent
     Subcommittee on Investigations, "Asian Organized Crime," Washington,
     DC (November 6).

Mydans, Seth (1992). "FBI Setting Sights on Street Gangs," *New York Times*,
     p. 8 (May 24).

Munch, R. (1986). "The American creed in sociological theory: Exchange,
     negotiated order, accommodated individualism, and contingency,"
     Sociological Theory, 4: 41-60.

Natemeyer, Walter E. and Jay S. Gilbert (1989). *Classics of Organizational
     Behavior*, Danville, IL: Interstate.

National Youth Gang Center (1997). 1995 National Youth Gang Survey.
     Summary. Washington DC: Office of Juvenile Justice and Delinquency
     Prevention.

National Youth Gang Center (1999a). 1996 National Youth Gang Survey.
     Summary. Washington DC: Office of Juvenile Justice and Delinquency
     Prevention.

National Youth Gang Center (1999b). 1997 National Youth Gang Survey.
     Summary. Washington DC: Office of Juvenile Justice and Delinquency
     Prevention.

National Youth Gang Center (2000). 1998 National Youth Gang Survey.
     Summary. Washington DC: Office of Juvenile Justice and Delinquency
     Prevention.

Needle, Jerome A. and William V. Stapleton (1983). "Police Handling of
     Youth Gangs," Washington, D.C.: U.S. Department of Justice, Office of
     Juvenile Justice and Delinquency Prevention, National Institute for
     Juvenile Justice and Delinquency Prevention (September).

O'Kane, James M. (1992). *The Crooked Ladder: Gangsters, Ethnicity, and the
     American Dream*, New Brunswick, NJ: Transaction Publishers.

Orton, J. Douglas and Karl E. Weick (1990). "Loosely coupled systems: A
     reconceptualization," *Management Review*, 15 (2): 203-223.

Ouchi, William G. and Alfred M. Jaeger (1978). "Social Structure and Organizational Type," in Marshall W. Meyer and Associates, Eds., *Environments and Organizations*, San Francisco: Jossey-Bass.

Padilla, Felix M. (1993a). *The Gang as an American Enterprise*, New Brunswick, NJ: Rutgers University Press.

Padilla, Felix M. (1993b). "The Working Gang" in Scott Cummings and Daniel J. Monti, Eds. *Gangs: The origins and impact of contemporary youth gangs in the United States*, Albany: State University of New York Press.

Parsons, Talcott (1987). "Suggestions for a Sociological Approach to the Theory of Organizations," in Jay M. Shafritz and J. Steven Ott, Eds., *Classics of Organization Theory*, 2nd edition, Chicago,IL: Dorsey Press.

Pennell, Susan et al (1994). "Down and Out for the Set: Defining and Describing Gangs in San Diego," San Diego: San Diego Association of Governments.

Pennings, Johannes (1980). "Environmental Influences on the Creation Process," in John R. Kimberly, Robert H. Miles and Associates, Eds., *The Organizational Life Cycle: Issues in the Creation, Transformation and Decline of Organizations*, San Francisco: Jossey Bass.

Pfeffer, Jeffrey and Gerald R. Salancik (1977). "Organization Design: The Case for a Coalitional Model of Organizations," *Organizational Dynamics*, Autumn: 15-30.

Polsky, Ned (1967). *Hustlers, Beats and Others*, Chicago: Aldine.

Popielarz, Pamela A. and J. Miller McPherson (1995). "On the Edge or In Between: Niche Position, Niche Overlap, and the Duration of Voluntary Association Memberships," *American Journal of Sociology*, Vol. 101, No. 2, 698-720.

Popper, Karl R. (1959). *The Logic of Scientific Discovery*, New York: Basic Books.

Potter, Gary W. (1994). *Criminal Organizations: Vice, Racketeering, and Politics in an American City*, Prospect Heights, IL: Waveland Press, Inc.

Powell, Walter W. (1990). "Neither market nor hierarchy: Network forms of organization," *Research in Organizational Behavior*, 12: 295-336.

Puffer, J. Adams (1912). *The Boy and His Gang*, Boston: Houghton-Miflin.

Rafferty, Frank T. and Harvey Bertcher (1963). "Gang Formation In Vitro," *Journal of Mental and Nervous Disorders*, Vol. 137, 76-81.

Rankin, Joseph H. and L. Edward Wells (1985). "From Status to Delinquent Offenses: Escalation?" *Journal of Criminal Justice*, 13: 171- 180.

Reckless, Walter C. (1967). *The Crime Problem*, 4th edition, New York: Appleton-Century-Crofts.

Renzetti, Claire M. and Raymond M. Lee, Eds. (1993). *Researching Sensitive Topics,* Newbury Park, CA: Sage Publications.

Reuter, Peter (1983). *Disorganized Crime: The Economics of the Visible Hand,* Cambridge, MA: The MIT Press.

Rojek, Dean G. and Maynard L. Erickson (1982). "Delinquent Careers: A Test of the Escalation Model," *Criminology,* 20: 5-28.

Rojek, Dean G. and Gary F. Jensen (1996). *Exploring Delinquency: Causes and Control,* Los Angeles, CA: Roxbury Publishing Co.

Rosenbaum, Dennis P. and June A. Grant (1983). "Gangs and Youth Problems in Evanston: Research Findings and Policy Options," Evanston, IL: Northwestern University Center for Urban Affairs and Policy Research.

Sale, R.T. (1971). *The Blackstone Rangers*, New York: Random House.

Salerno, Ralph F. and John R. Tomkins (1969). *The Crime Confederation: Costa Nostra and Allied Operations in Organized Crime*, Garden City, NY: Doubleday.

Sanders, William B. (1994). *Gangbangs and Drive-bys: Grounded Culture and Juvenile Gang Violence*, New York: Aldine De Gruyter.

Schein, Edgar H. (1985). Organizational Culture and Leadership, San Francisco: Jossey Bass Inc.

Schein, Edgar H. (1989). "Groups and Intergroup Relationships," in Walter E. Natemayer and Jay S. Gilberg, *Classics of Organizational Behavior*, Danville, IL: The Interstate Printers & Publishers, Inc.

Scott, W. Richard (1993). *Organizations: Rational, Natural, and Open Systems*. Englewood Clifts, NJ: Prentice Hall.

Shafritz, Jay M. and J. Steven Ott, Eds. (1987). *Classics of Organization Theory*, 2nd edition, Chicago,IL: Dorsey Press.

Shaw, Clifford R. and Henry D. McKay (1969). *Juvenile Delinquency and Urban Areas*, Chicago: University of Chicago Press.

Shoemaker, Donald J. (1990). *Theories of Delinquency*, 2nd edition, New York: Oxford University Press.

Short, James F. (1990). "New Wine in Old Bottles? Change and Continuity in American Gangs," in C. Ronald Huff, Ed., *Gangs in America*, Newbury Park, CA: Sage Publications.

Short, James F. and Fred L. Strodtbeck (1974). *Group Process and Gang Delinquency*, Chicago: University of Chicago Press.

Short, Martin (1984). *Crime Inc.: The Story of Organized Crime*, London: Thames-Methuen.

Silverman, David (1985). *Qualitative Methodology and Sociology: Describing the Social World*, Brookfield, VT :Gower.

Simel, Georg (1902-3). "The number of members as determining the sociological form of groups," I and II, *The American Journal of Sociology*, 8: 1-46, 138-96.

Singh, Jitendra V. (1990). *Organizational Evolution: New Directions*, Newbury Park, CA: Sage.

Singh, Jitendra V. and Joel A.C. Baum, Eds. (1994). *Evolutionary Dynamics of Organizations*, New York: Oxford University Press.

Skolnick, Jerome H. et al (n.d.). "The Social Structure of Street Drug Dealing," BCS Forum, Sacramento: Bureau of Criminal Statistics and Special Services.

Skolnick, Jerome H., Ricky Bluthenthal and Theodore Correl (1993). "Gang Organization and Migration" in Scott Cummings and Daniel J. Monti, Eds., *Gangs: The origins and impact of contemporary youth gangs in the United States*, Albany: State University of New York Press.

Smith, Dwight (1975). *The Mafia Mystique*, New York: Basic Books.

Smith, Dwight (1980). "Paragon, Pariahs and Pirates: A spectrum-based theory of enterprise," *Crime and Delinquency*, 26 (3): 358-386.

Smith, Mary Lee (1994). "Qualitative Plus/Vs. Quantitative: The Last Word" in Charles S. Reichardt and Sharon F. Rallis, Eds., *The Qualitative-Quantitative Debate: New Perspectives*, No. 61 (Spring), San Francisco: Jossey-Bass Publishers.

Snyder, Howard N. and Melissa Sickmund (1995). "Juvenile Offenders and Victims: A National Report," Washington, D.C.: Office of Juvenile Justice and Delinquency Prevention, U.S. Department of Justice (August).

Snyder, Howard N., Melissa Sickmund, and Eileen Poe-Yamagata (1996). "Juvenile Offenders and Victims: 1996 Update on Violence," Statistics Summary, Washington, D.C.: Office of Juvenile Justice and Delinquency Prevention, U.S. Department of Justice (February).

Spergel, Irving A. (1966). *Street Gang Work: Theory and Practice*, Reading, MA: Addison Wesley Publishing Co.

Spergel, Irving A. (1984). "Violent Gangs in Chicago: In Search of Social Policy," *Social Service Review*, 58 (2): 199-226.

Spergel, Irving A. (1990). "Youth Gangs: Continuity and Change," in Norval Morris and Michael Tonry, Eds., *Crime and Justice: A Review of Research*, Vol. 12, Chicago: University of Chicago Press (June).

Spergel, Irving A. (1995). *The Youth Gang Problem: A Community Approach*, New York: Oxford University Press.

Spergel, Irving A. et al (1991). "Youth Gangs: Problem and Response," Chicago: School of Social Service Administration, University of Chicago.

Spergel, Irving A. and G. David Curry (1993). "The National Youth Gang Survey: A Research and Development Process," in Arnold P. Goldstein and C. Ronald Huff, Eds., *The Gang Intervention Handbook*, Champaign, IL: Research Press.

Stafford, Mark (1984). "Gang Delinquency" in Robert F. Meier, Ed., *Major Forms of Crime*, Beverly Hills: Sage Publications.

Starbuck, William H. (1965). "Organizational Growth and Development," in James G. March, Ed., *Handbook of Organizations*, Chicago: Rand McNally.

State of California (n.d.). Organized Crime in California, 1989, California Department of Justice, Bureau of Organized Crime and Criminal Intelligence.

Staw, Barry M. and L.L. Cummings, Eds. (1990*). The Evolution and Adaptation of Organizations*, Greenwich, CN: JAI Press.

Steffensmeier, Darrell J. et al (1989). "Age and the Distribution of Crime," *American Journal of Sociology*, 94: 803 - 831.

Stinchcombe, Arthur L. (1965). "Social Structure and Organizations," in James G. March, Ed., *Handbook of Organizations*, Chicago: Rand McNally.

Sutherland, Edwin H. (1934). *Principles of Criminology*, Philadelphia: Lippincott.

Sutherland, Edwin H. and Donald R. Cressey (1970*). Criminology*, Philadelphia: J.B. Lippincott.

Tannenbaum, Frank (1938). *Crime and the Community*, Boston: Ginn.

Task Force on Juvenile Gangs (1993). "Reaffirming Prevention," Report on the Task Force of Juvenile Gangs, Rensselaer, NY: author.

Taylor, Carl S. (1990a). *Dangerous Society*, E. Lansing, MI: Michigan State University Press.

Taylor, Carl S. (1990b). "Gang Imperialism" in C. Ronald Huff, Ed., *Gangs in America*, Newbury Park, CA: Sage Publications Inc.

Taylor, Frederick W. (1911). *The Principles of Scientific Management*, New York: Norton.

Thornberry, Terence P., Marvin D. Krohn, Alan J. Lizotte and Deborah Chard-Wierschem (1993). "The Role of Juvenile Gangs in Facilitating Delinquent Behavior," *Journal of Research in Crime and Delinquency*, 30 (1): 55-87.

Thrasher, Frederic M. (1963*). The Gang: A Study of 1,313 Gangs in Chicago*, Chicago: University of Chicago Press (first published in 1927).

Tichy, Noel M. (1980). "Problem Cycles in Organizations and the Management of Change," in John R. Kimberly, Robert H. Miles and Associates, Eds., *The Organizational Life Cycle: Issues in the Creation, Transformation and Decline of Organizations*, San Francisco: Jossey Bass.

Tucker, David J. et al (1988). "Ecological and Institutional Sources of Change," in Glenn R. Carroll, Ed., *Ecological Models of Organizations*, Cambridge, MA: Ballinger Publishing Co.

Tushman, Michael L. and Elaine Romanelli (1990). "Organizational Evolution" in Barry M. Staw and L.L. Cummings, Eds., *The Evolution and Adaptation of Organizations*, Greenwich, CN: JAI Press.

U.S. Attorneys (1989). "Drug Trafficking: A Report to the President of the United States," Washington, D.C.: U.S. Attorneys and the Attorney General of the United States, U.S. Justice Department.

Vasu, Michael, Debra W. Stewart and G. David Garson (1990). *Organizational Behavior and Public Management*, 2nd edition, New York: Marcel Dekker.

Vigil, James D. (1988). *Barrio Gangs: Street Life and Identity in Southern California*, Austin: University of Texas Press.

Walker, Jeffrey T., Bill Watt and E. Ashley White (1994). "The Evolution of Gang Formation: Potentially Delinquent Activity and Gang Involvement," *Journal of Gang Re*search, Vol. 2, No. 2 (Winter).

Warr, Mark (1996). "Organization and Instigation in Delinquent Groups," *Criminology* 34 (1): 11-37.

Warren, Carol A. B. (1988). *Gender Issues in Field Research*, Newbury Park: Sage Publications.

Washington Crime News Service (1992). "USC Gang Report Sparks Controversy Among Calif. Narcotics Officers," *Narcotics Control Digest*, Vol. 22, No. 5 (February).

Weber, Robert Philip (1990). *Basic Content Analysis*, 2nd edition, Newbury Park, CA: Sage Publications.

Weber, Max (1947). *The Theory of Social and Economic Organization*, New York: The Free Press.

Webb, Sydney and Beatrice Webb (1932). *Methods of Social Study,* New York: Longmans, Green.

Weick, Karl E. (1969). *The Social Psychology of Organizing*, Reading, MA: Addison-Wesley.

Weisel, Deborah Lamm, Scott Decker and Timothy S. Bynum (1997). "Gangs and Organized Crime Groups: Connections and Similarities," Final Report, Washington, D.C.: National Institute of Justice.

Weisel, Deborah Lamm and Ellen Painter (1997*). The Police Response to Gangs: Case Studies of Five Cities*, Washington, D.C.: Police Executive Research Forum.

Weiss, Richard M. (1983). "Weber on Bureaucracy: Management Consultant or Political Theorist," *Academy of Management Review*, Vol. 8, No. 2, pp. 242-248.

Whyte, William F. (1969). *Organizational behavior: Theory and Application*, Homewood, IL: The Dorsey Press.

Whyte, William Foote (1981). *Street Corner Society*, 3rd edition, Chicago: University of Chicago Press.

Whyte, William F. (1984*). Learning from the Field: A Guide from Experience,* Newbury Park, CA; Sage Publications.

Whyte, William F. (1991). *Participatory Action Research*, Newbury Park: Sage Publications.

Williams, Frank P., III, and Marilyn D. McShane (1993). *Criminology Theory: Selected Classic Readings*, Cincinnati, OH: Anderson Publishing Co.

Wilson, James Q. and Richard Hernnstein (1985). *Crime and Human Nature,* New York: Simon and Schuster.

Wilson, William J. (1987). *The truly disadvantaged: The inner city, the underclass and public policy*, Chicago: University of Chicago Press.

Wolfgang, Marvin E., Robert Figlio and Thorsten Sellin (1972). *Delinquency in a Birth Cohort*, Chicago: University of Chicago Press.

Wright, Richard et al. (1992). "A Snowball's Chance in Hell: Doing Fieldwork with Active Residential Burglars," *Journal of Research in Crime and Delinquency*, Vol. 29, No. 2 (May): 148-161.

Yablonsky, Lewis (1962). *The Violent Gang*, New York: McMillan Publishing Co.

Yin, Robert K. (1984). *Case Study Research: Design and Methods*, Beverly Hills, CA: Sage Publications.

INDEX